Favorite Mittens

Best Traditional Mitten Patterns
from *Fox & Geese & Fences*
and *Flying Geese & Partridge Feet*

Robin Hansen

Down East

DOWN EAST BOOKS

ISBN: 0-89272-627-X   13-digit: 978-089272-627-1
Library of Congress Control Number: 2003113887
Cover design by Lurelle Cheverie
Page design by Faith Hague
Printed at P. A. Hutchison Co., Mayfield, Penn.

All photographs by the author unless otherwise noted in captions.

5 4

BOOKS·MAGAZINE·ONLINE
www.downeast.com

Distributed by National Book Network

To Nora and Janetta,
bearing our traditions into the present

To Hanne, Michele, and Adrienne,
carrying our traditions forward

Contents

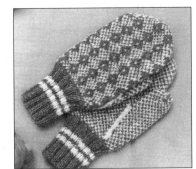

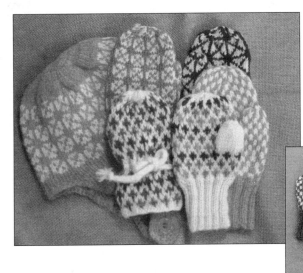

Introduction

Twenty-some years ago, Down East Books went out on a limb to publish its first knitting book—and my first book—*Fox & Geese & Fences: A Collection of Traditional Maine Mittens*. Before that, it was generally assumed that American knitters worked from patterns in books or magazines and that only European knitters carried patterns down in families and communities.

Since then, other researchers have found more knitting traditions that cross the North American continent and have documented sweater, mitten, and cap traditions in Native American, Anglo-American, and other ethnic communities in both North and South America.[1]

My father's family—the Halls and the Linscotts—were from Maine, but his father's parents went west to Missouri and Oklahoma. By an odd chance, my father was assigned to the U.S. Coast Artillery base on Great Diamond Island, Maine, when I was born. We lived there for perhaps six months, and my brother and sister and I were raised in almost every other state and three countries, but never came back to Maine as a family.

When my husband and I moved to Bath, Maine, I wanted deeply to be a native. I even bought Bert & I records to acquire the local accent, not knowing that the speaker, Marshall Dodge, was a Connecticut native caricaturing one of many Maine accents.

Then, in the late 1970s, I discovered a Maine mitten-knitting tradition different from anything I had ever seen—simple two-colored geometric patterns on the hands, and cuffs knitted in vertically striped stockinette. From Nora Johnson of Five Islands and Pat Zamore of Brunswick, I learned the pattern names—snowflake, fox and geese, stripes, compass, partridge—and I happily made mittens for my children, my husband, and myself, trying to root us more firmly in the landscape.

It occurred to me then that others who had returned to Maine after generations of wandering elsewhere might want to sink roots in this pleasant way. And so I wrote two articles, then a book of mitten and cap patterns—the first knitting patterns I had ever written. I used Gladys Thompson's 1960s collection of British fishermen's sweaters[2] as a model, expressing the directions mostly in words rather than in detailed charts, and including as much oral history about each pattern as I could, so that each pattern would carry its own stories into other families. Remembering my early efforts to follow published knitting patterns, I tried to simplify, to cut back on abbreviations.

Full of previously unrecorded lore and techniques, *Fox & Geese & Fences* (1983) became one of Down East Books' all-time best sellers and was followed by *Flying Geese & Partridge Feet* (1986), written with another knitting researcher, Nova Scotian Janetta Dexter, who had turned up an overlapping knitting tradition in Nova Scotia and New Brunswick.

I was encouraged that there were few complaints about the patterns and their format. Turns out, knitters were coping, and maybe even being kind about my directions and their homemade characteristics. Eventually, these two books went out of print—possibly every knitter in the world owned copies by then. Karin Womer at Down East Books contacted me a while ago to see if we could produce a collection of favorites from these two books. 'Twould be easy, we thought. Just combine sections, reproduce patterns, make corrections here and there, make the whole thing fit together.

'Twaren't easy.

We contacted a knit technical editor, Dorothy Ratigan, to be sure everything was as it should be. Dottie whacked me this way, then that way, told me how knitting patterns are written by real knitting designers, and insisted on my creating and sticking to a standard format—to be sure nothing was ever left out. Turns out, a lot had been left out all over the place on the first two books. We hope that it's all here now, and that these patterns will be easier to follow, while still enriched by oral history and chockerblock full of different and wonderful techniques of traditional mitten making.

If you live in New England or Atlantic Canada, we hope that you will feel roots sinking into our soil as you knit. These mittens and caps are all from the past, and can link you to our shared history and make you feel more "to home" in the Northeast even if you come "from away."

—*Robin Hansen*

1. Cynthia LeCompte, Priscilla Gibson Roberts, and Lizbet Upitis, among others.
2. Gladys Thompson, *Fishermen's Sweaters from the British Isles*, Dover Books, 1971.

Introduction from *Flying Geese & Partridge Feet*

Fox & Geese & Fences was a collection of mittens and mitten traditions from old Yankee families of Maine, mostly of British extraction. *Flying Geese & Partridge Feet* expands on that collection and includes other folk mitten traditions in Maine and Canada's Atlantic Provinces.

Fox & Geese & Fences contained all I knew about Maine mittens at the time. Since its publication in 1983, women from all over New England and eastern Canada have contributed more and more information about how people from the gentle coasts of Europe and Britain adapted their knitting to the unkind, bitter cold of eastern North America—and how they kept their hands and feet warm.

Lumberjacks in Maine—men alone in the woods—knit their own plain gray wool mittens and heelless tube socks. Women in both interior Maine and New Brunswick knit double-rolled mittens that carried thick strands of fleece along behind the knit. Logger John Richardson of Mariaville, Maine, covered plain white mittens with a thick, sewn-on wool pile, then dyed them black to hide the dirt and make them show up on snow.

Other women hooked half-inch-long yarn "fur" into cloth mittens. In hard times, old coating was laid out on a table, and a mother or grandmother traced around hands and made sewn mittens—"a perfect fit, and so warm," remembers a woman who grew up in northern Maine.

Many of the mittens here have other than English roots. Acadian women work fleurs-de-lis into their mittens, and knit the whole mitten differently from their Anglo neighbors. The hardy women of Newfoundland and Labrador knit waves and caribou designs into theirs, as well as a diamond pattern that has roots reaching straight across northern Europe to Estonia. The Moravian missionaries in Labrador taught Inuit women traditional Norwegian patterns; Inuit knitters still make them, using quick-fingered continental knitting, while most of the rest of the area uses the English technique, throwing the yarn with their right index finger.

In Nova Scotia and New Brunswick, women "double-knit" two-colored mittens covered with small geometric designs, like (and unlike) those known in Maine.

Here is the second collection of warm, traditional mittens, passed to you in the new tradition—by book—often in the words of the kind knitters who showed us how. They have been unearthed not by us but by people who make them or remember them and want the techniques remembered too and passed down. We have been a clearinghouse to receive and pass on information that other knitters have developed over generations.

Please try all that appeal to you, whether because they're from your province or state or because they intrigue you for one reason or another. But when you've sampled to your heart's content, we do hope you will choose one or two to make your own, ones you'll come to know inside out, to which you'll add your own little fillips and improvements. And we hope you will knit these one or two patterns for everyone in your family for a hundred years and teach them to your grandchildren.

In this way, you will become part of the folk process, and the good, warm patterns of our grandparents will be carried on in new generations.

—Robin Hansen and Janetta Dexter (1986)

General Instructions

■ Before You Start

The most general instructions I can give you are to ask you to *read the instructions and follow them*. These are old patterns that have been around for generations, and all the different ways of doing things here have a reason behind them. If you don't do it right, you'll probably do it wrong, waste your time and materials, and wonder what happened. So do read and study the charts and drawings carefully.

These patterns include many odd ways of doing things, which are usually only learned by sitting next to someone and watching. To simulate that immediacy, we've made picture series for some of the harder-to-explain ideas. Others, including some tricky increases, are charted. Don't let the charts frighten you. They're just another way of getting across an idea, another way of drawing. Study them closely and read the instructions that accompany them, and you'll see that they're usually easier to understand than the text.

Unusual techniques that apply to only one pattern are presented with that pattern.

Reading the Directions

It's said that after taking over a village from the Germans in World War II, the Allied military came across a knitting pattern written in pencil on lined paper and, thinking it was an encoded battle plan, sent it to their cryptographers, who spent hours trying to decipher it before a WAC leaned over the shoulder of one man and enlightened him.

In any handcraft—sewing, knitting, or building a dinghy—reading the entire instructions BEFORE you start is a good idea. Read the general instructions, which apply to all the mittens in this book, and read the specific directions for your project. When there are abbreviations—rampant in knitting—find out what they mean and try out any new techniques before you start. The abbreviations are keyed at the bottom of the first page of each pattern.

The more done in preparation, to a point, the better the resulting project will turn out. I don't mean you should procrastinate indefinitely, but rather that when you do start you should follow the Scout motto: "Be prepared!"

Reading the Charts

The charts are set up with one square equaling one stitch, with different colors represented by different shades of gray. Each set of charts has a key detailing symbols used in that chart.

Empty spaces (no squares at all): Charts of increases at the thumb gore and decreases at the tips of mittens typically show spaces between stitches. This is where stitches have been eaten up by the decrease or will appear in the increase. Knit directly from the last stitch on the right to the stitch on the left side of the space as if there were no space.

The thumb gore is never worked separately. Following the textual directions, you will see that you knit directly from the hand to the thumb gore to the next stitch of the hand.

Sizes—A Rule of Thumb

Sizes are pretty clearly defined at the beginning of each set of directions and are standard throughout the book. They are also named—Child's 4 to 6, for example. These names are only guidelines. Large children can wear adult-sized mittens, and small-handed men can wear women's and children's sizes, and so forth. I am comfortable in a man's medium (and I'm not a man).

More important than the name of the size is that mittens and hands have proportions that generally hold true for all hands. To determine which size to use, check the measurements of the hand you are knitting for—if you can—and compare with the measurements in the directions. If you can't get measurements of the actual hand, working from the names of the sizes is a good second best.

The thumb is key to the length of the mitten or glove. It is one-third the length of the hand. While it's hard to measure the length of the thumb—the inside or the outside? to which part of the knuckle?—it's easy to measure the length of the hand and divide by 3.

Measure from the tip of the middle finger to the crease at the base of the hand. I add half an inch to this measurement for ease and to allow for a little shrinkage. Write down this number and the results of dividing it by 3.

- A short but comfortable cuff is ⅓ of the hand length measurement.
- The thumb gore is (believe it or not) ⅓ of the hand length measurement.
- The thumb is ⅓ of the hand length measurement.
- The hand above the thumb hole is ⅔ the hand length measurement.

If this entire formula is followed, the mitten or glove will be ⁴⁄₃ the hand length, with the thumb hole exactly in the middle of the length.

Another proportion, useful for gloves, is that the little finger separates from the hand at about half the length of the hand, and the index finger takes off ¼" to ⅓" (6 to 8mm) after that.

The measurement around the hand, taken just above the knuckles and including the tip of the thumb is the other important measurement you need to determine size, or to launch out on your own design. Including the thumb tip in this measurement provides ease that adjusts with the size of the hand. (Small hands have small thumbs. Skinny hands have skinny thumbs.)

This measurement—say, 9½ inches (24cm)—will be the number you multiply by the number of stitches per inch to find out how many stitches you need to cast on.

The circumference of the thumb (not the thumb gore) will be 40% of the measurement around the hand. Translate the fractional inches around the hand to decimals (½ = .5; ⅛ = .125; and so forth) and multiply by .4, then multiply the result by the number of stitches per inch to find out how many stitches you will need around the thumb.

With these two measurements—length and girth—you can make a mitten for anyone in the world using any technique you choose.

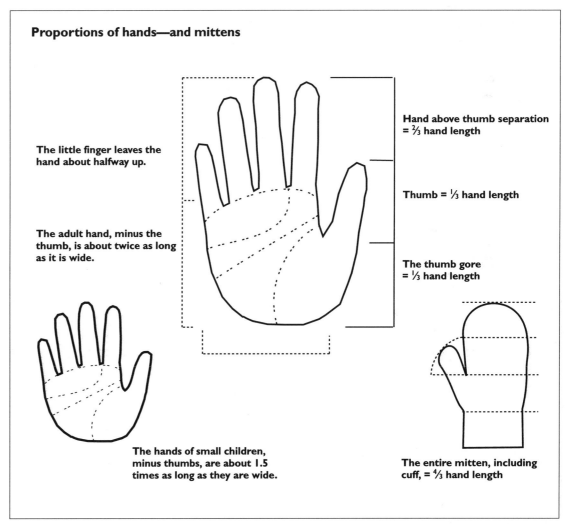

Proportions of hands—and mittens

The little finger leaves the hand about halfway up.

The adult hand, minus the thumb, is about twice as long as it is wide.

Hand above thumb separation = ⅔ hand length

Thumb = ⅓ hand length

The thumb gore = ⅓ hand length

The hands of small children, minus thumbs, are about 1.5 times as long as they are wide.

The entire mitten, including cuff, = ⁴⁄₃ hand length

Standard Sizes — in Inches *(Centimeters)* *

	Child Sizes			
	2–4	4–6	6–8	8–10
Hand Measurements:				
Hand Length	4½ (11.5)	5½ (14)	6 (15.25)	6½ (16.5)
Thumb (⅓ hand)	1½ (3.75)	1⅞ (4.75)	2 (5)	2⅛ (5.5)
Hand Circumference (incl. thumb tip)	6 (15.25)	7 (17.75)	7¼ (18.5)	8 (20.25)
Finished Mitten:				
Hand Length	4¾ (12)	6 (15.25)	6½ (16.5)	7 (17.75)
Thumb Length	1⅝ (4.13)	1⅞ (4.75)	2 (5)	2⅜ (6)
Width	3 (7.5)	3½ (9)	3⅝ (9.25)	4 (10.25)

	Adult Sizes					
	WS	WM	MM	WL	ML	XL
Hand Measurements:						
Hand Length	6½ (16.5)	7 (17.75)	7 (17.75)	7½ (19)	7½ (19)	8½ (21.5)
Thumb (⅓ hand)	2¼ (5.75)	2⅜ (6)	2⅜ (6)	2½ (6.25)	2½ (6.25)	2⅞ (7.25)
Hand Circumference (incl. thumb tip)	7½ (19)	9 (22.75)	9½ (24)	9 (22.75)	9½ (24)	10 (25.5)
Finished Mitten:						
Hand Length	7 (17.75)	7½ (19)	7½ (19)	8 (20.25)	8 (20.25)	9 (22.75)
Thumb Length	2⅜ (6)	2½ (6.25)	2½ (6.25)	2⅝ (6.75)	2⅝ (6.75)	3 (7.5)
Width	3¾ (9.5)	4½ (11.5)	4¾ (12)	4½ (11.5)	4¾ (12)	5 (12.75)

English measurements to nearest ⅛"; metric conversions rounded to nearest .25cm.

Directions for some mittens may vary slightly from these standard measurements to accommodate pattern repeats. This is noted in the specific pattern.

Knitting Needles and Yarn Sizes

All the mittens in this book are knitted in the traditional way—circularly on four double-pointed needles, three to hold the stitches and a fourth to knit onto. While it is possible to knit some of these mittens flat, doing so is more difficult and the results less pleasing than when the mitten is knit in the round.

Knitting needles come in different sizes that, along with the yarn thickness, determine the size of each stitch and of the entire piece of knitting.

It is important to use the correct size needle and the correct size yarn if you wish to get the finished-mitten sizes given in the directions. Don't guess about needle or yarn size! Metal needle gauges are available at all yarn stores, usually with an attached short ruler. Buy one and use it.

If you are a new knitter without an abundant supply of different sizes of needles, ask the store owner whether you can return the needles in their original packaging if they are not quite the right size. You may find that you knit more loosely or more tightly than the tension given in the directions. (See "Tension," page 15.)

Materials for Making Traditional Mittens

Most of the mittens and caps here are made with worsted weight (medium weight) wool yarns. Some are made with sport weight yarn, and one pair of gloves is made with fingering weight wool yarn.

Because we're doing a lot of border-hopping in this book, I've used both Canadian and American yarns. I've also tried to use wool from small mills in Canada and New England, as these yarns were most often used in traditional New England and Canadian knitting. Even today, many families with sheep take their fleeces to a mill in their state or province to be exchanged for spun yarn, and the mills rely on these family shipments to supply them.

You can use other yarns, wool or synthetic, that work well with the tensions given. If your project requires shrinking, though, DO NOT use Superwash™-treated sheep's wool or a synthetic.

On the subject of whether to knit in wool or synthetic yarn, I repeat a story told before:

In the first snowfall one winter, our children burst out of the house in whatever winter clothes they could find—last year's jackets, unmatched boot socks and mittens, and caps too big or too small. Christmas had not yet arrived with the new supplies.

About ten minutes later, my seven-year-old was back inside, in tears. "My hand is *so* cold!" he wept, shaking it splashily.

On that hand, he was wearing a mitten made of a synthetic yarn. It was soaked like a wet mop, it was heavy, and it was freezing cold.

The other hand, which emerged from its mitten rosy and steamy warm (I'm not exaggerating), was wearing a wool, double-knit mitten, like the ones you'll find in this book. The mitten was covered with caked-on wet snow. But it was warm inside.

Some knitters tell me wool is harsh to knit with. If you think so, choose a softer wool. Not all wool is scratchy. If ordering by mail, ask about softness. If you're buying in a store, touch the yarn to your lips. Scratchy will show.

Other women who love synthetics tell me you can throw the synthetic mittens in the washer, launder them, then throw them in the dryer. I haven't yet figured out why this should be an important feature for anything but a baby mitten. Winter is often over before mittens get washed in our house. If it's an issue with you, there are many Superwash™ treated wools on the market that can stand being laundered without shrinking. (Again, don't use Superwash™ treated wools for any project intended to be shrunk!)

Of course, wool does shrink. One project here calls for washing the yarn in the skein in hot soapy water and rinsing it in cold *before* knitting it, thus preshrinking it.

Shrinking is part of the wool's natural defense against cold and wet, and actually improves a garment's weather resistance. Fishermen's mittens, a tight, single-knit mitten once worn by seamen all along the North Atlantic coast, are meant to be fulled and shrunk both before

wearing and while in use. They are knit inches too long and quite wide. Most of the mittens here are about one-half inch longer than the hand, allowing a little for shrinkage but also a little ease.

See page 215 for sources of yarn and fleece used for the mittens in this book.

Starting a Mitten

Casting On

Every knitter has a favorite way of casting on stitches at the beginning of a project. If you can knit, you probably know how to cast on as well. However, I offer an old-fashioned cast-on shown to me by Nora Johnson, a traditional knitter from Five Islands, Maine, because it gives a firm, slightly elastic, and strong edge. This so-called Maine method of casting on is useful for any mittens (sweaters and socks, too), but it's essential for mittens with stockinette cuffs to help keep their edges from curling.

The Maine method is a long-tail cast-on with an extra half-twist that makes a little bead on the knit side, just below the loops of the new stitches. It's a little more time-consuming than many other cast-ons but its even, elastic, strong edge and fine appearance are worth a few minutes more.

Over the years of teaching knitting workshops from Texas to Surrey, England, I've come across a few people who consistently use this cast-on, which they always have learned from a grandmother or older relative. It is a standard cast-on for the archaic twined knitting (*tvåändssticking*) technique in the mountains of Norway and Sweden.

To cast on ten stitches using the Maine method, measure off yarn twice the length of your hand and start at that point. This should allow you about 10 sts and a tail roughly as long as your hand. Since your hand and mine are not the same size, see how this works on your own knitting and find a measure on your body that works for you for 10 stitches. With a little math, you can then determine how long a tail you'll need to cast on the stitches for any piece of knitting.

Follow the drawings, which are worth at least a thousand words.

Casting On the Maine Way

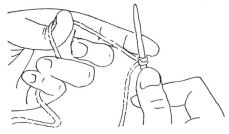

1. This is the third stitch. To make the first and all succeeding stitches, start with the yarn looped over the thumb, holding the short end in the left hand, tensioning the long end with the right lesser fingers, as if you were going to knit.

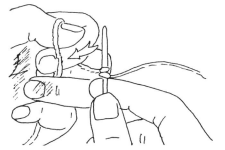 

2. Insert index finger into loop.

3. Slip thumb out of loop and turn index finger away as if pointing at someone.

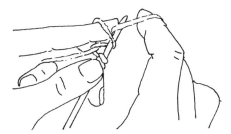 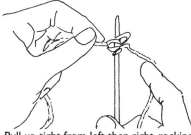

4. Knit stitch as if the left index were a knitting needle. Notice the twist.

5. Pull up tight from left then right, rocking back and forth until the stitch is snug on the needle. The twist provides the room to knit this off easily in the next round. Each cast-on makes one stitch.

Cuffs

In northeastern North America, cuffs come in several forms.

Cuffs at one time were a separate unit not even attached to the mittens. In Maine, these were called wristers and were made either in a color that harmonized with the mittens or in gray, with knit 2, purl 1 or knit 2, purl 2 ribbing. They were slipped on before the mitten. One woman told me she remembered as a child wearing wristers to her elbows over her winter jacket but under her mittens.

Cuffs nowadays are knit two ways, and they are usually part of the mitten. There is the ribbed cuff, sometimes striped to even out yarn consumption, almost invariably worked with knit 2, purl 1 ribbing or knit 3, purl 1 ribbing. I have met only one traditional knitter in the area who makes knit 2, purl 2 ribbed cuffs. The consensus is that the first two ribbings make a more elastic cuff. Some knitters say they don't have to change needle sizes when they reach the main body of the mitten if they use one of these two combinations.

The other kind of cuff is in stockinette stitch! Yarn is cast on in one color, using the Maine method shown at left. A two-color pattern is begun in the next round. One technique is to work the cuffs with stripes of knit 2 dark, knit 2 light or knit 1 dark, knit 1 light. By pulling the fabric up in widthwise ridges in a closer tension than the patterned stockinette that follows, the vertical stripe patterns snug the cuff close to the wrist like ribbing. The stripes even look a little like ribbing. Mittens with these striped cuffs look marvelously handmade and old-timey.

Sometimes, instead of stripes, the pattern used on the rest of the mitten is also knit on the cuff. Although such cuffs look loose, they generally fit quite snugly and don't let in any weather at all. Extra stitches are often added either in the thumb gore or on the little finger side to loosen up the fit around the hand.

The patterned cuffs are of course double-knit and hence warmer than a ribbed cuff. I don't think I would knit a cuff like these on any of the Newfoundland/Labrador mittens, but on the small geometric patterns from farther south, they look great.

A variety of cuffs. *Center:* Patterned cuff in Peek-a-Boo. *Clockwise from one o'clock:* Patterned stockinette cuff in three-color Fox & Geese; knit 2, purl 1 ribbing with Norwegian-style 3 stripes; Newfoundland-style stripes on a knit 2 purl 1 ribbing; knit 2, purl 2 ribbing with stripes on a Labrador Diamonds mitten; plain knit 2, purl 2 ribbing on a Maine Fisherman's mitten; Maine snug cuff with 2-stitch-wide vertical stripes.

Tension

The important thing about needle and yarn sizes is that they determine how many stitches you knit per inch vertically and horizontally. This is called "tension" or "gauge" and determines the size of what you are knitting. It is expressed thus: *Tension: 6.5 sts = 1"*, or sometimes *6.5 sts and 7 rnds = 1"*. (In metric measurements, 1" = 2.5cm.)

Most knitting directions tell you never to knit anything without first making a test swatch—a little square or tube more than two inches wide made with the same needles, the same yarn, and the same pattern as your project—so you can check your tension before you have knitted six inches of a sweater.

However, mittens are small projects, sometimes barely two inches wide, and for them only, I suggest that you use *them* as your swatch. If you have a ribbed cuff, make it on the suggested needles—a little tight or loose is not a catastrophe on a stretchy cuff. When you reach the stockinette portion of the knitting, use the suggested needle size and work the first inch (2.5cm) according to the pattern, then knit half the round and stop. Leaving the needles in place, fold the knitting in half, so that half the round is visible. Move the stitches around on the needles so they are relaxed—neither crowded together nor pulled hard apart. Gently flatten the piece on a flat surface.

Measure along the bottom points of a row of stitches, lining up a marker line on the ruler with the exact edge of one stitch. Count until you get to the next inch (or 2.5cm) line on the ruler. If that line falls in the middle of a stitch or at a quarter, count that as well, or keep going until you get to two inches (5cm). Write down how many stitches there are in that space, and check a couple of other places on the work, avoiding thumb gore increases. If you don't have the correct gauge anywhere, rip back to the round above the cuff and reknit on different size needles. DON'T change needle sizes in midstream.

If you have one-half stitch too many per inch (2.5cm), try the next larger needle size. If you have a half-stitch too few, try the next smaller needle size.

To determine your vertical gauge, count up from the point of one stitch. The trick is to count from point to point, not to the top of a stitch.

The coauthor of *Flying Geese*, Janetta Dexter, and I found that even when we knit the same number of stitches per inch widthwise, we knit a different number of rounds per vertical inch. Because of such differences among knitters, all vertical measurements here are given in inches or centimeters, although traditionally the measurements are given in bands of pattern, as in the directions given Nora Johnson by her mother for Fox & Geese mittens: "Knit three bands for the wrist, 3 for the thumb gore and 5 for the hand and don't worry about that little bit beyond the fifth band."

Working the Hand

Two-Color Knitting (Double-Knitting or Stranding)

For those who knit in only one color, creating beautiful patterns by knitting with two or even three colors must seem an esoteric skill living only in hands born to it. Perhaps Norwegian knitters have a double-knitting gene and need only to have it awakened at age six or seven to become wonderful knitters.

To the single-color knitters of the world, I say that nobody in my family double-knit anything, although all the women and little girls could knit, fast and smoothly, without mistakes. We loved Scandinavian sweaters, Norwegian mittens, Fair Isle sweaters, but it never occurred to us that we could knit them ourselves. And if it had, reasonable instruction in the art simply didn't exist in our neighborhoods until recently.

We were told everywhere to pick up the "new color" from underneath (Did "new color" mean the contrast color, or just the color we were about to use?), with the result that the two yarns steadily and inevitably became twisted around each other and *had* to be untwisted every few rounds—a bore at best. The result of this questionable method is a lumpy piece of knitting with an indistinct pattern.

I would like everyone to know that jacquard, stranding, or double-knitting is not something present in the genes of the elect, that it can be learned and done with skill by anyone who wants to do it. I am living proof of this. The fabric needn't be lumpy or strangely pulled up, and it can come off the needles perfectly flat, with even tension and a back side as neat as the front.

The first axiom is NEVER TWIST THE YARN. Its corollary, like unto it, is DON'T PICK UP BOTH COLORS THE SAME WAY.

Carrying One Color Ahead

"Carrying one color ahead" is a technique for organizing two strands of yarn so they neither tangle nor twist nor pull unevenly at each other. That curious expression is how traditional knitters say, "When changing colors, pick up Color A from beneath and in front of Color B, and bring Color B from above and behind Color A."

Color A, the one arriving on your needle from beneath and in front, is the one "carried ahead." It will actually lie beneath (south of) Color B in the row or round, and it will be emphasized on the front side of the fabric. It is usually the darkest color in your hand, unless you are knitting a pattern of fine light lines that need special emphasis.

Color B, the one arriving on your needle from above and behind like a small airplane, is the one "carried behind." It will lie above (north of) Color A in the row or round, and will be emphasized on the back side of the fabric. Because light, bright colors (particularly white) stand out by virtue of their lightness, Color B is almost always the lighter color.

(Try carrying white ahead sometime in a mitten where both colors are in equal abundance. You'll find you have a white mitten with a little added color. This too has its place.)

Now that you know this, how can it be applied to the knitting in your hands?

Knitters in the Continental tradition, who pick the yarn off the left index finger with the knitting needle, should place Color A (to be car-

Knit side of Checkerboard pattern with the dark strand carried ahead. Note the dominance of the darker color and the pulled-up effect caused by the vertical lines of color changes.

Purl side of the same Checkerboard pattern. Note how the lighter color dominates on the purl side, and there is no evidence of the pulled-up effect.

Knit side of wide stripes with the dark strand carried ahead. Because white is the lighter color, the dominance of the black strand is not so obvious, but if white were carried ahead, the dark color would recede greatly.

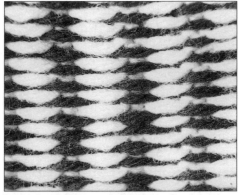

Purl side of the same wide stripes. On this side, the strand not carried ahead dominates, while the color carried ahead recedes.

ried ahead) in the crease of the left index finger, Color B nearer the fingertip (top illustration at right). The strand nearest the joint is being carried ahead and will be emphasized on the front of the work.

Pick both colors the same way, and don't go under either to get to the other—unless you have a long run of one color and have to weave in (see p. 18).

Knitters familiar with *both* right-handed Anglo-American knitting and left-handed Continental knitting can use both when working with two colors: Hold Color A (carried ahead) on your left forefinger and pick it *à la* Continental knitting; hold Color B with your right index finger and bring it to the needle *à la* American knitting. (See lower drawing at right.) The yarns never cross, never tangle, and Color A will be carried ahead and emphasized. This combination is called "stranding" and is most often seen in Norwegian knitting. When I use this method, color patterns that are meant to be ridgy flatten out. Because I like to have the pattern stand out a little, I almost never use this method. But I've never been very good at Continental knitting, either.

Position of the working yarns in Continental knitting, with Color B nearer the fingertip. Both colors are picked up the same way.

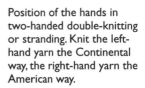

Position of the hands in two-handed double-knitting or stranding. Knit the left-hand yarn the Continental way, the right-hand yarn the American way.

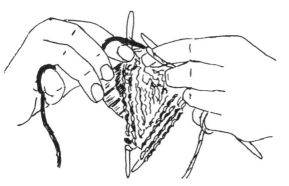

For those of us who knit in the Anglo-American tradition, with the yarn on the right index finger, carrying one color ahead is not as clear cut. If neat double-knitting is a problem for you, read carefully and study the drawings on p. 18, try it out, and I think you'll get it.

Here are some useful terms: *Above* and *over* mean "closer to the sky;" *Below* and *under* mean "closer to the earth."

For this lesson only, *in front* does not mean toward you, versus *behind* meaning away from you on the back side of your knitting. Instead, think of the knitting on your needles as a road, with the stitches not yet knitted as ahead or in front of you, and the stitches you've already knitted as behind you. You stand at the point where you are actually knitting, looking ahead to the left needle.

I tension both yarns together in the crooks of my right ring and little fingers, controlling them from that point. Only the yarn I am using at the time is on my right index finger.

To knit Color A (the yarn being carried ahead), I lift it with the back of my index finger FROM UNDER AND IN FRONT OF Color B, then knit with it as usual. Once Color A is in hand, you can continue knitting with it for 1 to 4 stitches without further gyrations.

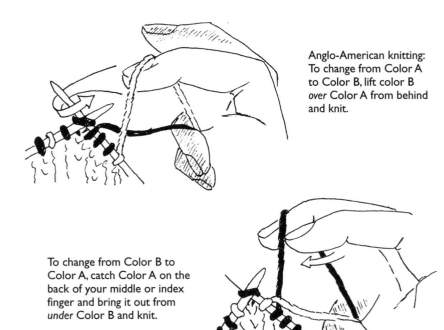

Anglo-American knitting:
To change from Color A
to Color B, lift color B
over Color A from behind
and knit.

To change from Color B to
Color A, catch Color A on the
back of your middle or index
finger and bring it out from
under Color B and knit.

To change to Color B, drop Color A or push it down with your
index finger or middle finger and, moving above Color A, catch Color
B on your index finger, bring it over Color A, and knit. Once Color B is
at work, you can knit 1 to 4 stitches without worrying about Color A.

To change back to Color A, push Color B back (down the road)
over Color A, catch Color A on the back of your middle or index
finger and bring it out from UNDER Color B, and knit.

Tension in Double-Knitting

The second axiom of double-knitting is: BE SURE TO CHECK THE
TENSION IN THE PATTERN YOU'RE USING. Don't assume that because you got seven stitches to the inch on Size 3 needles in Salt and
Pepper pattern that you will get the same tension on the same needles
when knitting Stripes or Checkerboard. Some of these patterns are
meant to pull up slightly, or even a lot, into ridges. These may have to
be knitted on larger needles to get the same tension as other patterns.

Joining a New Color and Weaving In

"Joining a New Color" and "Weaving In" are together because
they are essentially the same technique. In both cases, you are knitting
with one color and hitching another color on behind your work, so
that it is attached but invisible on the front of the work. The difference
is that when joining a new color, you have to anchor a loose end.

When you start a new color, either as a horizontal stripe or as a
second color in a double-knit pattern, it's nice to be able to start that
color as an ordinary stitch without having to worry about its becoming gigantic in the next round or pulling loose, and without having to
bother with working the end into the back of the knit later. By working it in *before* you start knitting with it, you make your knitting easier
and more even, and you'll save yourself a lot of sewing-in later. The
worked-in end of the new color will knit like any other knitting stitch,
without stress, from the get-go.

To join Color B, stop knitting 7 stitches before you need Color B.
Pinch the short end of Color B against the back of your knitting below
your most recent stitch, tail pointing down and long end up, and knit
1 stitch with Color A so that the working yarn goes around Color B,
catching its end against the knit. Knit the next 6 stitches alternately
over and under Color B, but never knitting it.

This action is called weaving in. It is also used for securing
"floats," where the color not in use is carried behind the worked
stitches for more than 4 stitches.

Most double-knitting patterns, if they are nice, have color changes
every one to three stitches. Some go on much longer. In this book, Partridge Feet, Double Irish Chain, Big Waves, and the Newfoundland
Diamond patterns have five or more stitches of one color in a row.
This means that on the back of your work, there is a 5-stitch-long
stretch of the opposite color floating along, blissfully unaware that
you're about to catch it on the back of your diamond ring or your fingernail, rip stitches out of place, and pucker your beautiful work. Multiply this by the number of repeats horizontally and vertically, and
your chances of messing things up just by wearing your mittens are
very good. Called floats, these loops should never be more than three

or four stitches long. Help these little guys not ruin your work by weaving in floats as you knit.

Each knitting method has its own way to knit over and under a strand being woven in.

If You Use Both Hands to Knit with Two Colors (Stranding)

To weave in the left strand, insert the needle into the next stitch, then lift the left strand so it rests above the right needle. Knit the right

Weaving in or joining a new strand, two-handed technique:

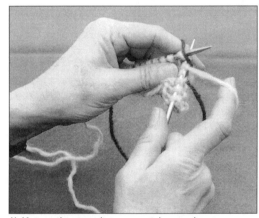

1) Knit under new (or woven-in) strand.

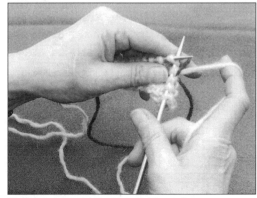

2) Knit *over* new (or woven-in) strand.

strand as usual. Knit the next right-hand stitch with the left strand in its usual position. The float yarn will be tacked to the back of the knit in two places, and the working yarn (from your right hand) will form a little V around the float yarn on the back of your work.

To weave in the right strand while knitting with the left, insert the needle in the next stitch, bring the right strand under both needles above the left yarn. Hold it (loosely) to the left of the left yarn while you knit the left yarn. Bring the right yarn back to its usual position and knit the next stitch as usual. You will have anchored the float yarn at two points and the working yarn will form a

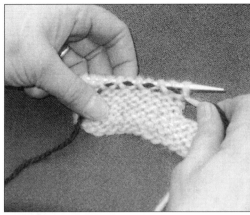

Weaving in the left (or carried ahead) strand forms inverted Vs on the purl side.

little inverted V around the float on the back of your work.

If You Carry the Yarns on Your Left Index Finger

To weave in the strand nearest your finger tip (Color B) while knitting the color nearer the joint of your finger tip (Color A), go over, then under, Color B to pick up and knit Color A. If the positions of the yarns switch when you do this, so that Color B now lies closer to the joint of your finger, go under it to get to Color A again. If not, just pick up Color A as usual. This tacks the float yarn to the fabric twice. The working yarn will cover it with a little inverted V on the back side.

To weave in Color A (closest to your index finger joint) while knitting Color B (closest to your finger tip), reverse the procedure. Dig under Color A to get to Color B. Knit Color B. In the next stitch, work Color B as usual. The working yarn (B) will hold the float yarn (A) to the fabric at 2 points and will look like a little V on the back of the fabric.

If You Carry the Yarns in Your Right Hand

Pick up the color you want to weave in from the *wrong* position—that is, to weave in Color B, go through the motions of changing colors but twist Color A (carried ahead) under and to the right of Color B, then over Color B. Knit color A. In the next stitch reverse this: bring Color A back over then under Color B and knit it. Reverse this to weave in Color A.

If this sounds impossibly complicated, just remember that you are giving the yarns a half-twist one way between two stitches and a half-twist back to where they were between the next two stitches. Like everything else in knitting, it gets easier after the first few times.

You will be tacking the float yarn to the back of the fabric with a little V or an inverted V of the working yarn.

Join a New Yarn by Sewing

When joining two colors at the same time with no attached working yarn in sight, don't weave in. Instead, grab your blunt-pointed yarn needle and thread the short end of one yarn you want to join. If it's convenient to turn the work inside out at this point, do. If not (as when you're joining two colors at the thumb hole of a double-knit mitten), work through the hole.

Starting quite near where you want to begin knitting, make a line of running stitches on the back side of the fabric to anchor the end of the yarn, using available floats or the tops of purl stitches (on the backs of your knit stitches). End by drawing the yarn needle (and yarn end) out through the fabric. Remove the yarn needle, and pull gently on the long end (the one you'll knit with) until only an inch or two is still sticking out.

Do the same with the second color. Now you have two yarns well anchored and can turn your attention to more important things than loose ends—how many stitches to pick up at the corners, things like that. When you finish the mitten and turn it inside out to work in and trim loose ends, check these ends to see if you like the way they're worked in. You can always re-do them at this point. Pull the short end through from the outside and re-do or, if you like the way it is already, trim close to the fabric.

Increasing for the Thumb

Mittens would be simple if it weren't for the human thumb. The thumb makes the hand wider where it begins at the wrist, wider and wider until it separates from the hand, leaving a gathered group of four fingers. This makes mittens not so simple.

Some mittens have no thumb gore at all and rely on a heavy increase at the top of the cuff to provide room for the thumb, but most

Ways of coping with the thumb, left to right: A New Sweden, Maine, mitten with all the increases in the first two rounds above the cuff. A Maine Fishermen's mitten with the thumb gore marked on each side with a line of purl stitches. A Norwegian-style mitten from Newfoundland with a triangular thumb gore set apart by two contrasting lines and a separate pattern. A Maine Compass mitten with an entire 8-stitch pattern element added in one (light) round. A Newfoundland mitten with typical palm and wedge-shaped thumb gore bounded by white lines. A Nova Scotia mitten with an unmarked wedge-shaped thumb gore. An Acadian mitten with no thumb gore but a sizable increase above the cuff to accommodate the base of the thumb.

of the mittens in this book have what is called a wedge-shaped thumb gore, although it is usually more like a top-heavy trapezoid.

Janetta and I have used several methods of increasing for the thumb, all of them taken from traditional knitters. Where and how they are used differs from region to region, mitten to mitten, knitter to knitter. These increases are fairly invisible, unlike those where one knits into the front and back of one stitch.

There are three options for a single increase, all of them in use throughout New England and Atlantic Canada.

1. Make One (M1)

Make One Left (M1L). This increase is the most common in this book. It is simple to make and nearly invisible. M1 means you make a stitch out of nothing, hanging it on nothing. At the point where you want to increase, wrap your *right* thumb away from you over the working yarn close to the knit, down, then up toward you under the yarn, as if digging into a pint of ice cream with your thumbnail. (This is also called a thumb cast-on.) Slip the loop off your thumb onto the right needle and continue to knit. In the next round, knit into the *front* loop as an ordinary stitch.

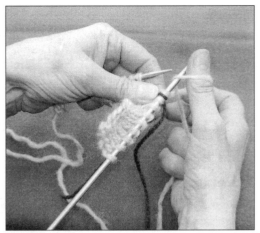
Make One Left

This version, twisted clockwise, leans left. When it is important that it do so, it is called M1L. Otherwise, it is called Make One (M1).

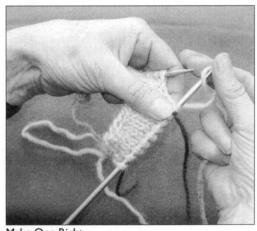
Make One Right

Make One Right is the same as Make One Left, but it leans the other way. You can exactly mirror the Make One Left by repeating the directions above on your *left* thumb. Or, you can pick up a little loop between thumb and forefinger, give it a half twist counterclockwise, and slip it onto the right needle, as shown in the photo. In the next round, knit into the *back* of this stitch.

This increase, twisted counterclockwise, leans right and is often paired with M1L for thumb gore increases.

2. Knit Both Colors into One Stitch

This increase can be only used in two-color knitting and at a point in the charted pattern where two colors change. Because the stitches are attached to the previous round, up to eight of these increases can be lined up next to each other without weakening the fabric. This decrease distorts vertical lines somewhat, so avoid involving vertical lines in the actual increase, although you can work it next to lines successfully. Remember that the increase must fit into the color sequence of the pattern.

Two regular stitches followed by four increases

To knit both colors into one stitch, place the increase at a point where the color will change in the second stitch. (This is worked out for you in the directions.) Insert the right needle in the front loop of the next stitch (as usual), place the color for the next stitch around the needle. Without moving the needles, wrap the opposite color around the needle as well, carrying the correct color ahead (p. 16). Knit both colors as one stitch. In the next round, knit each separately.

If you start with the color you are carrying ahead, be careful that the two colors don't change places as you knit. If you happen to start with the other color, bringing the carried-ahead color from underneath (as usual), locks the two colors in place in the correct order.

3. Step-Down Increase to Add One or Two Stitches

On mittens with strong vertical lines, such as Double-Rolled Mittens and Striped Mittens, emphasize these lines on the sides of the thumb gore with a Step-Down Increase in the darker yarn or the yarn carried ahead.

To work this increase, you must step down to the round below that on your left needle. Insert the right needle into the stitch *below* the next stitch on your left needle. To increase one stitch here, simply knit that lower stitch, then move back up to the next stitch on the left needle and knit it. To increase two stitches here, as you must to maintain the pattern in Striped Mittens, knit both colors (p. 21) into the lower stitch, then knit the next stitch on the left needle, keeping the color sequence in order.

You can make a left leaning step-down increase by reversing this procedure: Knit a carried-ahead stitch onto the right needle, then step down two rounds, pick up the top of the stitch from the right needle with the left, knit with one, or two, strands, settle these stitches comfortably on the needle, and work the next stitch as usual.

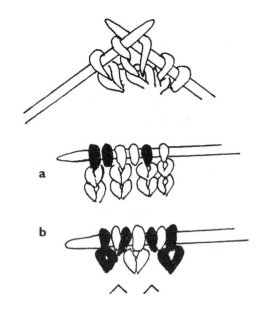

Top: Making an increase by stepping down one round and knitting into the *back* of the stitch, then knitting the next stitch on the left needle as usual.

(a) Two 1-stitch increases completed

(b) Two 2-stitches increases completed

A Wild Variety of Thumb Gores

The usual thumb gore, widely accepted for published knitting patterns, is a simple wedge shape, bounded by lines of color or purl stitches. If there is a color pattern on the rest of the mitten, the color pattern on the thumb gore is often different from or related to the pattern on the palm of the mitten. Increases are generally just inside the marking lines (see p. 20 photo), made either by Make One or by knitting both colors into one stitch.

An older style of thumb gore for double-knit mittens is much less adaptable but almost invisible. A whole pattern element is added at once, within the space of a few stitches, usually in the first round of a color pattern repeat, so that two units of pattern seem magically to

erupt from one. Because up to eight increases may be crowded together, knitters use combinations of several increases, usually Make-Ones and Knitting Both Colors into One Stitch on both sides of a center stitch.

This old-time thumb gore must have as many increase stitches crowded together as there are stitches in the repeat. In 2- to 4-stitch repeats, this can be almost invisible, even when 2-stitch increases are paired on opposite sides of a thumb gore. Five- to eight-stitch increases worked this way create a slight bulge in the knitted work, which, however, soon disappears when the mitten is worn.

It's almost impossible to transfer increase directions from one of these old-time mitten patterns to another because of the peculiarities necessary to make each whole-unit increase fit perfectly into the allover pattern. Knitters may simply use a different, smaller pattern for the thumb and thumb gore to avoid having to increase so many stitches in so little space.

In Chipman's Check, which is a bundle of clever tricks as well as a 6-stitch repeat, the bulge is avoided by increasing in 2 rounds. This is possible because within the 8-line repeat are pairs of Salt & Pepper rounds, which have only a 2-stitch repeat.

You may encounter these organic thumb gore increases in mittens from New England, Nova Scotia, and New Brunswick, often surrounded by amazed onlookers.

Keeping Your Place When There Are No Marking Stitches

The New Brunswick and Nova Scotia patterns provided by Janetta Dexter call for an increase of one stitch on each side of the thumb gore with no line of marking stitches. This can be confusing and difficult if you're not accustomed to it. Mark the edge of the thumb gore for your own benefit by laying a piece of contrasting waste yarn between the last stitch of the palm and the first stitch of the thumb gore in the very first round of the thumb gore. Keep your place here by flipping it from front to back (or vice versa) every few rounds. You will be in no danger of knitting this yarn and can remove it easily when you later need it to hold the thumb gore stitches.

Casting On over the Thumb—Twisted Make One

You have placed the thumb gore stitches on a piece of waste yarn and want to cast on stitches above the thumb hole so you can continue knitting the hand. It would be nice to be able to have the advantages of the Maine cast-on—elasticity, firmness, and so forth—but no: There's no second end, and the two strands you're using have to continue the two-colored pattern.

The answer is the Twisted Make One, a one-strand version of the Maine method of casting on. Follow steps 1 through 4 of the Maine cast-on drawings (p. 14), but instead of knitting the loop off, simply tighten it onto the right needle. Repeat for each stitch you need. If you are working a color pattern, use the strands in the pattern order, so that when you reach the other side of the thumb hole, both colors will be there to work with.

The resultant stitch, like a Make One or a thumb cast-on, is not anchored to anything at the bottom; it doesn't need to be. Like the Maine cast-on, it has a half-twist that gives it elasticity and makes it easy to knit into in the next round. When it's time to pick up stitches for the thumb, you will find the twist still shows as a little diagonal at the knit-side edge of the thumb hole, ready for you to pick up and knit. Neat.

This is not traditional from anywhere. I made it up. But how nicely it works!

◾ Ending the Mitten—About Decreasing

As with increases, so with decreases: Every knitter has a preferred layout for decreases. Decreasing along two edges will create a flat mitten that must be planned as either a left or a right. Decreasing with the pattern or decreasing at three points will produce an ambidextrous mitten that can be worn on either hand or trained to one.

Decreasing on Both Edges of the Mitten

The women in Labrador and Newfoundland usually decrease at both sides of a mitten: two stitches to a side every round, almost to the tip. At this point, the Norwegian-tradition Newfoundlanders part company with the Anglo-Celtic Newfoundlanders and keep ploddingly decreasing until they reach a point with one or two stitches on each needle. The tip of the finished mitten is like a housetop, what Maine knitters with a sniff call a "pickèd" tip (as in picket fence). The other knitters either begin decreasing in the center front and back when pickèdness threatens, pull the last 14 to 16 stitches in on the end for a rounded tip, or graft the last 16 to 20 stitches front to back to make a squared-off tip.

Decreasing on both edges is commonly used in modern printed patterns—with or without the pickèd tip.

Decreasing with the Pattern

In Maine, knitters are also divided. An old tradition exists of decreasing by whole pattern elements, knitting two stitches together as many times as are needed to eat up a single repeat (six times for a 6-stitch repeat), sort of the reverse of adding a whole pattern repeat on the thumb. Another old tradition is to decrease the repeat itself, by knitting stitches together within each element of the pattern.

These two modes of decreasing are associated with increasing by whole pattern elements. They both give a rounded mitten tip that maintains the integrity of the pattern all the way around. They're very organic endings for a mitten.

Decreasing at Three Points

A third old method, used both on single- and double-knit mittens, is to decrease by knitting two stitches together at both ends of all three needles either every round or every second round. You thus decrease six stitches in every decrease round. This too makes a nicely rounded tip and was once the nearly universal method of ending both mittens and socks throughout northern Europe and New England.

How to Decrease

There are two decreases used in this book, SSK2tog and K2tog, which lean in opposite directions. Both are used on almost all the patterns and sometimes both are used in tandem to complement a 2-color pattern. Using only one or the other, repeated on the same stitch in succeeding rounds, as in Maine Fisherman's Mittens, creates a subtle spiral of decreases that shows you really know what you're doing and are in control of your craft.

Knit Two Together (K2tog)

This is the most obvious decrease in knitting—simply knitting two stitches as if they were one. This decrease slants to the right.

On the entering side of a pair of decreases, K2tog makes a one-stitch-wide decrease band. On Norwegian mittens, this stitch is often followed by two or more additional stitches and given its own pattern, forming a decorative decrease band. You will find such a decrease band on Spruce mittens in this book.

Used on the leaving side of a pair of decreases, K2tog brings the pattern all the way to the "crack" between decreases, so that, matched with SSK2tog, the patterns from both sides meet, often with great visual effect. Striped mittens have this decrease layout.

In the most basic K2tog, the right needle is inserted as usual but through two stitches, starting with the second stitch on the left needle. These are knitted off as if they were a single stitch.

The K2tog called for in this book has a prep step: Slip the first stitch on the left needle purlwise (as if you were going to purl it) onto the right needle, then insert the left needle into the stitch back to front and replace it on the left needle. You have turned the stitch counterclockwise. Insert right needle into the second stitch and the twisted first stitch on the left needle and knit them as one stitch. This K2tog, which has no distinctive name, lies flatter and is less visible than the ordinary one above. Not necessarily a traditional decrease (although it may be), it came from Elizabeth Zimmermann's repertoire.

Slip, Slip, Knit Two Together (SSK2tog)

This decrease was invented, or found, by famous knitter Barbara Walker, whose several collections of knitting stitches and patterns have become classics. It leans to the left and lies flatter and is less visible

than the old Slip One, Knit One, Pass the Slipped Stitch Over (S1, K1, PSSO), which it has generally superseded.

SSK2tog involves a little fancy footwork on your needles and basically means that you turn *two* stitches around, one at a time, replace them on the left needle, and knit them through the back loop (right needle inserted from right to left) as if they were a single stitch.

On the entering side of a pair of decreases, it brings the pattern all the way to the "crack" between decreases, so that, matched with K2tog, the patterns from both sides meet neatly. In this book, Striped mittens have this decrease layout.

Used on the leaving side of a pair of decreases, it makes a one-stitch-wide decrease band. On Norwegian mittens, this is often emphasized with two or more preceding stitches with a separate pattern, forming a decorative decrease band. You will find such a decrease band on Spruce mittens in this book.

To work SSK2tog, slip the first stitch on the left needle knitwise (as if you were going to knit) onto the right needle, slip the next stitch purlwise, then start to replace both stitches on the left needle. As you do so, your right needle will be inserted through the two stitches from right to left. Knit the two stitches together from this position.

■ Winding a Center-Pull Ball

This is not strictly a knitting thing, but think how convenient it would be not to have to chase that ball of yarn around the room and not to have it tangling with other yarns and needles as it turns around in your knitting bag, seeking escape. A center-pull ball, where the working end comes from inside the ball, just sits there and hands you yarn as you need it. Only at the very end does it start to collapse and cause problems—and then you can wind a new little ball that will be just as handy as the first.

You can wind these on mechanical or electric yarn winders, but less expensively, you can wind them yourself by hand. What you need is a *nøstepinde* (pronounced "nusta pinna"; can you tell that this idea comes from a foreign country?), which has been called in English a "winding stick" or a "yarn dibble" (because it looks like a gardening

Nøstepinder, yarn winding sticks. This collection is from all over the United States and Scandinavia.

dibble, which you stick into the ground to make holes for seedlings).

A *nøstepinde* can be any smooth 8- to 12-inch stick, from a sanded and waxed ⅝" dowel or the end of a broomstick to a handsomely turned piece of mesquite or rosewood with an elaborate handle and a tapered end that will slip the finished ball of yarn off slick as a whistle.

Nøstepinder have been used for generations in Scandinavia for winding balls of yarn from skeins, and young men may still carve or turn them for their sweethearts. They traveled to this country in the 1980s with a knitting technique called twined knitting (or *tvåånds-sticking*), which necessitates a ball with both the center and the outside yarn ends accessible. They were taken up by American woodworking men who needed something creative to do while their wives and girlfriends were off knitting. You can find *nøstepinder* in yarn stores today, you can make one yourself, or you can bundle to-

gether some markers or knitting needles in your hand and use them as a *nøstepinde*. What works, works.

Mount your skein of yarn on a swift or someone else's hands, or lay it across your knees, carefully untwisted so that the end you have in hand is on top all the way around.

1) Tie the yarn end about halfway down the *nøstepinde,* using a knot you can get undone. I use two thumb cast-ons, also called a clove hitch.

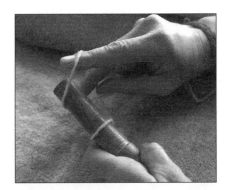

2) Take your yarn dibble, *nøstepinde,* in your left hand. Start winding around the undecorated end about an inch from the end, and wind straight across the stick until you have a pad of wound yarn 1 to 1½ inches wide and ¼ inch deep.

3) Now, wind diagonally, twisting the stick away from you a little all the time, to lay each turn of yarn parallel and close to the one before it. As the ball gets larger, place your left index finger toward the shoulder of the ball to guide the yarn there, so that the ball grows outward, not longer. It should look like a ball of string from the hardware store, not like an egg.

4) When all the yarn is wound, wind the last ten feet or so around the fat waist of the ball and tuck in the end. Remove

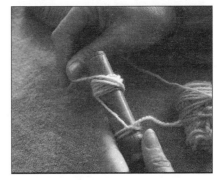

the ball from the stick, untie the knot, and give the ball a little squeeze from the sides. The hole will collapse slightly, giving the center end a little tension and re-laxing all the turns within to keep the yarn soft and manageable.

Place the ball in your bag or on the table, center-pull end up, and knit using the center end. The outside end will not be used until last, unless—as often happens—you need a short length for some other purpose. Then you can take off a piece without having to break the working end.

PART ONE

Practical Woolies from Up North and Down East

Wool mittens are warm, but a knitted fabric is a mesh, full of holes. The icy wind blows, and being a lazy wind, it will go right through, rather than around, the ordinary wool mitten. All the mitten patterns in this book are old-time inventions to deal with this very aspect of the knitted wool mitten.

One of the most widespread methods is to knit alternating two strands of yarn, so that every hole is backed by the other strand of yarn. In Dalarna, Sweden, this is done in one color, with a little twist behind, but in most places, it's done with two, and the colors are alternated to make patterns taken from patchwork and weaving, with names from the surrounding world. You will find these double-knit patterns in the second part of this book.

But there are other ways of getting rid of or covering the holes. The most usual in today's world is to cover the mitten with a yellow horsehide or Goretex™ mitten. This solution is like wearing a paper bag over the head to hide problem skin: it solves the problem but it isn't good looking. It covers up the beautiful mitten.

A mitten can be felted by washing it in hot, soapy water and rinsing it in cold, vigorously and repeatedly. The fishermen's mittens presented here are treated this way and shrink into dense, matted hand coverings that are worn wet, the wetness serving to make them even more windproof and dense.

In both Europe and America, knitted mittens have been covered

Elizabeth Berg, a Norwegian nurse who retired to Chebeague Island, Maine, in the 1970s, re-created the directions for fishermen's mittens from a mitten knitted by the late Minnie Doughty, an island native.
STEVE MUSKIE PHOTO

with pile or lined with pile, or lined with tufts or rolls of fleece or loops of wool yarn. All are handsome solutions. Some of these are offered here, as well as a mitten crocheted on a special homemade hook in a way that eliminates all the lacy holes one associates with crochet. "And don't call it 'crochet,'" I was told by Albert Miller of Turner, Maine, who taught me how. "Call them 'mittens hooked on a dowel'!"

Chebeague Island Fishermen's Wet Mittens

Time was, when a man went out in his boat in winter, he took his mittens off a nail on the boat, dipped them in the warm salt water cooling the engine, wrung them out good, and put them on wet. Then he began hauling and baiting his traps. His hands stayed warm in the wet wool mittens even working with wet traps dragged out of a frigid Casco Bay. When he peeled the mittens off later, his hands were so warm they

Two pairs of fishermen's mittens knitted by the late Minnie Doughty of Chebeague Island, Maine.

steamed in the cold air. Then he hung the mittens up again by little loops in their cuffs and went ashore.

The warm wool mittens had an amazing insulating quality—but only when wet, fishermen say. They may have been knit by his wife, or he may have bought them—hand knit—from the same store that sold him his trap stock, boots, netting shuttles, and other gear. Wherever he got them, they were big when new, maybe a third bigger than his hand.

He took them on his boat and wetted them in the cooling water, then threw them on deck, sometimes in fish gore, and walked on them as he hauled traps. When he had a moment, he laid them out on the hot engine manifold to dry, turning them carefully now and then to keep them from scorching. He did this over and over all day. The wool became thicker, the stitches tighter than can be knit. By the end of the

day, they were smaller and fit his hands and were marinated in the smell of the sea and fish and his boat.

As he wore them, wetting them in salt water each time, they shrank even more and became more matted, until they were molded to his hands and quite stiff when dry. Cod fishermen, handling oily fish, found the mittens never stopped shrinking and would finally have to be discarded or given to their children to wear.

Fishermen wore mittens like these in Maine and Nova Scotia for hundreds of years. Some still do, when they can get them. In Newfoundland, they are still used year-round. In many fishing communities, though, the art of knitting fishermen's mittens was lost after the introduction of the insulated rubber glove. Even those women who want to knit them for their husbands can't do so because there are no mittens left to measure, and no women left who know how to make them.

So it was also on Chebeague Island until a few years ago. Minnie Doughty, the one woman who had maintained the skill, had died, taking her knowledge with her. Like many other coastal women, Mrs. Doughty had a difficult life and lost several of her six sons to the sea. In her lifetime, she had knitted a great many pairs of fishermen's mittens—so many that when she died, her daughters treasured the single remaining new pair as a keepsake.

One of the expert knitters of the Chebeague Island Methodist Church Ladies' Aid, Elizabeth Bergh, took these mittens, counted stitches, measured, found a loose end to determine the thickness of the yarn, and put together instructions for fishermen's mittens. These follow.

This pattern makes a huge mitten, which *must* be shrunk to be usable. Although the mitten is designed to be used wet, in salt water, by fishermen, it makes a wonderfully thick, dry mitten for landlubbers, if shrunk according to the fulling directions that follow the knitting instructions.

Minnie Doughty's grandson, lobsterman Richard Ross, wrings out his mittens before heading out. STEVE MUSKIE PHOTO

Chebeague Island Fishermen's Wet Mittens

Yarn

Medium weight: Bartlettyarns 2-ply Fisherman Yarn

| | (oz) | 3 | 3½ | 6 |
| | (g) | 85.5 | 99.25 | 171 |

or other untreated, medium weight wool yarn. (Peace Fleece 2-ply knitting yarn, with some kid mohair, makes a wonderfully soft and shaggy fisherman's mitten.)

OR, *Heavy weight:* Barlettyarns 3-ply Fisherman Yarn

| | (oz) | 3½ | 5½ | 7 |
| | (g) | 99.75 | 156.75 | 199.5 |

or other untreated, heavy fisherman wool with lanolin.

The mittens are traditionally cream-colored in North America. Do not use Superwash™ wools or synthetics—they will NOT shrink.

Equipment 1 set Size 6 (4mm, Can. Size 8) double-pointed needles, or size you need to knit at correct tension • 1 Size F (4mm, Can. Size 8) crochet hook • 12" (30cm) contrasting waste yarn • blunt-tipped yarn needle. *For fulling:* Two large dishpans • Washboard or felting board • Scrub brush or pet slicker • Murphy's Oil Soap or other natural soap • Optional: 3 tablespoons (44ml) ammonia

Tension before shrinking In 2-ply yarn, 5 sts and 7 rnds = 1" or 2.5cm • In 3-ply yarn, 4 sts and 6 rnds = 1" or 2.5cm

Tension after shrinking In 2-ply yarn, 10½ sts and 8¾ rnds = 2" or 5cm • In 3-ply yarn, 8½ sts and 9 rnds= 2" or 5cm

---

ABBREVIATIONS beg: beginning • CC: contrast color • dec(s): decrease(s) • inc(s): increase(s) • k: knit • k2tog: knit 2 together • M1: make 1 stitch • M1L: make 1 stitch left • M1R: make 1 stitch right • MC: main color • p: purl • rep: repeat • rnd(s): round(s) • SSK2tog: slip, slip, knit 2 sts together • st(s): stitch(es) • twisted M1: twisted make 1 cast-on

Measurements—inches and *centimeters*

| | MEDIUM WEIGHT YARN | | | HEAVY WEIGHT YARN | | |
| | Child | Adult | | Child | Adult | |
	6–8	M	XL	6–8	M	XL
Hand length	5½	7	8½	5½	7	8½
	14	*17.75*	*21.5*	*14*	*17.75*	*21.5*
Hand circumference, incl. tip of thumb	7	9½	10	7	9½	10
	17.75	*24*	*25.5*	*17.75*	*24*	*25.5*
Mitten before shrinking Length of hand	8	10	12	8	10	12
	20.25	*25.5*	*30.5*	*20.25*	*25.5*	*30.5*
Thumb length (⅓ hand)	2⅝	3⅜	4	2⅝	3⅜	4
	6.5	*8.5*	*10.25*	*6.5*	*8.5*	*10.25*
Width	4	5	5⅜	3¾	4¾	5⅜
	10.25	*12.75*	*13.5*	*9.5*	*12*	*13.75*
Mitten after shrinking Length of hand	6	7½	9	6	7½	9
	15.25	*19*	*23*	*15.25*	*19*	*23*
Thumb length	2	2½	3	2	2½	3
	5	*6.5*	*7.5*	*5*	*6.5*	*7.5*
Width	3¾	4¾	5	3¾	4¾	5
	9.5	*12*	*12.75*	*9.5*	*12*	*12.75*

To make other sizes, use a simple one-color mitten pattern and allow 25 percent shrinkage lengthwise, about 6 percent widthwise.

Pattern Notes

This mitten is knit huge, and *must* be shrunk before wearing. It can be worn damp—dip in water and wring out—or dry. I have put my hand in a dry Fishermen's Mitten into our sheeps' drinking water in winter and lifted off an inch of ice without getting wet. If I do get wet, I give my hands a couple of hard shakes, and the wetness disappears.

Making the cuff

		MEDIUM WEIGHT YARN			HEAVY WEIGHT YARN		
---	---	Child 6–8	Adult M	XL	Child 6–8	Adult M	XL
Using the Maine method (p. 13), cast on		30 sts	36 sts	42 sts	24 sts	30 sts	36 sts.
Distribute sts:	Needle 1:	9 sts	12 sts	12 sts	6 sts	9 sts	12 sts
	Needle 2:	12 sts	12 sts	15 sts	12 sts	12 sts	12 sts
	Needle 3:	9 sts	12 sts	15 sts	6 sts	9 sts	12 sts
Join into a triangle, being careful not to twist sts around the needles. Work k2, p1 ribbing until cuff measures	(inches)	3	4	4	3	4	4
	(cm)	7.5	10.25	10.25	7.5	10.25	10.25

Starting the hand and thumb gore

Rnd 1: Place last p st on first needle. Slip this p st, k2, p1. These p sts mark the two sides of the thumb gore. K rest of rnd, increasing 2 sts on each needle by M1 (p. 26) between k sts of ribbing.

	Total:	36 sts	42 sts	48 sts	30 sts	36 sts	42 sts

Rnd 2: P1, M1R, k2, M1L, p1, k to end of rnd without further incs.

Rnds 3–5: Work even, maintaining the 2 p sts to mark outside of thumb gore.

Rnd 6: P1, M1R, k up to p st, M1L, p1. Continue even to end of rnd. Total between p sts: 6 k sts.

Rnds 7–9: Work even.

Rep Rnds 6–9 until there are _____ between p sts.	8 sts	10 sts	12 sts	6 sts	8 sts	10 sts

Taking off the thumb gore stitches

When thumb gore incs are complete, work even until thumb gore measures	(inches)	2⅝	3⅜	4	2⅝	3⅜	4
	(cm)	6.75	8.5	10.25	6.75	8.5	10.25
Place all thumb gore sts including the marking lines onto waste yarn.	Total:	10 sts	12 sts	14 sts	8 sts	10 sts	12 sts

		MEDIUM WEIGHT YARN			HEAVY WEIGHT YARN		
		Child	Adult		Child	Adult	
		6–8	M	XL	6–8	M	XL
Using twisted M1 (p. 23), cast on over the gap.		7 sts	7 sts	10 sts	5 sts	4 sts	7 sts
	Total:	39 sts	45 sts	54 sts	31 sts	36 sts	45 sts
K1 rnd even. Distribute sts:	Needles 1 and 2: each	13 sts	15 sts	18 sts	10 sts	12 sts	15 sts
	Needle 3:	13 sts	15 sts	18 sts	11 sts	12 sts	15 sts
K even until work above cuff measures	(inches)	6¼	7½	9	6¼	8	10
	(cm)	*16*	*19*	*23*	*16*	*20.25*	*25.5*

Closing the mitten tip

NOTE: Decs do not come out even in all sizes. If one or two sts are left over at the end of the rnd, work them even.

In medium weight yarn, largest size only:

Rnd 1: *SSK2tog, k7 sts; rep from * to end of rnd.
Total per needle, 16 sts.

Rnds 2 and 3: Work even.

In med wt yarn, two largest sizes:

Rnd 4: *SSK2tog, k 6 sts; rep from * to end of rnd.

Rnds 5 and 6: Work even.	Total per needle:	13 sts	13 sts	14 sts	10 sts	12 sts	15 sts

In all sizes but heavy weight yarn Child's 6–8,

Rnd 7: *SSK2tog, k5 sts; rep from * to end of rnd. Total per needle:	11 sts	11 sts	12 sts	—	12 sts	13 sts

Rnds 8 and 9: Work even.

Rnd 10: *SSK2 tog, k4 sts; rep from * to end of rnd. Total per needle:	9 sts	9 sts	10 sts	—	10 sts	11 sts

Rnds 11 and 12: Work even.

All sizes

Rnd 13: *SSK2tog, k3 sts; rep from * to end of rnd. Total:	21 sts	21 sts	24 sts	24 sts	24 sts	27 sts

		MEDIUM WEIGHT YARN			HEAVY WEIGHT YARN		
		Child	Adult		Child	Adult	
		6–8	M	XL	6–8	M	XL

Rnds 14 and 15: Work even.

Rnd 16: *SSK2tog, k2 sts; rep from * to end of rnd.

Rnds 17 and 18: Work even.	Total:	16 sts	16 sts	18 sts	18 sts	18 sts	20 sts

Rnds 19 and 20: Work even.

Rnd 21: *SSK2tog, k1 st; rep from * to end of rnd.	Total:	11 sts	11 sts	12 sts	12 sts	12 sts	14 sts

Check measurements against finished measurements at beg of directions. If you are satisfied, break yarn leaving a 6" (15cm) tail. With yarn needle, thread one end through the remaining sts and draw up firmly. Thread first end through drawn-up sts again, darn a few sts to secure it and draw it to inside of mitten.

Working the thumb

Needle 1: Pick up from cast-on sts above the thumb hole.		7 sts	7 sts	10 sts	5 sts	4 sts	7 sts
Needle 2: Pick up from thumb gore		5 sts	6 sts	7 sts	4 sts	5 sts	6 sts
Needle 3: Pick up from thumb gore		5 sts	6 sts	7 sts	4 sts	5 sts	6 sts
Pick up and twist onto needle from each corner of thumb hole		1 st	1 st	1 st	1 st	2 sts	2 sts
	Total:	19 sts	21 sts	26 sts	15 sts	18 sts	23 sts

Join yarn by sewing (p. 20) into back of fabric starting at the right side of the thumb hole.

Rnd 1: Work even.

Rnd 2: Needle 1: Work even.
Needle 2: K2tog, k to end of needle.
Needle 3: K to last 2 sts of needle, SSK2 tog.

Total (about 40% of total hand sts):		17 sts	19 sts	24 sts	13 sts	16 sts	21 sts.
Work even until thumb measures	(inches)	2	2⅜	3	2	2¼	2⅞
	(cm)	*5*	*6*	*7.5*	*5*	*5.75*	*7.25*

Closing the thumb

Rnd 1: *K2tog, k2; rep from * to end of rnd.
16 sts

Rnds 2 and 3: Work even.

Rnd 4: *K2tog, k1; rep from * to end of rnd.

	MEDIUM WEIGHT YARN			HEAVY WEIGHT YARN		
	Child 6–8	Adult M	XL	Child 6–8	Adult M	XL
Rnd 1 Total:		13 sts	15 sts	18 sts	10 sts	12 sts
Rnd 4 Total:	9 sts	10 sts	12 sts	7 sts	8 sts	11 sts

Break yarn leaving a 6" (15cm) tail. With yarn needle, thread one end through the remaining sts and draw up firmly. Thread end through drawn-up sts again, darn a few sts to secure it, and draw to inside of thumb.

Finishing the mitten

Crochet a loop on edge of cuff with the tail from casting on to hang the mitten up to dry. Minnie Doughty also buttonhole-stitched the loop for extra strength. Or, work a loop on one cuff and sew a button or a wooden toggle to the second mitten cuff.

Turn mitten inside out and darn all ends into the back of the fabric. Repair possible holes at corners of the thumb hole with nearby tails. Trim ends closely.

Make another identical mitten. This mitten can be worn on either hand.

When both mittens are completed and finished, shrink them according to the fulling directions on pps. 34–35 until they shrink one quarter of their length.

Fulling Fishermen's Mittens

Fulling means shrinking and brushing knitted or woven fabric, as contrasted to *felting*, which starts with loose wool fibers. The shock of cold to hot and hot to cold temperature changes, oil (either as codfish oil or soap), and agitation (on a washboard or in a washing machine or dryer) are what cause wool to shrink. You probably will not shrink your mittens by simply boiling them in a pot of water.

It's good to do this project outdoors, where water can be splashed or poured onto the ground as you work. Otherwise, use a laundry tub or the kitchen sink.

This is how you proceed:

1. Prepare two large dishpans, one of very cold water (tap water can be cold enough, but add ice if you wish) and one of hot water (a mix of boiling and tap water, just cool enough to put your hands in). The hot water will be the wash and rub water; the cold water will be the rinse. Keep refreshing both baths as you work, keeping the hot very hot and the cold clear and cold.

Shrinking mittens is a good group project. Women have been known to sing to the rhythm of scrubbing. Here, three Maine women—Diane Calder of Chebeague, Robin and Hanne Hansen of West Bath—work together at the Maine Festival to shrink mittens. CHARLES FREIBURG PHOTO

Plenty of soap and agitation, together with sharp changes from hot to cold and back again, will cause the wool to shrink. CHARLES FREIBURG PHOTO

2. Work both mittens of a pair at the same time, alternating throughout the process. Apply soap to the mitten, submerse it completely in hot water, then scrub and rub on the washboard, dipping it continually in the hot water.

3. When you are tired of scrubbing, plunge the mitten into cold water and squeeze the water through quickly, to shock the fibers. Get the whole mitten cold.

4. Repeat back and forth between hot and soapy water and

You will need two large dishpans, supplies of ice cold water and almost boiling water, plenty of soap, and a washboard. CHARLES FREIBURG PHOTO

cold rinse water. The fabric will relax in the hot water and pull together in the cold, until the mitten suddenly gives up, shrinks, and doesn't relax.

5. When the mittens have shrunk to your satisfaction, rinse once more, optionally adding 3 tablespoons of ammonia to the rinse water. Ammonia is said to whiten and soften the wool. Usually a lot of gunk will come out of the wool if you add ammonia to the rinse water. (This is the lanolin. Whether you want it in your mitten is up to you, but it does help make the mitten water- and wind-resistant.)

6. If you used ammonia in Step 5, rinse the mittens once more in clear water.

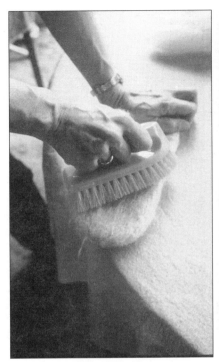

When the mitten has shrunk adequately, brushing it with a scrub brush or a fine wire brush brings up a fine nap.
CHARLES FREIBURG PHOTO

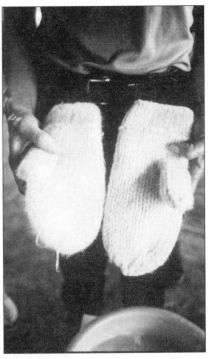

One mitten of an identical pair has been shrunk to demonstrate the difference.
CHARLES FREIBURG PHOTO

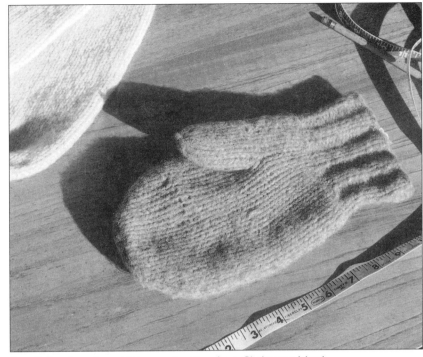

A well-shrunk, well-used fishermen's mitten from Chebeague Island.

7. Brush thoroughly toward the tip on both sides (and, optionally, widthwise on the inside) using a scrub brush or fine wire brush, or a pet slicker. Put the mittens in the washer on the spin cycle (only!), then brush again and spread them in a warm spot to dry.

You can also dry the mittens in the dryer with other clothes, but be aware that this might shrink and stiffen them more than you wish. You no longer control the process when you offer your lovely handwork to an uncomprehending machine. But I do it sometimes anyhow.

The shrinking/fulling process may take up to 45 minutes of your hard labor, but will probably take less. Should you despair halfway through, you can always quit and throw the mittens in with a load of laundry. With a little brushing afterward, they should look handfulled. If you start with the washing machine, however, you may end up with a less nappy, less long-haired mitten. On the other hand, you will have less actual hard work. There are many such trade-offs in life.

In Bartlettyarns 2-ply Fisherman yarn or Peace Fleece 2-ply knitting yarn, the mitten will lose about 25 percent (one quarter) of its length and less than 5 percent widthwise. In Bartlettyarns 3-ply Fisherman yarn, the mitten should lose 16 to 20 percent of its length and 10 percent of its width.

Double-Rolled Mittens

I had spread my mittens under a tree at the Norlands Living History Center Heritage Days Festival to excite interest and conversation and to show off the marvelous warmth and good looks of old-time Maine mittens. But the reception at Norlands—near Livermore, Maine—was different from the reception at other places, where people exclaim at the mittens' thickness or remember the patterns of their childhoods. In the Norlands area, people still knit traditional mittens, and the response is always, "Oh, I know someone who knits mittens like that."

At Norlands I met Beulah Moore, who found my collection of mittens incomplete. "Don't you have any double-rolled mittens?" she asked, after looking them over. Double-rolled mittens? I'd never heard of them.

Double-Rolled Mittens are knit in one color with a narrow roll of unspun fleece carried behind the work, caught up between sts, just as one weaves in long floats of yarn in double-knitting (p. 18). Mrs. Moore showed me how to carry the fleece so that the knitting progresses rapidly, flipping the little bit of fleece over and under the knitting strand with each stitch.

She was unwilling to make me a pair right then, but she did teach me the technique. I was able to play with what she had shown me, so when I saw my first real pair of Double-Rolled Mittens in the Maine State Museum, I knew immediately what they were. With Curator Paul Rivard's permission, Mrs. Hattie Stover Brown's mittens are shown here in a black-and-white photo. They were knit in a somewhat finer yarn than I have used, at a tension of seven sts per inch.

I had just decided that this technique was truly extinct when I met Edna Mower of Merrimack, New Hampshire, who told me she still knits double-rolled mittens and socks. "I can't imagine why it should be extinct," she told me. "It's really a simple procedure."

Mrs. Mower grew up on a farm in Sevogle, New Brunswick, seventeen miles upriver from New Castle, in a large family that combined

Double-Rolled Mittens with shagged cuffs made by Hattie Stover Brown.
COURTESY OF MAINE STATE MUSEUM

French, Irish, Scottish, and English traditions. Her father was the ranger for the region. Her mother was a schoolteacher.

"We learned to do everything," Mrs. Mower remembers. "You learned to milk cows and churn butter and knit and crochet and hoe the garden and clean the barns and everything else." She grew up making several well-known double-knit patterns that her family taught her, but she learned to make Double-Rolled Mittens from a neighbor.

"I remember learning it very well. I probably was about twelve. I watched an elderly woman in the neighborhood making them. I watched her, and she said, 'Wouldn't you like to learn to do these too?' I said yes. She said, 'Well, it's a very simple procedure. I card the rolls myself with a pair of cards, then I pull it out very, very thin, you know, and long.' And she said, 'Fine. I'll give you a handful, a great handful, of the wool you put on the inside, and you try it yourself and see how you do.'

"I knit them for my father first, and he showed them around, and everyone seemed to want them."

Mrs. Mower soon thought of a way to simplify the process: "I'd watched this woman taking these pieces of wool and pulling them and knitting and stopping every little while to make a dozen or so rolls, and I thought, 'It's silly to stop and pull these apart when you can do the same thing with pencil roving.'"

Pencil roving is the carded fiber that forms the plies of machine spun yarns, a long strip of carded but unspun wool that is very thin and light. Some people spin it; others knit it without spinning. Some women who work at Briggs & Little in New Brunswick knit short bits of pencil roving into Newfoundland-style Fleece-Stuffed Mittens (described on p. 54).

Both women who showed me the double-rolled technique have used the over-and-under, weaving-in method that produces something of a thick lattice of unspun wool on the inside of the mitten and reverses the twist of fleece with every stitch. This reversal is visible on the outside as well if you look closely.

On Mrs. Brown's mittens in the Maine State Museum, however, the twists are all in the same direction, and the lining looks as if each loop between sts were *wrapped* with a twist of fleece. The twists of fleece lie close, side by side, each fitting neatly against the next and those above and below. To get this effect, you must throw the yarn with your right forefinger as you knit, flipping the fleece over the yarn after every stitch. You cannot use a continuous strand, as it would reverse twist hopelessly around the long end of the yarn; you must use a short bit, as Mrs. Brown must have, as Mrs. Moore said one must, and as Mrs. Mower's neighbor did.

My private theory is that the one-way twist with short bits of fleece is the ancestor of the other, and that when clever knitting methods—two-handed stranding and Continental left-handed knitting—came into vogue, not many knitters figured out how to adapt the old technique to their new way of knitting, and double-rolled knitting fell into disuse and nearly disappeared. A pity, as the mittens are soft and thick and strong.

When Mrs. Moore first told me about making these mittens, she said to use Size 1 or Size 0 needles, but I (1) disbelieved and (2) decided there were better things to do with my time than knitting mittens on Size 0 needles. I assumed that anything knit on such tiny needles must have a tension of about 11 (or more) sts to the inch, which in this case turned out to be a wrong assumption. In fact, the twist of fleece forces the sts apart slightly, so that one *must* use tiny needles to get even a fairly loose tension of, say, 6 sts to the inch.

There's no way to keep the fleece from showing through here and there on the outside, and in fact, this is part of the mitten's charm. The slightly raggy look is folksy, like gray ragg socks, and tells the world you know a better way of keeping warm.

The shag cuff is a touch hard to pass up. Easy to apply, it looks smashing, as well as old-fashioned in a very nice way, like the fur blankets in the film *Doctor Zhivago*.

Although Edna Mower knitted double-rolled mittens and socks until shortly before her death, Beulah Moore hadn't knit a pair in forty-one years when I met her. If you knit a pair, you will be helping to revive a nearly vanished craft, like making Clovis knife blades or writing in hieroglyphs. They are special.

Double-Rolled Mittens

Measurements—inches and *centimeters*

	Child Sizes				Adult Sizes				
	2–4	4–6	6–8	8–10	WS	WM	WL	MM	ML
Hand length	4½	5½	6	6½	6½	7	7½	7	7½
	11.5	*14*	*15.25*	*16.5*	*16.5*	*18*	*19*	*18*	*19*
Hand circumference, incl. tip of thumb	6	7	7¼	8	7½	9	9	9½	9½
	15.25	*18*	*18.5*	*20.25*	*19*	*23*	*23*	*24*	*24*
Mitten hand length	4¾	6	6½	7	7	7½	8	7½	8
	12	*15.25*	*16.5*	*18*	*18*	*19*	*20.25*	*19*	*20.25*
Mitten thumb (⅓ hand)	1⅝	2	2¼	2⅜	2⅜	2½	2⅝	2½	2⅝
	4.25	*5*	*5.75*	*6*	*6*	*6.5*	*6.75*	*6.5*	*6.75*
Mitten width	3	3½	3½	3¾	4½	4¾	4¾	4¾	4¾
	7.5	*9*	*9*	*9.5*	*11.5*	*12*	*12*	*12*	*12*

Materials

Knitting yarn. This mitten breaks my rule of using only wool yarns for mittens. Edna Mower knitted her mittens with synthetic yarn, which she felt was easier on the knitting hands than wool and lasted longer without wearing out or shrinking. She "double-rolled"—lined—her mittens with wool, the only fiber that came in contact with the skin. If you want to do this, go for it with my blessing. I use medium or DK weight wool yarns for this pattern.

Fiber for the lining. The lining is the most distinctive part of this mitten. Ideally, it should be wool or another animal fiber, for maximum warmth and water absorption. One can use loose fleece, lengths of split 1-inch roving, or pencil roving for the rolled lining. I confess that for my first double-rolled mitten, I had neither. Instead, I picked

apart Bartlettyarns Fisherman's Bulky, a heavy Lopi-type yarn, and recarded it, so that too is a possibility.

Mrs. Moore recommended loose fleece rather than unspun carded yarn or products like Icelandic Lopi yarn. This is only necessary if you are using the first method, flipping the fleece continually in the same direction around the yarn. As every action has an equal and opposite reaction, after a round of flipping, a long, fragile, unspun wisp of fleece will be thoroughly spun—around the working yarn. By using little bits of loose fleece, no more than 8" long, one can flip easier and the end will go along for the ride without ensnaring the working yarn.

To use washed, loose fleece right from the sheep, you will need hand carders, those 4-by-8-inch rectangular tools spinners use that look like giant cat combs. If you don't know a spinner or a place where you can buy carders, write or call Halcyon Yarn or another spinning tools supplier (see Sources, p. 215). Or, use two cat combs, available in the pet department of your supermarket.

Card a handful of fleece.

Follow the drawings: Card a handful of fleece until the fibers are lined up in the direction of the action. Then pick off a piece about a half inch (1.25cm) wide, pull it out about 8" (20cm) long and rub it briefly between your palms to make it long and rounded with the fibers still parallel. Make quite a few of these if you're taking your knitting with you somewhere.

Pick a strip about ½ inch (1 cm) wide off the hand carder.

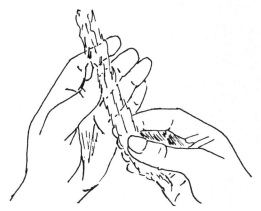

Pull it out smooth, about 8 inches (20cm) long.

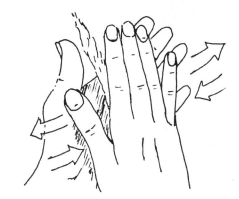

Roll it lightly between your hands.

They can be kept safely in a plastic bag and are easier to carry along than the carders.

To use roving instead of fleece. Roving is carded, unspun wool, ready to spin into yarn by machine or by hand. Pencil roving is about the diameter of a pencil, thus the name, and wound into big, flat, 4 oz or 100g wheels, sometimes called "cheeses" because of their shape. It is the raw material of machine-spun yarn and is generally available at spinning mills and sometimes at yarn shops (see Sources, p. 215).

One-inch (2.5cm) roving is wider than pencil roving and comes wound into huge balls for handspinners and felters. It is usually sold by the ounce at fine yarn stores (Sources, p. 215).

Because they are organized by winding, both types of roving are more convenient to deal with than loose fleece. If you blanch at buying 4 ounces or 100 grams of something you need only 20 grams of, consider that you can also use roving to make Stuffed Mittens (p. 54), you can spin it into yarn, or, lacking a spinning wheel, you can knit pairs of pencil rovings without further processing, and split and knit one-inch roving as well.

To prepare one-inch roving, break off a chunk about 3 inches (7.5cm) long. Split it lengthwise into 4 equal parts and stretch each to about 8 inches (20cm) long. Roll each briefly between your palms to make a long, round snake.

To prepare pencil roving. This can be used without further processing, in short lengths for the one-way wrapping method of double-rolled knitting, or in a continuous strand for the over-and-under method.

To line your mittens with other things. When you have gotten the hang of double-rolled knitting, it may occur to you, as it did to me, that you can attach almost anything to the back of your knitting with this technology, from dryer lint and dust balls from under the bed to yarn scraps, string, rabbit fur, milkweed silk, or musk ox wool. They will all show through on the front of your work and look intriguing. Play with it.

Yarn To knit a pair of mittens with medium weight wool yarn, you will need about:

		Child Sizes				Adult Sizes				
		2–4	4–6	6–8	8–10	WS	WM	WL	MM	ML
MC	(oz)	1½	1¾	2¼	2½	3	3½	3½	4	4
	(g)	40	50	60	70	80	100	100	110	110
CC [for shag on cuff]	(oz)	¼	¼	¼	¼	½	½	½	½	½
	(g)	4	5	6	7	8	10	10	11	11
Fleece or roving	(oz)	½	½	¾	¾	¾	1	1	1¼	1¼
	(g)	10	12.5	15	18	20	25	25	30	30

Equipment 1 set No. 2 (2.75mm, Can. Size 11) double-pointed needles, or size you need to knit in pattern at correct tension • 6" (15cm) length of contrasting waste yarn • blunt yarn needle • pencil or ballpoint pen as a spacer for the optional shag

Tension 5½ sts = 1" or 2.5cm

ABBREVIATIONS beg: beginning • CC: contrast color • dec(s): decrease(s) • inc(s): increase(s) • k: knit • k2tog: knit 2 together • M1: make 1 stitch • M1L: make 1 stitch left • M1R: make 1 stitch right • MC: main color • p: purl • rep: repeat • rnd(s): round(s) • SSK2tog: slip, slip, knit 2 sts together • st(s): stitch(es) • twisted M1: twisted make 1 cast-on

Pattern: Double-Rolling Your Knitting

The term *double-rolled knitting* probably comes from the fact that this technique creates a lined mitten that is doubly thick. The "rolled" part refers to the thin rolls of fleece, not to any rolling action of the knitting process itself.

The pattern comprises one st and the space between it and the next st. It's worked either by (1) flipping a thin, short roll of unspun fleece over the yarn between sts, always in the same direction so that, inside the mitten, the fleece appears to twine around the yarn; or (2) by knitting sts alternately over and under a strand of pencil roving or unspun fleece in every st in every rnd to create a soft lining that looks like a yarn latticework over a fleece background.

Because the fleece shows through as contrasting vertical stripes on the outside of the mitten, the Step-Down Increase (p. 21) is used to emphasize the vertical lines, making the actual stitches branch off from the base of the thumb gore in Ys.

To start each new bit of fleece or roving:

1. Lay the fleece across the yarn, close to the stitch just knitted, holding the long end down with the left index finger.

2. Knit around it, anchoring the fleece.

If you knit holding the yarn in your right hand, you're in luck. This is one of a few knitting techniques developed by right-hand knitters. Study the instructional drawings at right and you should do fine. The result will be the old-style, short-piece double-rolled knitting of Mrs. Brown's mittens, which twines consistently in the same direction.

If you would rather knit over and under, using a continuous strand, refer to the drawings on p. 41 instead.

If you knit the American way:

1. Flip the long end toward you, under the yarn, then over it and away. Hold it in place behind the work with the left index finger

2. Knit around the fleece.

3. Repeated with each stitch, this process produces a lining with this appearance, like the double rolled mittens made by Hattie Stover Brown, which are now at the Maine State Museum.

If you knit by picking the yarn off your left index finger, this pattern is possible but not easy. I haven't found any way to do double-rolled knitting quickly or easily while picking the yarn off my left index finger. Continental knitting seems designed to keep things from getting twisted. You must alternate going over and under the fleece, as shown below. This will not give the same density as Mrs. Brown's technique, but has the advantage of allowing you to use a continuous strand.

In stranding, anchor the end as in right-hand knitting, then carry the fleece on your left index finger, just as you would carry a CC strand ahead in color knitting, but never knit it! Carry the working yarn on your right index finger.

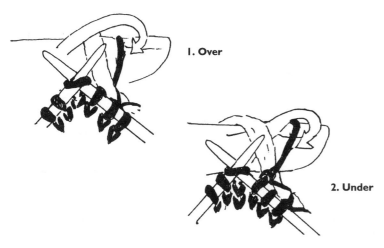

1. Over

2. Under

In left-hand (Continental) knitting, hold the yarn on tip of left index finger, the fleece closer to the knuckle. Knit one stitch as usual, and go under the fleece to pick up the next stitch.

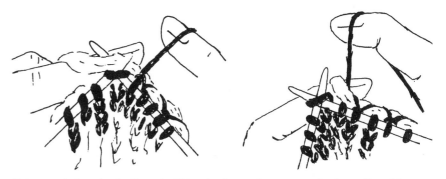

Knit one stitch *under* the fleece by lifting the fleece above one or both needles while knitting with the yarn as usual. Knit the next stitch *over* the fleece by lowering the fleece under the needle and knitting.

If you knit with both hands, *à la* Norwegian stranding, you will find the over-and-under method of double-rolled knitting quick and very easy. Follow the drawings at right.

You can use a continuous strand, but you needn't. You will not get the dense coverage of the first method, but you will still have a very warm, wonderful, lined mitten.

I have watched Edna Mower use the over-and-under technique and, with a quick movement of her left index finger, pinch little bunches or mini-loops of fleece against the fabric with every second stitch, probably on the knit-over-the-fleece step. I have yet to master that, but it thickens the lining considerably.

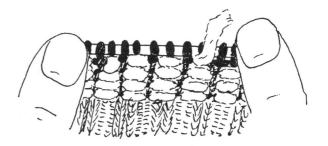

This is the look of over-and-under double-rolled knitting—not as closely covered as the old short-piece double-rolled knitting but still much warmer than ordinary mittens. Both Edna Mower and Beulah Moore used this technique.

Off the Cuff

Surprisingly, the shagged cuff is worked in ordinary k2, p1 ribbing. After the mitten is completed, the shag is applied to the two loops in the center of the knit ribs. The method is described at the end of the directions.

		Child				Adult				
		2–4	4–6	6–8	8–10	WS	WM	WL	MM	ML

Making the cuff

With a single strand of wool yarn, and using the Maine method (p. 13), cast on — 33 sts, 39 sts, 39 sts, 42 sts | 42 sts, 48 sts, 48 sts, 51 sts, 51 sts

Join, being careful not to twist sts around the needles. Distribute sts on 3 needles approximately equally with a multiple of 3 on each needle. This distribution means that each needle begins a new rib and makes ribbing easier.

Work k2, p1 ribbing in MC for (inches): $1\frac{5}{8}$, 2, $2\frac{1}{4}$, $2\frac{3}{8}$ | $2\frac{3}{8}$, $2\frac{1}{2}$, $2\frac{5}{8}$, $2\frac{1}{2}$, $2\frac{5}{8}$
(cm): 4.25, 5, 5.75, 6 | 6, 6.5, 6.75, 6.5, 6.75

Starting the pattern and thumb gore

Change to pattern stitch. Start thumb gore immediately:

Rnd 1, Needle 1: In pattern, k1, lay a piece of waste yarn before the next st as a marker, k1, inc by M1 (p. 20): 1 st, —, 1 st, 1 st | 1 st, 1 st, 1 st, —, —
then: k1, k2, k1, k1 | k1, k1, k1, k2, k2

Lay another piece of waste yarn as a marker before the next st. The base of the thumb gore is the 3 sts between waste yarn markers.

Continue in pattern to end of rnd, increasing by M1 at beg of Needle 2 (or 2 and 3): —, —, 1 st, 2 sts | —, 1 st, 1 st, 1 st, 1 st
Total: 34 sts, 39 sts, 41 sts, 45 sts | 43 sts, 50 sts, 50 sts, 52 sts, 52 sts

Rnd 2: K1, use Step-Down Increase (p. 21) in the next st, adding only 1 st; k1; work Step-Down Increase in next st (add only 1 st), continue in pattern to end of rnd.

		Child				Adult				
		2–4	4–6	6–8	8–10	WS	WM	WL	MM	ML
Rnd 3: Work even in pattern. You should now have 2 little Ys with the beginning of a fleecy vertical stripe between them.										
Rep Rnds 2 and 3, working Step-Down Incs in the outermost branch of the outermost Y on both sides of the thumb gore until there are on the thumb gore, including the outside branches.		7 sts	11 sts	11 sts	13 sts	13 sts	15 sts	15 sts	17 sts	17 sts
Work even until thumb gore measures	(inches)	1⅝	2	2¼	2⅜	2⅜	2½	2⅝	2½	2⅝
	(cm)	*4.25*	*5*	*5.75*	*6*	*6*	*6.5*	*6.75*	*6.5*	*6.75*

Taking off the thumb gore stitches

		Child				Adult				
Place of the thumb gore on a piece of waste yarn. Using twisted M1 (p. 23), cast on 3 sts over the gap.		7 sts	11 sts	11 sts	13 sts	13 sts	15 sts	15 sts	17 sts	17 sts
	Total:	33 sts	38 sts	40 sts	44 sts	42 sts	50 sts	50 sts	52 sts	52 sts
Work even until hand above cuff measures	(inches)	4	5	5½	6	5⅞	6¼	6¾	6¼	6¾
	(cm)	*10.25*	*12.75*	*14*	*15.25*	*15*	*16*	*17.25*	*16*	*17.25*

Closing the mitten tip

		Child				Adult				
Shift some sts from Needle 3 to Needle 1 so that the sts above the thumb gore are exactly centered on Needle 1. Now move sts to Needles 2 and 3 so that there are	Needle 1:	11 sts	12 sts	13 sts	14 sts	14 sts	16 sts	16 sts	17 sts	17 sts
	Needle 2:	11 sts	13 sts	13 sts	15 sts	14 sts	17 sts	17 sts	17 sts	17 sts
	Needle 3:	11 sts	13 sts	14 sts	15 sts	14 sts	17 sts	17 sts	18 sts	18 sts
Work in pattern to end of Needle 3.										
Rnd 1: Needle 1: K1, SSK2tog (p. 24), work in pattern to 2 sts from end of needle, k2tog. Needles 2 and 3: Rep Needle 1. This makes a 3-st-wide dec band at 3 points, placed so that the mitten will look balanced on either hand.										
Rnd 2: Work even on all needles.										
Work Rnds 1 and 2		2 X	2 X	2 X	2 X	3 X	3 X	3 X	3 X	3 X

	Child 2–4	4–6	6–8	8–10	Adult WS	WM	WL	MM	ML
Then work Rnd 1	1½X	2½X	3½X	4 X	3½X	4½X	4½X	5½X	5½X

On the half dec rnd, there will be 12 sts in 3 dec bands, each 3 sts wide, with only 1 st left to dec, except in Child's 8–10, which will have 15 sts. Work decs only at beg of each needle, except in Child's 8–10, where you work Rnd 1 as usual. 9 sts remain.

Check measurements against finished measurements at beg of directions. If you are satisfied, break fleece with a very short tail and push it into the hole at the tip of the mitten. Break yarn, leaving a 6" (15cm) tail.

With a yarn needle, thread end through remaining sts and draw up firmly. Thread end through drawn-up sts again, darn a few sts to secure it, and draw to inside of mitten.

Working the thumb

	2–4	4–6	6–8	8–10	WS	WM	WL	MM	ML
On Needles 1 and 2, pick up from waste yarn	7 sts	11 sts	11 sts	13 sts	13 sts	15 sts	15 sts	17 sts	17 sts

On Needle 3, pick up 3 sts from cast-on sts at top of thumb hole, and twist 1 st onto the needle from each side of thumb hole.   Total:

	2–4	4–6	6–8	8–10	WS	WM	WL	MM	ML
Total	12 sts	16 sts	16 sts	18 sts	18 sts	20 sts	20 sts	22 sts	22 sts

Join yarn by sewing (p. 20) into back of fabric starting at the right side of the thumb hole.

Working in pattern, k even until thumb measures	(inches)	1⅛	1⅞	2	2¼	2¼	2⅜	2½	2⅜	2½
	(cm)	3	4.75	5	5.75	5.75	6	6.5	6	6.5

Closing the thumb

Rnd 1: Needle 1: SSK2tog, work in pattern to 2 sts before end of needle, k2tog.
Needles 2 and 3: Rep Needle 1.

Rnd 2: Work even on all sts.

	Child				Adult				
	2–4	4–6	6–8	8–10	WS	WM	WL	MM	ML
Work Rnds 1 and 2 more.	1 X	1 X	1 X	2 X	2 X	2 X	2 X	2 X	2 X
Total:	6 sts	10 sts	10 sts	6 sts	6 sts	8 sts	8 sts	10 sts	10 sts

Break fleece, leaving almost no tail, and stuff end into thumb.
Break yarn with a tail about 6" (15cm) long. With yarn needle,
thread one end through the remaining sts and draw up firmly. Thread
end through drawn-up sts again, darn a few sts to secure it and draw
to inside of thumb.

Finishing the mitten

Turn mitten inside out and darn all ends into the back of the fabric.
Repair any holes at corners of the thumb hole with nearby tail. Trim
ends closely.

Make another identical mitten. These mittens fit either hand. When both
mittens are finished, work shag on the cuffs, if you wish (see p. 46).

Woolly Shag on the Cuff

Shag is applied to ordinary knitting by stitching it into the fabric in an overhand stitch around a spacer like a pencil or a knitting needle. The shag I've seen has not been knotted or even anchored by anything but the tension of the knitting and the spread of the cut ends of the yarn. It is an act of faith to cut such shag and expect it to stay in place, but neither of the examples I saw at the Maine State Museum had any bare patches, although one had been well used and the other was designed for work in the woods.

Sewing in Shag

Thread a yarn needle with a double strand of medium weight yarn—the same yarn you knitted with is fine. You will stitch along the center of a knit rib, through the two inward facing loops of two knit sts. (If you hold the mitten cuff down, these 2 loops appear as an inverted V in the middle of the rib.) This puts the short, stubby bits of shag in the position of least tension, so they're not pulled loose by stretching the cuff in ordinary use.

Lay a pencil or ballpoint pen along the rib and stitch over and over around it; going through 2 half-sts, one inverted V, each time. When you reach the base of the hand, stop, and remove the pencil. Don't clip the shag open until you've done all the knit ribs this way: the clipped ends tend to get caught in the working yarn.

Alternate MC and CC from rib to rib or make the bottom half one color and the top half another. If you want vertical stripes to come out even, there must be an even number of ribs. If there is not, start the al-

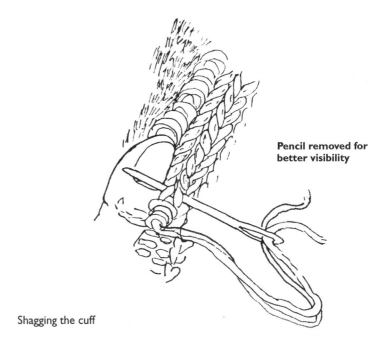

Pencil removed for better visibility

Shagging the cuff

ternation on the palm and work around. You will have two stripes the same color on the palm side of the wrist—making your folk mitten look even more old-timey. *Alternatively*, shag both knit sts of one rib only to make an even number of stripes.

When you're all finished, pull out the pencil for the last time, slip scissors through the lines of loops, and clip them open. They will fluff out to the sides to form a thick fur. Steam the cuff lightly over the nozzle of a boiling teapot or over a pan of boiling water to encourage the ends to fluff apart and fill the entire cuff area, then carefully shear any ends that stick out.

Mittens Hooked on a Dowel

I wanted to bring Maine folk mittens to the Washburn-Norlands Annual Heritage Days, to show them to people, but the person I called there told me it wasn't necessary. "We have our own kind of mittens up here—and a man who hooks them," she said.

Wild horses couldn't have kept me away.

He was in his seventies and sat at a card table, talking across a display of his mittens and a couple of those reels mounted with baby food jars that some people think are a convenient way to store nails or spices.

He was making a mitten, quickly, deftly, using a funny little hook that was sharp and flattened on the end but otherwise resembled a crochet hook. I watched. The mittens on the table were clearly synthetic ("Wool wears out too fast," he told me later, smiling. "This is warmer than wool."), but were they thick! and solid!

When he finished that mitten, the second, he opened a little notebook and wrote "257" under "256." It was his 257th pair that year, he said. It was June.

I asked him to show me how, but he said I needed a cuff first. He himself had a boxful of paired cuffs ready to work on, behind the table. I hurried back to my display to knit a cuff.

Albert Miller comes from central Maine and was for years a schoolteacher in one-room schoolhouses, accustomed to applying discipline firmly where it was needed. He learned to make "hooked" mittens from his mother, who brought the little-known technique with her when she emigrated from Poland. He'd been making them off and on as a hobby for 70 years, and until recently had kept the method a secret. In the last five or six years, however, he changed his mind and decided it would be better to teach people the technique—which he thought his mother had invented—in hopes that it would be carried on.

Albert had a set of instructions printed up and began making more hooks. He had more cuffs knitted by neighbor women. "You

Mitten hooked on a dowel by Albert Miller (back). Hooked mitten in two colors made by the author (front).

can't do this with a crochet hook," his son Lowell told me, and he's right. I've tried.

At one workshop at the Livermore Falls Senior Citizens Center, he expected two or three people to show up. No fewer than 63 men and women came to learn to make Albert's wonderful mittens, and Albert managed to teach them all. One man completed his first mitten before he left that evening.

For years, one could get a set of instructions and a handmade hook by sending him a dollar-fifty. "I have to charge that," he explained, "because it takes time to make them."

Albert Miller died in the winter of 1984–85, but Lowell, who can also hook mittens, though he is less busy at it, gave me permission to share the technique in this book. "He would have wanted it that way," Lowell assured me.

Mittens Hooked on a Dowel

Yarn Albert's mittens were worked in a sturdy, medium weight acrylic yarn, called "Knitting Worsted, 100% Virgin Acrylic," on the package. He vowed that wool neither held up as well nor was as warm. Although I don't agree with him about the warmth, there are many people in central Maine who wouldn't use anything but synthetic yarn for these mittens. It's up to you. I use Bartlettyarns Homespun, a medium weight wool yarn tending to heavy—about half again as thick as Albert's acrylic, but loftier.

For a pair you will need, MC (oz)   3   4   4   5   5
                              (g) 85.5 114   114 142.5 142.5

CC (for cuffs)   (oz)   ½   ¾   ¾   1   1
                      (g) 14.25 21.5 21.5 28.5 28.5

Equipment The dowel hook (see below) • 1 set Size 4 (3.5mm, Can. Size 9) double-pointed needles, or size you need to work k1, p1 ribbing at correct tension • blunt-tipped yarn needle • 1 medium size safety pin and 1 smaller (but not tiny) safety pin

Tension 6.5 sts = 1" or 2.5cm in k1, p1 ribbing
6 sts = 1" or 2.5 cm in slip-st crochet worked through the front of the st only

ABBREVIATIONS beg: beginning • CC: contrast color • dec(s): decrease(s) • inc(s): increase(s) • k: knit • k2tog: knit 2 together • M1: make 1 stitch • M1L: make 1 stitch left • M1R: make 1 stitch right • MC: main color • p: purl • rep: repeat • rnd(s): round(s) • SSK2tog: slip, slip, knit 2 sts together • st(s): stitch(es) • twisted M1: twisted make 1 cast-on

Measurements—inches and *centimeters*

		Child 8–10	WM	WL	MM	ML
				Adult		
Hand length	(inches)	6½	7	7½	7	7½
	(cm)	*16.5*	*18*	*19*	*18*	*19*
Hand circumference, incl. tip of thumb	(inches)	8	9	9	9½	9½
	(cm)	*20*	*23*	*23*	*24*	*24*
Mitten hand length	(inches)	7	7½	8	7½	8
	(cm)	*18*	*19*	*20*	*19*	*20*
Length of mitten thumb	(inches)	2⅜	2½	2⅝	2½	2⅝
	(cm)	*6*	*6.25*	*6.75*	*6.5*	*6.75*
Mitten width		4	4½	4½	4¾	4¾
		10.25	*11.5*	*11.5*	*12*	*12*

The sizes of Albert's mittens were less precise than those for the other mittens in this book. Roughly they were Small (about child size 8–10), Medium (woman's medium), and Large (about man's large). I have finessed them a little to bring them into line with the sizing in this book.

The Hook

The hook has been the problem with these mittens. Albert is gone, and two wooden knitting needle companies who offered to make the hooks have also expired. If you are interested in making these superior mittens, you will need the correct tool. As these hooks are no longer available (anywhere, apparently), put a dollar-fifty's worth of time in and make one yourself—or get someone else to make one for you.

Albert's hooks are made from birch dowels, ¼", ⁵⁄₁₆", or ⅜" in diameter (6, 8, or 9.5mm), cut in 5½" (14cm) lengths. This is filed or sanded to a 1¼"-long (3.25cm-long) flat taper on one end, with the taper on both sides. The point is sharp and very flat compared to a crochet hook (see top and side views in lower half of diagram below).

I found an alternative hook in Ingebjørg Gravjord's work on Norwegian mittens, *Votten i norsk tradisjon*. She gives bone or metal as the material of choice for the hook, including the handle of an old silver spoon. Because these materials are already quite flat, she makes no note of the need for flatness, but emphasizes the shape: the old Norwegian hooks are all long triangles, rounded at the back end and tapering to a narrow hook (top version in diagram below). The taper is to force the stitch apart horizontally, loosening up the very tight

mesh slightly. The flatness and the tinyness of the hook itself makes it possible to wiggle into a very tight spot—the front loop of a firm slip stitch. The Swedish name for this technique is *"pota,"* or *"to poke,"* which is what you will be doing.

Experiment with different crochet hooks to get an idea of the size you need before you start cutting up your grandmother's silver spoons. A tongue-depressor-sized piece of hardwood from the hobby store might substitute for bone or metal anyhow.

I find that making Albert's hooks is pleasant and goes quickly. If making your own hook seems too daunting, I will make you one. Ten dollars will cover shipping and my costs. (I'm not as dedicated as Albert.) Write me c/o this publisher, and be sure to tell me the size dowel you want—diameter ¼", ⁵⁄₁₆", or ⅜".

Make your own dowel hook. You will have a tool you will like a great deal because you made it yourself. Or, you may establish a new relationship with the person who agrees to do this for you. Study the drawing at left as you carve and abrade the material into shape.

To make one of Albert Miller's dowel hooks, you will need:

    a dowel, diameter ¼", ⁵⁄₁₆", or ⅜" (6, 8, or 9.5mm)
    ¼ sheet coarse sandpaper
    ¼ sheet medium grit sandpaper
    ¼ sheet fine grit sandpaper
    sharp knife
    medium-cut half-round wood file
    ruler
    pinch of solid wax (beeswax, Johnson's or Butcher's floor
        wax, or other)

I have found that sandpaper on a flat surface is the most easily controlled abrading tool for flat planes on small objects. If you are good at whittling or prefer to use a file, don't let me deter you.

1. Don't cut the dowel until you have a satisfactory tip. Place coarse sandpaper on a work surface and rub one side of the tip at an angle comparable to the point of a sharpened pencil until the wood is removed up to the center of the dowel. Repeat on the op-

Poking Hooks

Two styles of hook. *Top:* Made from flat piece of wood, bone, or metal. *Bottom:* Made from a dowel.

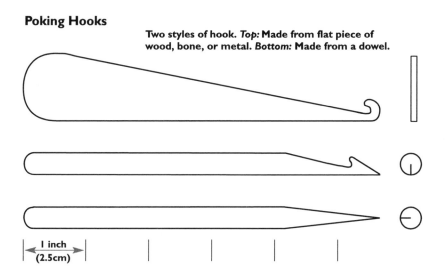

I inch
(2.5cm)

posite side, so that you have a fine, squared edge at the end of the dowel. Smooth with medium grit sandpaper.

2. Turn the dowel exactly 90 degrees and rub one of the edges at a slightly wider angle (about 45°) until you get a sharp point at the far edge of the dowel. Smooth with medium-grade sandpaper.

3. Now the cutting part: Lay the dowel with the last angle cut up. About ⅜" (9.6mm) from the point, use your well-sharpened knife to cut down toward the table, angling your cut *just slightly* toward the pointed end. (This is meant to be a *hook*.) Cut no more than halfway through the remaining wood.

4. *Carefully* and controlledly, cut or shave from the top of the 45° taper toward the cut, stopping in the nick of time at your cut. Cut only as deep as the bottom of the cut in Step 3. Use medium-grade sandpaper or a wood file to trim and slightly round the inside of the hook.

5. Saw or cut the dowel 5½" (14cm) from the point. Round the back end with coarse sandpaper or a wood file.

6. Smooth the entire surface with fine sandpaper, rounding sharp points just a little. Rub with a dab of wax. Nice, eh?

If you destroy the hook or the handle at any point, cut off the damaged part and start over. You should have plenty of length to work with.

(You can also use the sandpaper method to make your own knitting needles from dowels. Check the diameters on a knitting needle gauge. Wooden needles are ideal for teaching small children to knit.)

Pattern

Called Special Hooked Mittens by Albert Miller, these are known in rural Sweden as *potad* (poked) mittens, referring to the technique by which they are made. Everyone everywhere who makes them objects to their being called "crocheted mittens." This may be because they are much denser than most crocheted fabric, which one expects to be full of little holes. These mittens have no little holes anywhere and, done in steel wool, could probably repel machine gun bullets.

The mittens are worked in a crocheted (yes) slip-stitch through the front loop of each st in the preceding rnd. To make the work easy (or even possible), you must have the kind of sharp, flattened, and *tapered* needle that Albert Miller's mother used, and you must push the needle deeply into each new loop as it is formed. This push regulates the tension and makes a loop the needle can get into in the next rnd.

Because you work continually in the front loop of the sts, the fabric has an enormous penchant to curl outward, which you prevent by continuing doggedly upward, decreasing, and finally fastening the whole thing together at the tip. You will find that the finished mitten still wants to curl outward, and may have strange bends and leanings in the fabric. Forcing the fabric to vertical makes the mitten very dense, as rnd after rnd of the back side is pushed tight against the preceding rnd and the rnd above it.

To increase, slip st twice into the same loop of the preceding rnd.

To decrease, poke the needle through two sts from the preceding rnd, make a slip st, pulling it to the usual tension.

Design possibilities: Alternating colors in one- to three-rnd stripes creates an interesting effect. A textured design, even a motif, can be created by hooking into the back of single sts every second rnd or by hooking into the back of single rnds. This leaves the front loop on the outside surface. Both techniques are used in European *potning*.

Off the Cuff

The cuff is knitted on four needles in ordinary ribbing, then bound off. Albert had friends knit cuffs for him, as he was not interested in knitting.

Last aside: Albert Miller demonstrated his method of making mittens to many groups in his last years and sold hooks he made of birch dowels with a typewritten set of directions. These directions are reproduced here with only such additions as he made when teaching in person. I've added directions for a basic ribbed cuff; Albert's directions commence with the hand.

	Child 8–10	Adult WM	WL	MM	ML

Making the cuff

Using the Maine method (p. 13), cast on	38 sts	40 sts	40 sts	42 sts	42 sts

Join, being careful not to twist sts. Distribute sts among 3 double-pointed needles. K1, p1 for 3" (7.5cm). Bind off loosely in ribbing.

Starting the pattern and the thumb gore

Place the larger safety pin vertically through the sts in the cuff directly above the beg of the rnd. Place the smaller safety pin vertically into the ribbing exactly opposite the beg of the rnd. These are the inc and dec points.

Right mitten

Hook 2 rnds, hooking into every st of the cuff in the first rnd.

Rnds 3, 5, 7, and 9: Inc. Add a st above each marker, while hooking in pattern.

Rnds 4, 6, 8, and 10: Work even. (If you have trouble counting rnds on the outside, look on the inside, where they are quite apparent.)

Work even until thumb gore measures (inches)	2⅜	2½	2⅝	2½	2⅝
(cm)	*6*	*6.25*	*6.75*	*6.25*	*6.75*

A little too much is better than a little too little if you are working with wool.

Taking off the thumb gore stitches

Beginning at the smaller safety pin, hook through both front and back of the next st, then crochet a chain of	6 sts	8 sts	8 sts	10 sts	10 sts

Fasten this down 8 sts from the small safety pin by hooking into *both front and back* of the 9th st. This forms a slot for the thumb.
Hook around as usual. Remove the small safety pin.

		Child 8–10	Adult			
			WM	WL	MM	ML

Working the hand

Hook 7 rnds even. On the 8th rnd, dec 1 st at the safety pin. This and the following decs will make the mitten curve in on the little-finger side, just as your hand does.

Hook 6 rnds and dec 1 st at the marker. Hook 5 rnds and dec 1 st at the marker. In the next 6 rnds, dec 1 st every other rnd.

Closing the mitten tip

		Child 8–10	WM	WL	MM	ML
The mitten should reach to the end of the index finger before the final dec. This is roughly	(inches)	6½	7	7½	7	7½
	(cm)	*16.5*	*18*	*19*	*18*	*19*

If the mitten is already longer than the end of the index finger (or longer than the measurements for your size), pull it out to that point and continue from there.

	Child 8–10	WM	WL	MM	ML
Rnd 1: General dec. *Dec 1, hook and rep from * to end of rnd.	5 sts	6 sts	6 sts	7 sts	7 sts
Rnd 2: General dec. *Dec 1, hook and rep from * to end of rnd.	4 sts	5 sts	5 sts	6 sts	6 sts
Rnd 3: *Dec 1, hook and rep from * to end of rnd.	3 sts	4 sts	4 sts	5 sts	5 sts

Continue to reduce the number of sts between decs by 1 st in every rnd until you are decreasing in every st.

When only 7 or 8 sts remain, break the yarn, pull the tail through the last st and thread it onto a yarn needle. Catch up all the remaining sts on the tail and pull them up firmly. Pull the tail to the inside of the mitten.

Working the thumb

	Child 8–10	WM	WL	MM	ML
Pick up 5 more sts than double your chain. That will be	17 sts	21 sts	21 sts	25 sts	25 sts

adding 3 of these on the palm side of the thumb hole and 1 on each of
the outside corners of the thumb hole. (Albert thought that mittens with
even a tiny hole on the palm side of the thumb were no good. In general,
he had no use for any of my mittens because of this and because they
were made of wool!)

Closing the tip of the thumb

Hook 3 rnds with the same number of sts, then dec 1 st on the palm side in
the 4th and 5th rnds.

		Child 8–10	WM	WL	MM	ML
				Adult		
Continue even to the end of the thumb, roughly	(inches)	1⅛	2⅜	2½	2⅜	2½
	(cm)	2.75	6	6.5	6	6.5

Dec every other st for 2 rnds. Dec every st for one rnd.

Break yarn, thread it through the last st, then onto a yarn needle. Pick up the
remaining sts and draw them up firmly. Draw the tail to the inside.

Finishing the mitten

Turn the mitten inside out, and work all tails into the fabric. Trim closely.

Left mitten

Follow directions for the right mitten, but place the thumb hole on
the last 8 sts *before* the small safety pin.

Fleece-Stuffed Mittens

Fleece-Stuffed Mittens, also called thrummed (or drummed) mittens, come from Labrador and northern Newfoundland, but they belong to the same tradition as Maine Fishermen's Wet Mittens. They are often knit large and shrunk to size, and they appear to be made according to the same set of directions, except that twists of unspun fleece are knit into the fabric every few stitches every few rounds in a distinct pattern. The ends of the bits of fleece, fluffing to the inside, are thick and woolly and mat into an almost continuous lining with wear, imitating the lining formed by fur on the inside of skin mittens.

They are beautiful mittens. Like Fishermen's Wet Mittens, they are knit of oily natural yarn, often in natural sheep's colors. In dark brown and white fleece, they seem to show large flakes of snow falling softly against the night.

The pattern is no newcomer in Canada. Hazel McNeill, of Belleville, Ontario, wrote me that her mother and grandmother knit these mittens for their men, who used them both as a general outdoor mitten for dogsled travel and as a wet mitten for hauling nets in winter. She dates the pattern tentatively to the early 1800s.

In the areas where these mittens are used, icebergs float in the sea in August, and fishermen use a light wet mitten through the summer. Stuffed mittens are a logical extension of the wet-mitten concept.

The word *thrummed*, or *drummed*, refers to the warp ends left over on the loom after a piece of weaving is completed—thrums. (Newfoundland dialect often pronounces *th* as *d*.) These may have once been knitted into mittens and hats as additional insulation. *Them Days*, an interview magazine about Labrador's past, speaks of stuffed or "thrummed mitts" as children's mittens.

In North America today, only fleece or rovings are used in these mittens. In Sweden they are stuffed with short loops of heavy yarn, wrapped around the finger and locked around the stitch (*100 Landskapsvottar*, Stockholm, 1982). They're called "mittens with batting" in Sweden, indicating that they too were once stuffed with fleece.

Two kinds of Fleece-stuffed Mittens

Fleece-Stuffed Mittens have only a tenuous place in Maine folk knitting. In 1980, I had heard of only one Maine woman who knitted them. I had never met her or learned her name, and she was unwilling to discuss the mittens with my informant (Pat Zamore, in Brunswick), other than to say that they had come down in her family. She did, however, make me a pair, and they are the basis of this pattern.

Since I first learned of stuffed mittens, I've found that northern knitters seem to like them and like to knit them. Sheep farmers appreciate them as a use for unspun fleece—always in excess on sheep farms. And everyone seems to have a way to make them better. These directions pass on techniques I learned from Judith McGrath in Happy Valley, Labrador, and are the original directions presented in *Fox & Geese & Fences* (Down East Books, 1983).

Like other mittens in this book, Fleece-Stuffed Mittens call for techniques you may find nowhere else in the world. Read all the directions carefully and study the pictures. Stuffed mittens aren't hard to knit once you've made the first pair—a little tedious, perhaps, but not difficult.

Fleece-Stuffed Mittens

Yarn Bartlettyarns 2-ply Fisherman Yarn or other medium weight natural wool yarn • loose fleece, pencil rovings, or 1-inch rovings

For a pair, you will need yarn,

(oz)	3	4	5	6
(g)	*85.75*	*114*	*142.5*	*171*

stuffing, about

(oz)	½	¾	1	1¼
(g)	*14.3*	*21.5*	*29*	*36*

Equipment 1 set Size 5 (3.75mm, Can. Size 9) double-pointed needles, or size you need to knit stockinette at the correct tension • 1 set Size 3 (3.25mm, Can. Size 10) double-pointed needles for ribbed cuff • 6" (15cm) length of contrasting waste yarn • Blunt-tipped yarn needle

Tension 4½ sts = 1" (2.5cm) measured across rnd with fleece

ABBREVIATIONS beg: beginning • CC: contrast color • dec(s): decrease(s) • inc(s): increase(s) • k: knit • k2tog: knit 2 together • M1: make 1 stitch • M1L: make 1 stitch left • M1R: make 1 stitch right • MC: main color • p: purl • rep: repeat • rnd(s): round(s) • SSK2tog: slip, slip, knit 2 sts together • st(s): stitch(es) • twisted M1: twisted make 1 cast-on

Measurements—inches and *centimeters*

	Child 6–8	Adult S	Adult M	Adult L
Hand length	6 *15.25*	6½ *16.5*	7 *18*	7½ *19*
Hand circumference, incl. tip of thumb	7 *18*	8 *20.25*	9 *23*	10 *25.5*
Mitten hand length*	6¾ *17.25*	7¼ *18.5*	7¾ *19.75*	8¼ *21*
Mitten thumb (⅓ hand)	2¼ *5.75*	2½ *6.5*	2⅝ *6.75*	2¾ *7*
Mitten width*	3¾ *9.5*	4¼ *10.75*	4½ *11.5*	5¼ *13.25*

**These measurements allow an additional quarter inch (6mm) in length and an additional half-inch (1.3cm) in circumference to accommodate the stuffing.*

Pattern

A folded bit of fleece is knit into the fabric along with the yarn in a regular pattern. Fleece sts can be arranged to form vertical lines (on the left in the photograph opposite) or short or long diamonds (on right in photograph). The Long Diamonds pattern was taken from a mitten knitted by an unidentified knitter in Kennebunk, Maine, which has a warmer climate than Newfoundland, where a closer stuffing pattern is used.

Note: When stuffing mittens for children, particularly when stuffing the thumb, be careful not to make the stuffing so big that there is no room inside for the child's hand. After the mitten is completed, force your fingers into the mitten and the thumb and mash down the fleece to make room for the child's hand. Warmth, not gangrene, is the goal.

To prepare the bits of stuffing from 1-inch roving, follow the photo sequence at right.

To work with sheep's fleece, which can be used "in the grease" (unwashed) or washed, card a small handful and lift half-inch-wide (1.25cm) lengthwise strips off the carder. Fluff, roll, and fold, as in the photo sequence.

To prepare pencil roving, cut 3" (7.5cm) lengths. Use in pairs, with the ends loose.

Make enough bits of stuffing for at least one rnd—6 to 8, depending on the size mitten you're making—and store them in a plastic sandwich bag to keep them neat if you're taking them with you somewhere.

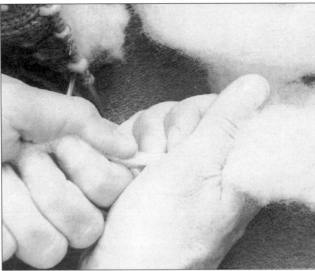

1. Pull off a 5-inch (12.75cm) length of 1-inch (2.5cm) roving.

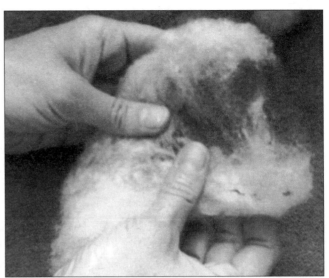

2. Split this in half lengthwise, then split the halves in half.

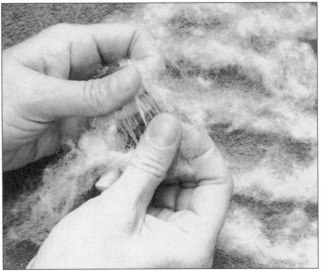

3. Finally, split the quarters in half lengthwise, ending with 8 very wispy 5- to 6-inch (12.75 to 15.25cm)-long pieces.

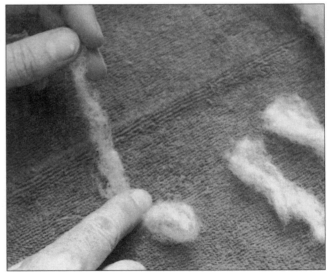

4. Roll each piece slightly between the palms, then fold the ends over the center. Give each piece a little twist in the middle.

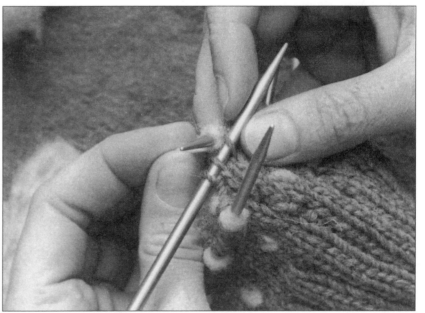

Knitting in the Fleece: Stuffing

Two methods of knitting in the bits of fleece are used in Maine and Newfoundland/Labrador. The first method (bottom photo in left column) produces a little blob of fleece on the outside of the mitten. The second method (photo below) produces a little heart-shaped fleece stitch on the outside of the mitten. There is no danger of the fleece bits falling out.

Wrap twisted bit of fleece over index finger with ends down.

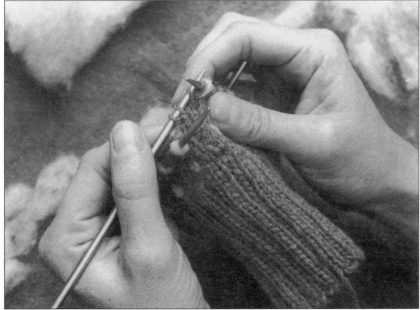

To produce a little fleece blob on the knit side: Insert right needle into next stitch. Lay the twisted bit of fleece over the right needle with ends to the inside of the mitten, then wrap yarn as usual, knitting both fleece and yarn in the same stitch.

To produce a little fleecy heart on the knit side: Insert the right needle into the next stitch. Lay the twisted bit of fleece over the right needle with ends to the inside of the mitten. Knit the fleece as if it were the working yarn. Knit the *next* stitch with yarn, bringing the yarn behind the fleece stitch to lock it in. In the next round, work both fleece sts and yarn sts with yarn. At the end of the round, go back and give each fleece stitch a little downward tug by its beard to settle it in place.

Making the cuff

With smaller needles, and using the Maine method (p. 13), cast on

Distribute on 3 needles, each needle starting a new k rib.
Join into a triangle, being careful not to twist sts around the needles.
Work k2, p1 ribbing for   (inches)
                                                              (cm)

	Child 6–8	Adult S	Adult M	Adult L
cast on	33 sts	39 sts	42 sts	48 sts
Work k2, p1 ribbing for (inches)	2¼	2½	2⅝	2¾
(cm)	5.75	6.5	6.75	7

Starting the hand and thumb gore

Rnd 1: Change to larger needles and shift the last p st from Needle 3 to Needle 1. Slip it to the right needle, then k3, p1. Work in stockinette to end of rnd. The area marked off with p sts is the base of the thumb gore. The p sts should line up with p sts from the cuff. Maintain them as marking sts to the top of the thumb gore.

Rnd 2: Begin pattern by inserting fleece in the middle st of the thumb gore. Follow the chart with your choice of stuffing patterns. All those shown are a 6-st rep. If you don't have a multiple of 6 sts on your needles (the two smaller sizes), make the adjustment on the palm, placing more fleece there.

Stuffing patterns for Fleece-Stuffed Mittens

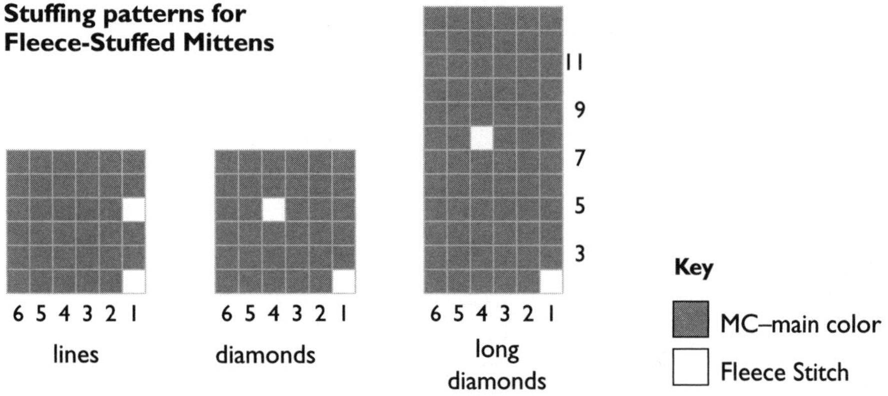

6 5 4 3 2 1
lines

6 5 4 3 2 1
diamonds

11
9
7
5
3
6 5 4 3 2 1
long
diamonds

Key

MC–main color

Fleece Stitch

	Child 6–8	Adult S	Adult M	Adult L

Be sure there is fleece covering every square inch of the inside, especially the tips of the fingers and thumb. This will mean inserting fleece along lines of dec and other unlikely places.

Rnd 3: Inc: P1, M1L (p. 20), k to p st, M1R, p1; work to end of rnd (in pattern).

Rnd 4: In pattern, p1, k to p st, p 1, k even to end of rnd.

Rep Rnds 3 and 4		3 X	4 X	4 X	6 X
Total between p sts:		9 sts	11 sts	11 sts	15 sts

Work even, maintaining p sts, until thumb gore measures	(inches)	2¼	2½	2⅝	2¾
	(cm)	5.75	6.25	6.75	7

Taking off the thumb gore stitches

Place all sts between (but not including) the p sts onto waste yarn. Using twisted M1 (p. 23), cast on 3 sts over the gap. Discontinue the p marking sts (k them) and work even until hand above cuff measures	(inches)	5¼	5½	5¾	6¼
	(cm)	13.25	14	14.5	16

Stop halfway through Needle 2 to set up the dec.

Closing the mitten tip

Lay the mitten flat with the thumb gore sticking out to one side. The first 3 sts of Needle 1 will be the 3 sts directly above the thumb gore. You will dec on both sides of these 3 sts. Slip the first st onto Needle 3.

Now find the 3 sts exactly opposite these 3 sts on the little-finger side. Place a piece of waste yarn between Sts 1 and 2 of these 3 sts. Lay it back and forth every couple of rnds to mark the second dec band.

	Child 6–8	Adult S	Adult M	Adult L
Rnd 1: Dec (always in pattern): K2, SSK2tog. Work to end of needle. Work Needle 2 to waste yarn marker, K2tog, k2, SSK2tog, work to end of needle. Work Needle 3 up to 2nd to last st. K2tog.				
Rnd 2: Work even in pattern.				
Rep Rnds 1 and 2 until there are End after Rnd 2.	13 sts	15 sts	18 sts	16 sts

Bind off all sts. Break yarn with an 18" (46cm) tail. Place all sts on two needles, one holding all the palm sts, one holding all the back sts. With a yarn needle, weave tail back and forth between the front and back to simulate a row of stockinette knitting (Kitchener stitch), removing sts from needles as necessary. Draw tail to the inside.

Picking up the thumb stitches

		Child 6–8	Adult S	Adult M	Adult L
Needles 1 and 2: Pick up from waste yarn		9 sts	11 sts	11 sts	15 sts
Needle 3: Pick up and twist 1 st onto needle from each corner of thumb hole. Pick up 3 sts above thumb hole.	Total:	14 sts	16 sts	16 sts	20 sts
Join yarn by sewing (p. 20) into back of fabric, starting at the right side of the thumb hole. Work even in pattern until thumb measures	(inches)	1¾	2	2⅛	2¼
	(cm)	4.5	5	5.5	5.75
Dec sharply (never forgetting to stuff, of course):					
Rnd 1: K2tog, k2 on all needles.	Total:	10 sts	12 sts	12 sts	15 sts
Rnd 2: K2tog, k1 on all needles.	Total:	7 sts	8 sts	8 sts	10 sts
Rep Rnd 2		—	—	—	once
	Total:	7 sts	8 sts	8 sts	7 sts

Break yarn leaving a 6" (15cm) tail. With yarn needle, thread end through the remaining sts and draw up firmly. Thread end through drawn-up sts again, darn a few sts to secure it, and draw to inside of thumb.

Finishing the mitten

	Child 6–8		Adult S	Adult M	Adult L

Turn mitten inside out, and darn all ends (except cast-on tail) into the back of the fabric. Repair any holes at base of thumb with nearby tails. Trim ends closely.

While mitten is inside out, work the stuffed bits a little to fluff them to the sides, spreading them to cover any empty spaces. They will mat further in use.

Using the cast-on tail, crochet a loop on edge of cuff for hanging the mitten up to dry. Or, work a loop on one cuff and sew a button or a wooden toggle to the second mitten cuff.

Make another identical mitten. This mitten can be worn on either hand.

Shag on the Inside: A Mystery Mitten from Massachusetts

Erin Pender, of Hampton, New Hampshire, wrote me about these special mittens in response to my request for information about fleece mittens in an article in *Down East* magazine. "I know what fleece mittens are," she wrote. "These mittens were in Lowell, Mass., the winter of '54 or '55. I had borrowed them from a playmate for the afternoon. They were the warmest mittens I've ever worn, before or since. They were multicolored, as if the knitter had snippets of various colors of worsted weight yarn such as are used for markers, and had knitted them in with the mitten so that the tails were inside to create a warm 'fleece.'"

Erin checked back with her now grown-up playmate and her friend's mother, but the mother didn't remember the mittens, and the friend didn't know where the mittens had come from, whether from a local person or from someone of recent European extraction, only that her mother had given them to her. Mittens matching this description, but with loops rather than ends inside, are knitted in Sweden (*100 Landskapsvottar*, 1982) and in the Baltic countries, perhaps Latvia (Leszner, *Vottar från När och Fjärran*, 1982).

I made a mitten based on Erin's description, but like the European women, I didn't dare cut the loops to make an inside shag. And surprisingly, it didn't matter, because the loops don't catch fingers after all. Just don't try to pull on the mittens over a ring with a fancy setting.

I took my inside-shag mitten to Erin Pender, whom I arranged to meet at the Portsmouth Circle Howard Johnson's. Over coffee, I proudly whipped out my mitten. She shook her head. "Mm, no," she said. "It didn't look like that at all." There were no bumps on the outside of the mitten she remembered, and the shag on the inside hadn't shown through to the outside at all. The mitten itself was multicolored, perhaps of ombre yarn, with cut snippets rather than loops. She also thought the snippets might have been knotted in.

So there you have it. With a firm basis in European tradition but little more than a rumor to support it in this country, this pair of mittens is at best marginally a New England folk mitten. But—it's warm and squashy and funny looking, and it uses up scraps. Maybe it will become a folk mitten.

A mitten shagged on the inside, based on a description by Erin Pender and comparison with similar European mittens.

Shag on the Inside: A Mystery Mitten from Massachusetts

Yarn 3–6 ounces (85.5–171g) medium-weight wool yarn. About 2 ounces (57g) vari-colored wool scraps, each at least 4 inches long. For the mitten shown, size Adult Medium, I used Bartlettyarns 2-ply Fisherman Yarn and scraps of Persian wool crewel embroidery yarn that had been sitting around for years waiting for my interest in embroidery to revive. Of course, I ran out of real scraps and had to go buy more. You needn't be so lavish unless you want to be. This pattern was probably designed to use up scraps thriftily.

Equipment 1 set Size 4 (3.5mm, Can. Size 9) double-pointed knitting needles, or size you need to knit at the correct tension

- Blunt-pointed yarn needle

Tension 4½ sts = 1" (2.5cm), measured in the round with shag

ABBREVIATIONS beg: beginning • CC: contrast color • dec(s): decrease(s) • inc(s): increase(s) • k: knit • k2tog: knit 2 together • M1: make 1 stitch • M1L: make 1 stitch left • M1R: make 1 stitch right • MC: main color • p: purl • rep: repeat • rnd(s): round(s) • SSK2tog: slip, slip, knit 2 sts together • st(s): stitch(es) • twisted M1: twisted make 1 cast-on

Measurements—inches and *centimeters*

	Child Sizes		Adult Sizes		
	2–4	6–8	S	M	L
Length of hand	4½ *11.5*	6 *15.25*	6½ *16.5*	7 *18*	7½ *19*
Hand circumference, incl. tip of thumb	6 *15.25*	7¼ *18.5*	7½ *19*	9 *23*	9½ *24.25*
Length of mitten hand	4¾ *12*	6½ *16.5*	7 *18*	7½ *19*	8 *20.25*
Mitten thumb (⅓ hand length)	1⅝ *4.25*	2⅛ *5.5*	2⅜ *6*	2½ *6.5*	2⅜ *6*
Mitten width* a little more than	3 *7.5*	3⅝ *9.25*	4 *10.25*	4½ *11.5*	4¾ *12*

**These sizes allow extra room inside to accommodate the yarn loops.*

Pattern

A multiple of 2 sts and 2 rnds. The scraps are knit in every second st of every second rnd. Because I had no access to the person who made the original mittens (or even to the mittens themselves), I experimented and came up with this.

1. Knit 1 rnd in stockinette, working the thumb gore sts according to the directions.

In the second rnd, k 1 st, then join the scrap yarn (2 strands of medium weight yarn or 4 of finer yarns). Insert the right needle into the next st. Hold the end of the scrap yarn against the back of the knit with the third finger of the left hand, leaving a 1- to 2-inch tail pointing down.

Do this each time you start a new scrap.

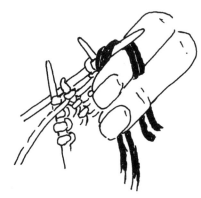

2. To work a shag stitch, wrap the long end of the scrap yarn around the left index finger and over the needle as if to knit. Hold the long end out of the way behind the knit with the left index finger. This will form the loop.

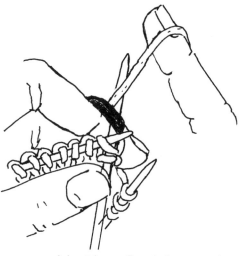

3. Wrap the knitting yarn around the right needle only (not around your finger).

4. Knit both together. Remove the left index finger from its loop and work one more plain knit stitch.

Note: Do not work a shag st in the line of p marking sts. Instead, when entering the thumb gore, catch up the strand of scrap yarn by knitting under it the st before the first p st, then purling over it. Leaving the thumb gore, p over the scrap yarn strand, then k the next st under it, unless the next st is a shag st. If it is, don't worry about catching it up near the p st.

Off the Cuff

The cuffs are k2, p1 ribbing. You may wish to add stripes if your yarn scraps blend with the mitten color, but otherwise, stripes may make the mitten look too busy.

Making the cuff

		Child		Adult		
		2–4	6–8	S	M	L
Using the Maine method (p. 13), cast on		30 sts	33 sts	36 sts	39 sts	45 sts
Distribute sts on 3 needles:	Needle 1:	9 sts	12 sts	12 sts	15 sts	15 sts
	Needle 2:	12 sts	12 sts	15 sts	15 sts	18 sts
	Needle 3:	9 sts	12 sts	12 sts	15 sts	18 sts

This distribution has each needle begin a new k rib so that you can rib without too much difficulty in the car at night or in the movie theater.

Join into a triangle, being careful not to twist sts around the needles.

		Child		Adult		
Work k2, p1 ribbing for	(inches)	2"	2½"	3"	3"	3"
	(cm)	*5*	*6.5*	*7.5*	*7.5*	*7.5.*

Starting the pattern and thumb gore

When working this pattern, a 2-st, 4-rnd rep, you will need an even number of sts *only above* the thumb hole, where the pattern wraps around the hand. Follow the thumb gore chart to shag the thumb gore effectively and don't worry about making the pattern continuous from the hand to the thumb gore.

Shag Pattern

Shag Thumb

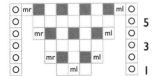

Key

☐ MC–main color

■ Shag Stitch

Ⓞ purl

ml make 1 left

mr make 1 right

		Child		Adult		
		2–4	6–8	S	M	L

Rnd 1: On Needle 1, start thumb gore and charted pattern (Line 1 is plain stockinette.). P1, k3, p1. Maintain the 2 p sts to the top of the thumb gore as markers. Work to end of needle in pattern.

Needle 2: Work in pattern increasing by M1 (p. 20) evenly spaced	2 sts	1 st	2 sts	3 sts	1 st
Needle 3: Work to end of needle in pattern. **Total:**	32 sts	34 sts	38 sts	42 sts	46 sts

Rnd 2: Work Line 2 of pattern and inc for thumb gore: P1, M1L, k in pattern up to p st, M1R, p1. Work to end of rnd in pattern.

Check after the first shag rnd that the rep comes out even. A mistake here can throw everything else off and take the fun out of the project.

Rnd 3: Work even in pattern, maintaining p marking sts.

Rep Rnds 2 and 3 until there are between (but not including) the 2 p sts.	9 sts	11 sts	11 sts	13 sts	13 sts

Work even until thumb gore measures (inches)	1⅝	2⅛	2⅜	2½	2⅜
(cm)	4	5.5	6	6.5	6

Taking off the thumb gore stitches

Complete Line 1 or Line 3 of the chart. Place all the thumb gore sts between (but not including) the marking lines onto waste yarn.

Using twisted M1 (p. 23), cast on 3 sts in pattern over the gap. **Total:**	32 sts	34 sts	38 sts	42 sts	46 sts

Discontinue p marking sts (k them) and work even in pattern until work above the cuff measures (inches)	3½	4¾	4¾	6	6½
(cm)	9	12	12	15.25	16.5

	Child		Adult		
	2–4	6–8	S	M	L

Closing the mitten tip

The first 3 sts on Needle 1, directly above the 3 sts bridging the thumb hole, will form a dec band. The first and last sts of the band are actually part of the dec. Set up the dec by moving the first st on Needle 1 to become the last st on Needle 3.

Set up another 3-st dec band on Needle 2, directly opposite the first one. Mark the dec band on Needle 2 by laying a piece of (clearly different) waste yarn between the first and 2nd st of these 3 sts.

Rnd 1: Dec, maintaining pattern:
    Needle 1: K1, SSK2tog (p. 24), work to end of needle.
    Needle 2: Work to 2 sts before marker, k2tog, k1, SSK2tog,
       work to end of needle.
    Needle 3: Work even to 2 sts before end of needle, k2 tog.

Rnd 2: Work even.

Rep Rnds 1 and 2					
	4 X	4 X	5 X	6 X	7 X
Total remaining:	16 sts	18 sts	18 sts	18 sts	18 sts

End with Line 1 of chart.

Divide the sts between 2 needles, with all the palm sts on one needle and all the back sts on the other. Graft the two sides together, sewing from front to back with a yarn needle in imitation of a row of stockinette stitch (Kitchener stitch).

Making the thumb

Join yarn by sewing (p. 20) into back of fabric starting at the right side of the thumb hole.

Pick up from waste yarn	9 sts	11 sts	11 sts	13 sts	13 sts

Pick up 3 sts above thumb hole, and 1 st from each corner.

Total:	14 sts	16 sts	16 sts	18 sts	18 sts

		Child		Adult		
		2–4	6–8	S	M	L
Work even in pattern for	(inches)	1¼	1½	1⅝	1⅝	1¾
	(cm)	*3.25*	*3.75*	*4.25*	*4.25*	*4.5*

End with Line 2 of chart.

Closing the tip of the thumb

	2–4	6–8	S	M	L
Dec sharply. K2tog, k1 in MC on all 3 needles until there remain	9 sts	11 sts	11 sts	9 sts	9 sts

Break yarn, leaving a 6" (15cm) tail. Cut off looped yarn with a
tail about 2" (5cm) long and stuff it inside mitten. Thread end through
drawn-up sts again, darn a few sts to secure it, and draw to inside of
thumb.

Finishing the mitten

Turn mitten inside out and darn all ends into the back of the fabric.
Repair possible holes at corners of the thumb hole with nearby tails.
Trim ends closely. Snip any longish ends of the shag to about 1" (2.5cm).

Make another identical mitten. This mitten can be worn on either hand.

Two Kinds of Wristers

At one time most Maine mittens were knit without ribbed cuffs, or without any attached cuff at all. The cuff was separate, a wrister, and stayed on even when a man had to take off his mittens in the woods to do a fine adjustment on a bit of harness or a tool.

Wristers are cuffs without mittens, usually about 5 inches (12.75cm) long, extending in under the sleeve and out under the mitten. Sometimes a little loop secures them to the crotch of the thumb.

Wristers have also been called "pulse warmers," "half-mitts," "half-handers," and "fingerless gloves," which pretty much sums up their function and shape.

Wristers are still used by Maine coastal fishermen. Even fishermen who have gone over to insulated rubber gloves often still use wristers underneath to protect their wrists from chafing by the edges of their frozen oilskin jackets. Laura Ridgewell, wife of West Point fisherman Bob Ridgewell, says that wristers prevent "pin boils" on the wrists.

Wristers are useful under loose, cuffless mittens for any outdoor occupation requiring occasional fine work—delivering mail or newspapers, working on cars, horseback riding—or as an indoor glove—working (typing, playing the piano) in a chilly home or workplace.

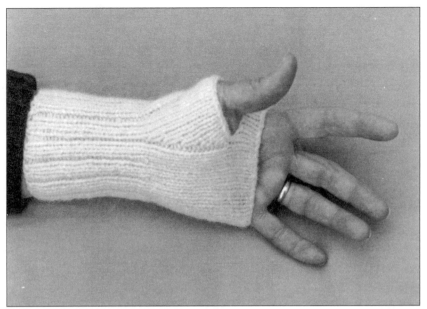

One style of wrister

Laura Ridgewell's Wristers

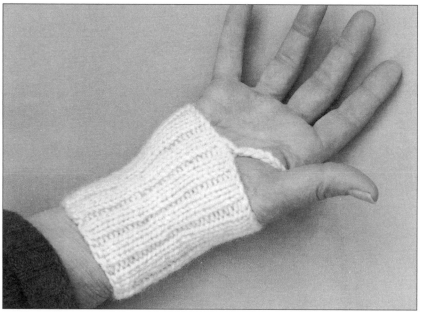

Laura Ridgewell's wristers

Yarn Laura knits her wristers of Bartlettyarns 3-ply Fisherman Yarn, a naturally oily cream-colored yarn. The sample here was made of Halcyon Yarns Deco, which is less oily and has a longer staple than Fisherman Yarn.

For each pair you will need	(oz)	1¾	2	2	2¼
	(g)	50	57	57	65

Equipment 1 set Size 4 (3.5mm, Can. Size 9) double-pointed knitting needles, or size you need to knit in stockinette at correct tension • Size F (4mm, Can. Size 8) crochet hook • Blunt-tipped yarn needle

Tension 6 sts = 1 inch (2.5cm) in k2, p1 ribbing (Measure from the center of a k rib without stretching the ribbing.)

ABBREVIATIONS beg: beginning • CC: contrast color • dec(s): decrease(s) • inc(s): increase(s) • k: knit • k2tog: knit 2 together • M1: make 1 stitch • M1L: make 1 stitch left • M1R: make 1 stitch right • MC: main color • p: purl • rep: repeat • rnd(s): round(s) • SSK2tog: slip, slip, knit 2 sts together • st(s): stitch(es) • twisted M1: twisted make 1 cast-on

---

Measurements—inches and *centimeters*

		Child 6–8	Adult S	Adult M	Adult L
Around hand including tip of thumb	(inches)	7½	8	9	9¾
	(cm)	*19*	*20.25*	*23*	*24.75*

Note: These wristers fit quite snugly and easily transcend sizes. Adult M should be wearable by medium-sized children's hands through medium adult hands.

Making the cuff

	Child 6–8	Adult S	Adult M	Adult L
On 3 needles, cast on	33 sts	36 sts	39 sts	42 sts

Join into a triangle, being careful not to twist sts around the needles.

		Child 6–8	Adult S	Adult M	Adult L
Work k2, p1 ribbing for	(inches)	3½	4	4½	5
	(cm)	*9*	*10.25*	*11.5*	*12.75*

Finishing

Bind off in ribbing. Without breaking yarn, use a size F crochet hook to make a loop for the thumb. Start with a slip st into the first k st of bind-off rnd

		Child 6–8	Adult S	Adult M	Adult L
to create a firm base, then crochet a chain measuring	(inches)	2	2½	3	3½
	(cm)	*5*	*6.25*	*7.5*	*9*
Attach this at a point	(inches)	1½	2	2	2½
	(cm)	*4*	*5*	*5*	*6.25*

from its starting point on the top edge. Some knitters go over this with buttonhole stitch in a finer yarn to improve strength and durability.

Make another identical wrister. This wrister can be worn on either hand.

Phyllis Wharton's Scallopers' Wristers

Some years ago, Phyllis Wharton of Seal Harbor sent me another kind of wrister, which she knitted for her grandson and other scallop fishermen. This is the wrister shown in the photograph, essentially a close fitting mitten without thumb or finger coverings. It will fit men's and women's medium and large hands.

This is a work garment, and no effort has been made to prettify it by working the top edge in ribbing or garter stitch, or by introducing all-over color or stripes. Of course, you are not bound by any of these limitations.

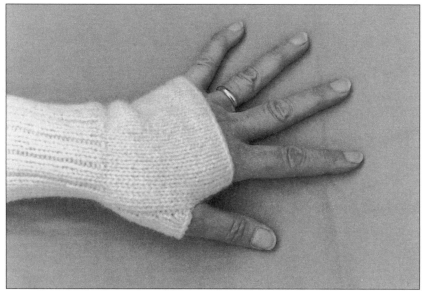

Phyllis Wharton's scallopers' wristers

Yarn Mrs. Wharton uses Bartlettyarns 2-ply Fisherman Yarn with No. 4 double-pointed needles. You can use any natural, oily medium weight yarn.

For each pair, you will need	(oz)	2	3
	(g)	57	85.5

Needles Although Mrs. Wharton, like many traditional mitten knitters, used Size 4 (3.5mm, Can. Size 9) double-pointed needles throughout, knitting the cuff with Size 3 (3.25mm, Can. Size 10) needles improves the appearance and the fit. Likewise, binding off with a smaller needle will prevent the top edge from rolling. For the hand of the wrister, use Size 4 double-pointed needles or the size you need to knit stockinette at the correct tension.

Tension 5½ sts = 1" (2.5cm) in stockinette on larger needles

Other supplies Blunt-tipped yarn needle

ABBREVIATIONS beg: beginning • CC: contrast color • dec(s): decrease(s) • inc(s): increase(s) • k: knit • k2tog: knit 2 together • M1: make 1 stitch • M1L: make 1 stitch left • M1R: make 1 stitch right • MC: main color • p: purl • rep: repeat • rnd(s): round(s) • SSK2tog: slip, slip, knit 2 sts together • st(s): stitch(es) • twisted M1: twisted make 1 cast-on

---

Measurements—inches and *centimeters*

		Woman's M/L	Man's M/L
Around hand including tip of thumb	(inches)	9	9¾
	(cm)	22.75	24.75

Making the cuff

	Woman's M/L	Man's M/L
Using smaller needles, cast on	39 sts	45 sts

Join into a triangle, being careful not to twist sts around the needles.
Divide equally onto 3 needles. K2, p1 for 30 rnds (about 4" or 10cm).

Making the thumb gore

Rnd 1: Change to stockinette and larger needles. Transfer the last p st
to Needle 1. Slip it, M1L (p. 20), k2, M1R, p1, k to end of rnd.
These p sts mark the two sides of the thumb gore.

Rnds 2 and 3: Work even.

Rnd 4: P1, M1L work up to next p marking st, M1R, p1. K to end of rnd.

	Woman's M/L	Man's M/L
Work Rnds 2–4 altogether	4 X	5 X
Total between p sts:	12 sts	14 sts

Work 2 more rnds even, maintaining p marking sts.

Finishing the top edge

	Woman's M/L	Man's M/L
Rnd 1: Bind off on thumb gore and k to end of rnd.	13 sts	15 sts
Rnd 2: K1 (discontinue p marking sts), then using twisted M1, cast on 4 sts over the gap and k to end of rnd. Total:	40 sts	46 sts
Rnd 3: SSK2tog at beg of thumb hole and complete rnd. Total:	39 sts	45 sts

Work 5 rnds even and bind off tightly, *ideally* using a smaller needle.

Turn wristers inside out and darn all ends into the back of the fabric.
Trim ends closely.

Make another identical wrister. This wrister can be worn on either hand.

PART TWO

Double-Knit Mittens from Maine's Up-Country

The beautiful designs on these mittens and gloves are not my patterns, nor are they new. They come from men and women in New England and Atlantic Canada who learned them by sitting next to a friend or a mother or an aunt, and watching. They learned the little peculiarities of increasing and decreasing that go with each mitten, learned the stories associated with it: how the mitten came into the family, what its colorful name means in relation to its geometric design.

In other words, these patterns are as much folklore as songs such as "Springfield Mountain" and "Calico Bush," as much folk art as patchwork quilt patterns. In fact, many of them parallel patchwork patterns.

The people they come from are the early settlers of the coast, the French, the English, Scots, Channel Islanders, the Irish, and the Norwegians and Swedes. Those who came later—the Finns, the Italians, the Portuguese, the Russians, and others—seem to have dropped their own knitting traditions in favor of local ones, or simply gone over to purchased mittens.

A yearlong inquiry in the Maine Finnish community produced not one Finnish mitten, although Finland certainly has knitting traditions distinct from the rest of Scandinavia. What the Finns brought to Maine was the art of making cross-country skis! Old people from the interior still remember learning to ski on locally made Finnish skis, and Finnish women skiing into town, without poles, while knitting! What they knitted, I haven't learned.

Nora Johnson brought her family knitting traditions to Five Islands, a village in Georgetown, Maine, from her native Farmington and shared these traditions and techniques with me and so with all knitters. Nora's family patterns include Stripes, Salt and Pepper (which she called Snowflake) and Fox and Geese. Here she knits a three-colored Fox and Geese mitten, holding both yarns in her right hand as is common among American knitters of Yankee ancestry. The third color, used singly every sixth round, hangs loose below her left hand.

These patterns all have ties to Europe and the British Isles, often surprising ones. Many of the more esoteric qualities of the mittens knit by old Yankee families showed up in a book on double-knit patterns from the island of Gotland in Sweden (*The Swedish Mitten Book*, Lark, 1984). Some of the Newfoundland/Labrador patterns are known in Estonia, although Estonian immigration was not noteworthy in Labrador. A Norwegian star pattern showed up in the pattern bag of a knitter of English/German descent, who said it was British.

This doesn't mean that English settlers picked up their knitting traditions in Gotland on their way to Maine, or that someone from Estonia settled in Newfoundland and set up a knitting school for young girls. Instead, it reflects the seagoing tradition of earlier centuries, the trade and codfishing links between all the North Atlantic communities. Mittens are not a drawing room tradition. They come from plain, hardworking people—fishermen, woodsmen, and farmers.

If women in Maine and Gotland knit the same mitten, it's because a once widespread pattern has survived in these two places. Because no one told these knitters that stockinette cuffs were no longer *de rigueur* in mitten fashions, they continued to knit them and pass them down, while knitters in other more trafficked areas invented and passed around another kind of cuff—ribbed.

The British Isles and Scandinavia have a rich tradition of fishermen's and farmers' sweaters. Not so North America. When this country was being settled, these sweaters were still underwear and unremarkable in Europe, thus we wear woolen jackets woven of black and red, orange, or blue. The old knitting traditions that have survived and grown here are for smaller garments like mittens, socks, gloves, and caps, possibly because the handmade item is so superior to anything available commercially.

The mittens and gloves presented here are from my first two books, *Fox & Geese & Fences* and *Flying Geese & Partridge Feet,* and from Janetta Dexter's booklet, *Nova Scotian Double-Knitting Patterns.* They are only some of many double-knit patterns in New England and Atlantic Canada. There are perhaps half as many again as there are knitters—other patterns, endless combinations of patterns, endless stories.

These are a few that Janetta and I and our readers like. Some are widespread, still actively knitted. Others are on the verge of extinction. But all of them fit well into today's northern life and fashion.

Fox and Geese Mittens

In Anglo-Saxon farm lore, foxes and geese go together as easily as crackers and cheese or cats and mice. We own an old baby spoon decorated on the handle with the incised figures of a goose frantically fleeing a pursuing fox. There are quilt patterns and mitten patterns called Fox and Geese, which seem to have no pictorial relation to either animal.

My friend Tony Cary, of Bath, pointed to the back wall of her fireplace and told me the weather—rainy for a week—would clear, because there were no fox and geese there. She explained that Mainers call the moving sparks on the back of the fireplace and the bottom side of the woodstove lids fox and geese and say that they portend bad weather. As a girl, Tony imagined light catching on the wings of night-flying geese in the waving movement of the sparks, but she has no other explanation of the expression.

In the prairie states and provinces of North America, children stamp a crossed circle into the snow, then play a chasing game called Fox and Geese. The crossed circle also shows up in an old board game in Appalachia and the Maritime Provinces called Fox and Geese. The Fox and Geese mitten pattern, rendered in two colors as it is in Canada, looks like the crossed circles of both Fox and Geese games.

Mainers, not knowing the game, were inventive. Nora Johnson of Five Islands, who learned to knit these mittens as a girl in the Farmington area, told me the *only* real Fox and Geese Mittens have three colors: red for the horizontal lines, black for the verticals and crosses, and white for the background.

Knitting the design in three colors completely destroys any resemblance to the Fox and Geese games, but makes possible the story Mrs. Johnson's grandmother told her—that the design actually depicts foxes and geese. To see them, you must allow your fantasy free play.

The red lines are fences—to keep foxes and geese apart, of course. The little black dots forming the Xs are worried little geese with their wings flapping. At the corner of each box, looking through the fences is a fox's head, its ears (which could also be geese) pricked diagonally

Nora Johnson's Fox and Geese Mittens in three colors

up, and its nose (which could also be a fence post) pointing straight down. Work on it. If you want to, you'll be able to see them.

These directions are based entirely on Mrs. Johnson's pattern, although I have worked out more sizes based on her oral instructions and have given the two-colored version of the pattern as well.

Roughly, you add one more horizontal rep widthwise and one more band lengthwise for each size increase. The thumb grows from three reps around for very young children to five reps around in men's sizes. There must be some compromise when this increase is a minimum of three-quarters of an inch. Florence Nowell of Newport, Maine, reduces a too-wide thumb by ripping it out and reknitting with needles one size smaller.

In two colors, this pattern is also called Compass Work or Compass in some parts of Nova Scotia and in Harpswell, Maine. In New Brunswick, it's called Naughts and Crosses (tic-tac-toe). These too are mind games: In two colors, you can see needles pointing north, east, south, and west, or the grid and Xs and Os of tic-tac-toe, as you choose.

Fox and Geese Mittens

Yarn In Maine, Fox and Geese Mittens are traditionally knit with black or navy verticals and crosses (MC), a white background (CCa), and red fences (CCb). Today knitters use whatever color combination appeals to them, with the third color often only slightly different from the color of the other lines.

Knit with medium weight yarn. I use Bartlettyarns 2-ply Fisherman, or similar 2-ply wool yarns, but softer, commercial medium weight wool (or acrylic) yarn that knits at the stated tension can also be used.

In Bartlettyarns 2-ply Fisherman, one 4-oz (114g) skein each of MC and CCa and about 1 oz (28.5g) of a third color (CCb) will make two pairs of Woman's Small mittens or one pair of Man's Medium and a pair of child's 2–3 or 6–8. Man's Large uses most of two skeins.

Equipment 1 set Size 4 (3.5mm, Can. Size 9) double-pointed needles, or size you need to knit in pattern at correct tension • 1 set Size 2 (2.75mm, Can. Size 12 or 11) double-pointed needles for optional ribbing • 6" (15cm) length of contrasting waste yarn • Blunt-tipped yarn needle

Tension 6 sts and 7 rnds = 1" (2.5cm) in pattern

ABBREVIATIONS beg: beginning • CC: contrast color • dec(s): decrease(s) • inc(s): increase(s) • k: knit • k2tog: knit 2 together • M1: make 1 stitch • M1L: make 1 stitch left • M1R: make 1 stitch right • MC: main color • p: purl • rep: repeat • rnd(s): round(s) • SSK2tog: slip, slip, knit 2 sts together • st(s): stitch(es) • twisted M1: twisted make 1 cast-on

---

Measurements—inches and *centimeters*

	Child Sizes		Adult Sizes					
	2–4	6–8	WS	WM	WL	MM	ML	MXL
Hand length	4½	6	6½	7	7½	7	7½	8½
	11.5	*15.25*	*16.5*	*18*	*19*	*18*	*19*	*21.5*
Hand circumference, incl. tip of thumb	5	7¼	7½	9	9	9½	9½	10
	12.75	*18.5*	*19*	*23*	*23*	*24.25*	*24.25*	*25.5*
Mitten hand length	4¾	6½	7	7½	8	7½	8	9
	12	*16.5*	*18*	*19*	*20.25*	*19*	*20.25*	*23*
Mitten thumb (⅓ hand)	1⅝	2⅛	2⅜	2½	2¾	2½	2	3
	4.25	*5.5*	*6*	*6.5*	*7*	*6.5*	*5*	*7.5*
Mitten width	2½	3½	3¾	4½	4½	4¾	4¾	5
	6.5	*9*	*9.5*	*11.5*	*11.5*	*12*	*12*	*12.75*

Fox and Geese Chart 1

5
3
1

6 5 4 3 2 1

Fox and Geese Chart 2

5
3
1

6 5 4 3 2 1

Fox and Geese Mitten Decrease

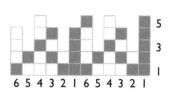

5
3
1

6 5 4 3 2 1 6 5 4 3 2 1

Fox and Geese Thumb Decrease

5
3
1

6 5 4 3 2 1

Fox and Geese Thumb Gore Increases

Increase group A

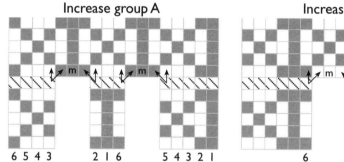

6 5 4 3   2 1 6   5 4 3 2 1

Increase group B

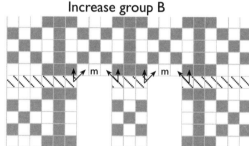

6   5 4 3   2 1

Key

■ MC–main color
□ CCa–contrast color a
▨ CCb–contrast color b
m Make 1 stitch
Ⅴ Knit both colors into 1 stitch

Pattern

Fox and Geese is a rep of 6 sts and 6 rnds. Incs are made only in the first pattern rnd. For clarity, 1 band means all 6 rnds; 1 rep means all 6 sts. Carry MC ahead at all times (p. 16).

Simplify carrying the third color by using a bobbin, a fisherman's netting needle, or a tight little center-pull ball (p. 24). After the first CCb rnd, drop the ball/bobbin down inside the mitten and pull it out only to knit the sixth rnd. Fox and Geese—both versions—works best as a circular pattern. Because of the single-color row and the odd number of 2-colored rows, knitting it flat may cause you to weep.

Off the Cuff

The cuff shown is worked in stockinette stitch with the Fox and Geese pattern. Cuffs can also be knitted in stockinette stitch with vertical stripes (k1MC, k1CCa) following the same directions as for the patterned cuff.

Cuffs in k2, p1 ribbing are another alternative (see directions on ps. 80–81, following directions for patterned cuff).

Making the patterned cuff

	Child		Adult					
	2–4	6–8	WS	WM	WL	MM	ML	MXL

With MC, larger needles, and using the Maine method (p. 13), cast on tightly onto 3 needles.

	2–4	6–8	WS	WM	WL	MM	ML	MXL
	36 sts	42 sts	48 sts	54 sts	54 sts	60 sts	60 sts	66 sts
Total per needle	12 sts	14 sts	16 sts	18 sts	18 sts	20 sts	20 sts	22 sts

Join, being careful not to twist sts around the needles. Join CCa by sewing (p. 20) and start Fox and Geese chart at lower right.

Note: Carry MC ahead throughout (p. 16). Check after the first rnd that the rep comes out even. A mistake here can throw everything else off and take the fun out of the project.

Work Fox and Geese chart on all sts, joining optional CCb 6 sts before beg of rnd 6 of band. (Twisting in CCb at beg of Line 3 of pattern will prevent long vertical floats.)
Work
Finish Line 6 (solid-color rnd).

	2–4	6–8	WS	WM	WL	MM	ML	MXL
Work	2 reps	2 reps	3 reps	3 reps	3 reps	3 reps	3 reps	3 reps

The vertical lines (foxes' noses or fence posts) will now be visible behind the horizontal fences as well as groups of 5 little CCa geese fluttering nervously in an X formation.

Alternative: Making a ribbed cuff

With MC, smaller needles, and using the Maine method (p. 13), cast on tightly

	2–4	6–8	WS	WM	WL	MM	ML	MXL
	36 sts	42 sts	48 sts	54 sts	54 sts	60 sts	60 sts	66 sts

Distribute sts among 3 needles:

	2–4	6–8	WS	WM	WL	MM	ML	MXL
Needle 1:	12 sts	12 sts	15 sts	18 sts	18 sts	18 sts	18 sts	21 sts
Needle 2:	12 sts	15 sts	18 sts	18 sts	18 sts	21 sts	21 sts	24 sts
Needle 3:	12 sts	15 sts	15 sts	18 sts	18 sts	21 sts	21 sts	21 sts

With this distribution, every needle starts with a k st and ends with a p st.

In MC, k2, p1 to end of rnd. Continue this ribbing until work measures

	2–4	6–8	WS	WM	WL	MM	ML	MXL
(inches)	1½	2	2¼	2½	3	2½	3	3½
(cm)	*4*	*5*	*5.75*	*6.5*	*7.5*	*6.5*	*7.5*	*9*

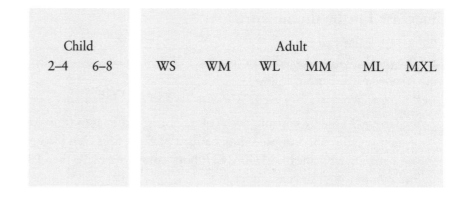

Child		Adult					
2–4	6–8	WS	WM	WL	MM	ML	MXL

Change to larger needles and stockinette and work 1 rnd MC
to 6 sts before end of rnd.

(*If you are using 3 colors for the Fox and Geese pattern*, join CCb
[p. 18], and complete rnd. Work 1 rnd CCb to 6 sts before end of rnd.)

Join CCa and complete rnd. Start chart at lower right on Rnd 1.

Starting the hand and thumb gore

The Fox and Geese thumb gore is unusual in that 6 sts are added in
each inc rnd, and inc rnds occur only every six rnds. This unique inc is
a feature of this mitten throughout New England and Atlantic Canada,
and a bragging point, if you care to brag!

Before you start working the first rnd of thumb gore incs, study the
photo at right and the charts on p. 79. Note that all incs are made in
Rnd 1 of chart and match pattern *2 rnds earlier* (Line 5 of chart).
There are 6 incs in each inc rnd, 3 incs on each side of st 1 or st 4 of
chart. In this way, the pattern continues undisturbed, with a whole rep
arising intact from the solid-color horizontal line.

The thumb gores are placed so that the joint between rnds lies on
the palm side of the mitten and a continuous MC line flows up the
back of the hand alongside the thumb.

Incs are worked by knitting both colors into the front loop of a st
to make 2 sts above 1 st (p. 21) and by M1 left or right (p. 20). Although all this sounds challenging, the inc is so logical and simple that
after you have done it once you probably won't have to refer to these
directions ever again.

Note: Carry MC ahead throughout (p. 16). Check after the first
rnd that the rep comes out even. A mistake here can throw everything
else off and take the fun out of the project.

The unusual Fox and Geese thumb gore increase, 6 stitches close together in 1 round
in Line 1 of each pattern repeat, is part of a set of oral mitten instructions passed down
for generations.

Increase for the thumb gore

Inc Rnd 1 (Line 1 of chart):

Right mitten: Work charted pattern to St 5 of next to last rep. Work inc Group A (directions follow).

Left mitten: Work Sts 1–4 even. Work Inc Group A as follows.

Inc Group A: Inc by knitting both colors one at a time into front loop of next st (above St 5 in preceding band, a MC st), first CCa then MC, still carrying MC ahead. M1R MC; k both colors, first MC then CCa, into front loop of next st (above St 6).

Work next st (the center st of the inc group) even in CCa (above St 1). K both colors, one at a time, into front loop of next st (above St 2), first CCa then MC. M1L in MC; K both colors, first MC then CCa, into front loop of next st (above a St 3 of preceding band).

In the present band of pattern, you should be ready to work St 4, which will be directly above St 4 in Line 5. If you are, you have increased 6 sts in the space of 5 sts, while maintaining Rnd 1 of the chart.

Work to end of rnd in pattern. Work Rnds 2 through 6 of chart even.

Inc Rnd 2 (Line 1 of chart):

Right mitten: Work charted pattern to beg of next-to-last rep. Work St 1. Work Inc Group B (directions follow).

Left mitten: Work first rep even. Work St 1 of 2nd rep. Work Inc Group B.

Inc Group B: Inc by knitting both colors one at a time into next st (above St 2, a MC st), first MC then CCa, still carrying MC ahead. M1R CCa. K both colors, first CCa then MC, into next st (above St 3, a CCa st).

Work next st (the center st of the inc group, above St 4, CCa) even in MC. K both colors, one at a time, into next st (above St 5, a CCa st), first MC then CCa. M1L CCa; k both colors, first CCa then MC, into next st (above St. 6, a MC st).

You should be about to work St 1 of chart in MC, and there should be a MC st, the base of a vertical line, directly above the center st (St 4) of Rnd 5.

Congratulations! These incs are the hardest part of Fox and Geese mittens. From here on, it's a piece of cake.

	Child		Adult					
	2–4	6–8	WS	WM	WL	MM	ML	MXL

	Child		Adult					
	2–4	6–8	WS	WM	WL	MM	ML	MXL
Work in pattern to end of rnd. Work Rnds 2 through 6 even. For the two child sizes, the thumb gore is complete.								

For Man's Medium, Large, and Extra Large:

Right mitten: Work even to third-to-last rep. Work Sts 1 through 4. Work Inc Group A once more.

Left Mitten: Work Rnds 2 through 6 even. Inc rnd: Work two reps even. Work Sts 1 through 4. Work Inc Group A once more.

For Woman's Small, Medium, Large, and Man's Large: Work 1 band of pattern even, ending after Rnd 6.

For Woman's and Man's Large: Additionally work Rnds 1–3 of chart even.

	Child		Adult					
	2–4	6–8	WS	WM	WL	MM	ML	MXL
In the thumb gore area, there are now bands of pattern and a total of:	2	2	3	3	3½	3	3½	4
	12 sts	12 sts	12 sts	12 sts	12 sts	18 sts	18 sts	18 sts

Taking off the thumb gore stitches

	Child		Adult					
	2–4	6–8	WS	WM	WL	MM	ML	MXL
Right mitten: Work in pattern up to St 1 of to-last rep.	3rd-	3rd-	3rd-	3rd-	3rd-	4th-	4th-	4th-
Left mitten: On Needle 1, work	1st rep	1st rep	Sts 1–4	Sts 1–4	Sts 1–5	Sts 1–5	Sts 1–5	Sts 1–5
On 2nd rep, work	St 1	St 1	—	—	—	—	—	—
Put thumb gore sts on a piece of waste yarn: Take needed sts (beyond incs) from side of thumb hole toward palm. This placement of the thumb hole keeps intact the MC vertical next to the thumb on the back of the hand.	11 sts	11 sts	14 sts	14 sts	14 sts	17 sts	17 sts	19 sts
Using twisted M1 (p. 23), cast on over thumb hole, in correct color order for Line 1 of chart,	5 sts	5 sts	8 sts	8 sts	8 sts	5 sts	5 sts	7 sts
Total:	42 sts	48 sts	54 sts	60 sts	60 sts	66 sts	66 sts	72 sts
Work even in pattern for bands of pattern, or about	2	3	3	4	4½	4	4½	5
(inches)	1¾	2½	2½	3½	4	3½	4	4¼
(cm)	4.5	6.5	6.5	9	10.25	9	10.25	10.75

Stop at end of Rnd 6.

The unusual mode of decreasing in the Fox and Geese pattern: Knit 2 sts together in 12 adjacent stitches to reduce by an entire pattern repeat at once. This decrease has been passed down for generations as part of the Fox and Geese Mitten directions.

Closing the mitten tip

	Child		Adult					
	2–4	6–8	WS	WM	WL	MM	ML	MXL
Dec group A: Dec on little finger side:	—	—	—	—	—	6 sts	6 sts	6 sts

Rnd 1: On side opposite thumb about the middle of Needle 2, above St 1 of chart, k2tog (p. 24) 4 times. Continue in pattern to end of rnd.

	Child		Adult					
Rnd 2: Working Line 1 of chart, k up to the 4 decs in Rnd 1, k2tog twice. Total:	—	—	—	—	—	60 sts	60 sts	66 sts

Complete pattern band, ending after Rnd 6.

	Child		Adult					
Dec group B: Dec on *both* little finger and index finger sides:	—	—	6 sts	6 sts	6 sts	6 sts	6 sts	6 sts

Needle 1: K2tog CCa, k2tog CCa, k2tog MC. Work even in pattern to end of needle.

Needle 2: Locate center two reps on needle. Work in pattern to first St 1. K2tog 6 times, maintaining order of sts on pattern chart Line 1 no matter what lies beneath. End with St 6 matching St 6 in Line 5 of the preceding band.

	Child		Adult					
	2–4	6–8	WS	WM	WL	MM	ML	MXL

Work to last 6 sts. The next st should be a St 1 of chart.
K2tog MC, k2tog MC, k2tog CCa.
Complete band to end of Line 6.

Total: — — 42 sts 48 sts 48 sts 48 sts 48 sts 54 sts

In all sizes:
Rnd 1: Work Rnd 1 of chart, *but* as you do so, k2tog, k1 to
end of rnd.

Total: 28 sts 32 sts 28 sts 32 sts 32 sts 32 sts 32 sts 36 sts

Work Mitten Decrease Chart, starting with Line 2: Dec in each rep
as indicated, by working SSK2tog only (p. 24). Follow dec chart
religiously even when rnd does not come out in even 6 st units.
K extra sts even.

Total: 13 sts 14 sts 13 sts 13 sts 13 sts 14 sts 14 sts 18 sts

Check measurements against finished measurements at beg of directions.
If you are satisfied, break yarns leaving three 6" (15cm) tails. With yarn
needle, thread one tail through remaining sts and draw up firmly. Draw
other ends to inside of mitten. Thread end through drawn-up sts again,
darn a few sts to secure it, and draw to inside of mitten.

Working the thumb

Note: Because of the 6-st pattern, the choice of thumb widths is limited.
If the thumb seems slightly too narrow or too wide when completed,
take it out and re-knit with needles one size larger or smaller. *Man's
Medium* should be knitted on one size larger needles at a tension of
6½ sts = 1 inch

	Child		Adult					
	2–4	6–8	WS	WM	WL	MM	ML	MXL
Needle 1: Pick up from top of thumb hole.	5 sts	5 sts	8 sts	8 sts	8 sts	5 sts	5 sts	7 sts
Needles 2 and 3: Pick up from waste yarn. Pick up and twist from each corner of thumb hole	11 sts	11 sts	14 sts	14 sts	14 sts	17 sts	17 sts	19 sts
	1 st	1 st	1 st	1 st	1 st	1 st	1 st	2 sts
Total:	18 sts	18 sts	24 sts	24 sts	24 sts	24 sts	24 sts	30 sts

Join MC by sewing (p. 20), starting at right corner of thumb hole. Work Needle 1 in MC (CCb). Join CCa by sewing. Start chart at Rnd 1 or Rnd 4 on Needle 1, continuing pattern from thumb gore. (The vertical lines—St 1—should continue perfectly from thumb gore to thumb.) Work chart, matching pattern to thumb gore pattern. You should have

	Child		Adult					
	2–4	6–8	WS	WM	WL	MM	ML	MXL
You should have	3 reps	3 reps	4 reps	4 reps	4 reps	4 reps	4 reps	5 reps
Work even in pattern for pattern bands, or until ¾ inch (2cm) less than total thumb length. In Woman's and Man's Medium and Large, complete Rnd 3. In all other sizes, end with Rnd 5 completed.	1	2	2	2½	3	2½	3	3

Closing the tip of the thumb

Dec Rnd 1: K2tog, k1 on all 3 needles, using *one* color—MC or CCb, whichever best fits the pattern—or *alternating* MC and CCa:	1 color	1 color	1 color	alt	alt	alt	alt	1 color
Total:	12 sts	12 sts	16 sts	16 sts	16 sts	16 sts	16 sts	20 sts

Rnd 2: Work even, fudging creatively to make the pattern look approximately right.

Dec Rnd 3, adult sizes only: K2tog, k1, either in MC (CCb) or alternating MC and CCa, whichever fits the pattern.	—	—						
Total:	12 sts	12 sts	11 sts	11 sts	11 sts	11 sts	11 sts	14 sts

Break yarn leaving a 6" (15cm) tail. With yarn needle, thread one end through the remaining sts and draw up firmly. Draw other end to inside of thumb. Thread end through drawn-up sts again, darn a few sts to secure it, and draw to inside of thumb.

Finishing the mitten

Turn mitten inside out and darn all ends into the back of the fabric. Repair possible holes at corners of the thumb hole with nearby tails. Trim ends closely.

This mitten is a right- or a left-handed mitten. Make another, being careful that it is for the opposite hand. (Although there is a left and right mitten, these *can* be worn on either hand. The handed directions place the joint between rnds at the palm.)

Striped Mittens

One of the first Maine double-knit mittens I ever saw was a Striped Mitten, but the pattern is less popular than either the Fox and Geese pattern or the Salt and Pepper pattern. I don't know why.

To the careful knitter, the sharp lines of this pattern are its best asset, because they emphasize perfection and yield a fine mitten with enough fashion pizzazz to be at home in London or Boston.

The pattern itself, a simple one-one alternation of two colors, pulls the mitten fabric up into fine ridges, making it appear that one color has been knit above the other. They are traditionally knit with a dark color "on top"—that is, carried ahead—and a very bright, warm color showing through from beneath.

This pattern was shown to me by Nora Johnson of Five Islands, who learned it as a girl in the Farmington area. It was until recently also knit by Elma Farwell of the Dromore area of Phippsburg. I once thought it was unknown outside of Maine, but have since seen it, exactly like this mitten, in a collection of traditional mittens from Gotland, Sweden, where it is called the Pole Pattern (*The Swedish Mitten Book*, Lark, 1984). I have seen similar mittens from other parts of Sweden, where the color carried ahead is changed once or twice in the length of the mitten so that first the dark color, then the light color, then the dark again, rise to the surface, creating the effect of waves of color. A blue and white striped mitten in the color photos shows this effect. If you want to try it, allow at least 10 rnds between changes.

Striped Mitten from Maine

Striped Mittens

Yarn Medium (worsted) weight yarn in two colors, either contrasting or close. Striped mittens were traditionally knitted in black or navy and white, but more recently are made with a dark MC carried ahead (p. 16) and a glowingly bright "under color." The samples were knitted in Bartlettyarns 2-ply Fisherman yarn (white) and Rangeley (red or blue) yarn. For one pair you will need

MC (oz)	1	1½	1¾	2	2	2½	2½	3
(g)	*28.5*	*42.75*	*50*	*57*	*57*	*71.25*	*71.25*	*85.5*
CC (oz)	1	1½	1¾	2	2	2½	2½	3
(g)	*28.5*	*42.75*	*50*	*57*	*57*	*71.25*	*71.25*	*85.5*

Equipment 1 set Size 5 (3.75mm, Can. Size 9) double-pointed needles, or size you need to knit in Stripes pattern at correct tension • 6" (15cm) length of contrasting waste yarn • Blunt-tipped yarn needle

Tension 6¾ sts and 5½ rnds = 1" (2.5cm) in narrow Stripes pattern.

ABBREVIATIONS beg: beginning • CC: contrast color • dec(s): decrease(s) • inc(s): increase(s) • k: knit • k2tog: knit 2 together • M1: make 1 stitch • M1L: make 1 stitch left • M1R: make 1 stitch right • MC: main color • p: purl • rep: repeat • rnd(s): round(s) • SSK2tog: slip, slip, knit 2 sts together • st(s): stitch(es) • twisted M1: twisted make 1 cast-on

---

Measurements—inches and *centimeters*

	Child Sizes		Adult Sizes					
	4–6	8–10	WS	WM	WL	MM	ML	XL
Hand length	5½	6½	6½	7	7½	7	7½	8½
	14	*16.5*	*16.5*	*18*	*19*	*18*	*19*	*21.5*
Hand circumference (incl. tip of thumb)	7	8	7½	9	9	9½	9½	10
	18	*20.25*	*19*	*23*	*23*	*24.25*	*24.25*	*25.5*
Mitten hand length	6	7	7	7½	8	7½	8	9
	15.25	*18*	*18*	*19*	*20.25*	*19*	*20.25*	*23*
Mitten thumb (⅓ hand)	2	2⅜	2⅜	2½	2⅝	2½	2⅝	3
	5	*6*	*6*	*6.5*	*6.75*	*6.5*	*6.75*	*7.5*
Mitten width	3½	4	3¾	4½	4½	4¾	4¾	5
	9	*10.25*	*9.5*	*11.5*	*11.5*	*12*	*12*	*12.75*

Note: Although these directions as originally published included Size 2–4 for small children, I find the resulting mitten is really too rigid for toddlers and babies. See Baby Foxes and Goslings section for traditional mittens in soft yarns and small sizes.

Pattern

A multiple of 2 sts and 1 rnd, this vertically striped pattern is a simple one-one alternation of two colors worked on an even number of sts. It wraps perfectly around the hand with no obvious break.

Wide stripes on the cuff split apart into narrow stripes on the hand and thumb. An unusual method of increasing keeps the stripes continuous through incs on the thumb gore. At the tip of the thumb and the hand, the stripes meet neatly at three dec points.

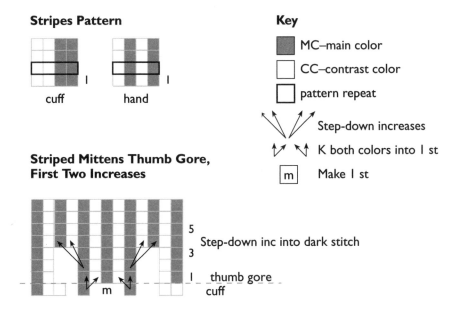

Stripes Pattern

cuff   hand

Key

MC–main color

CC–contrast color

pattern repeat

Step-down increases

K both colors into I st

m   Make I st

Striped Mittens Thumb Gore, First Two Increases

5
3
I
m   thumb gore
            cuff

Step-down inc into dark stitch

The stripes of the thumb gore branch from one MC rib of the cuff in a treelike pattern—the kind of detail that intrigues traditional knitters and keeps handwork precious and impossible to reproduce by machines.

This pattern can be knitted flat, but add one additional st each side for a seam and purl every other row. Check that you are still carrying MC ahead even when you purl. CC will seem to dominate on the p side of the work.

Knitted densely with MC carried ahead throughout (p. 16), the Stripes pattern pulls up the fabric of the knitting and, in the narrow stripe, causes the MC to stand up in ridges, like corduroy. The effect is not obvious until you have knitted several rnds. Failure to carry MC ahead shows prominently, so take care.

Off the Cuff

The 4-st, 1-rnd stockinette pattern of the cuff is unique to Maine and Gotland, Sweden. A similar pattern is knit in Shetland, but the off color is purled, and the result is called "corrugated ribbing." In Maine, the cuff is frequently used with other simple color patterns.

Although MC is also carried ahead on the cuff and the fabric is pulled up widthwise by the vertically aligned color changes, the MC doesn't dominate here as much as in the narrow stripe on the hand. However, there is still enough pull-up effect to make the cuff snug and warm on the wrist.

		Child		Adult					
		2–4	6–8	WS	WM	WL	MM	ML	MXL

Making the cuff

		Child		Adult					
With MC, and using the Maine method (p. 13), cast on		40 sts	44 sts	44 sts	52 sts	52 sts	56 sts	56 sts	64 sts
Distribute sts on 3 needles	Needle 1:	12 sts	12 sts	12 sts	16 sts	16 sts	16 sts	16 sts	20 sts
	Needle 2:	12 sts	16 sts	16 sts	16 sts	16 sts	20 sts	20 sts	20 sts
	Needle 3:	16 sts	16 sts	16 sts	20 sts	20 sts	20 sts	20 sts	24 sts

Join into a triangle, being careful not to twist sts around the needles.

Join CC and immediately begin wide stripes for cuff: k2 MC, k2 CC.

		Child		Adult					
Work even for	(inches)	2	2⅜	2⅜	2½	2⅝	2½	2⅝	3
	(cm)	5	6	6	6.5	6.75	6.5	6.75	7.5

Starting the hand and thumb gore

Nora Johnson makes a striking beginning to her striped thumb gore, which looks as if 5 narrow stripes branch out from one wide dark stripe on the cuff. To get this effect, you'll have to cheat a little, as follows:

Rnd 1: K both colors (MC then CC) into the first MC st on the left needle (p. 21). M1 MC (p. 20). K both colors (CC then MC) into the second MC st on the left needle. You have increased 3 sts.
The cheating part is that you now have an uneven number of sts, and the pattern won't work—so, k the next 2 sts tog in CC, and everything's all right again.

Continue to k1MC, k1CC to middle MC stripe (on cuff) of Needle 2. *K both colors, MC then CC, into front loop of next st. Rep from * in next st. (This adds 2 sts on the little finger side for ease.) Continue k1MC, k1CC to end of rnd. Check after the first rnd of pattern that the rep comes out even. A mistake here can throw everything else off and take the fun out of the project.

		Child		Adult					
Total on Needle 2:		14 sts	18 sts	18 sts	18 sts	18 sts	22 sts	22 sts	22 sts

Rnds 2 and 3: Work even in pattern.

Rnd 4: Inc 4 sts, 2 in each outside MC stripe of the thumb gore, using double Step-Down Inc (p. 21): *K both colors (MC then CC) into the

MC st UNDER the next st on the left needle. K1 MC into the MC st on the left needle. Continue in pattern to the last MC st of the thumb gore and rep from *. You'll be able to see the beginning of 2 Y- shapes in MC, with a CC st emerging in the middle of each. Finish rnd in pattern.

		Child		Adult					
		2–4	6–8	WS	WM	WL	MM	ML	MXL
Rnds 5 through 7: Work even in pattern.									
Work Rnds 4 through 7 altogether		2X	3X	2X	3X	3X	4X	4X	4X
Between the 2 outside MC sts of the thumb gore there should be		13 sts	17 sts	13 sts	17 sts	17 sts	21 sts	21 sts	21 sts.
Work even until thumb gore measures	(inches)	2	2⅜	2⅜	2½	2⅝	2½	2⅝	3
	(cm)	5	6	6	6.5	6.75	6.5	6.75	7.5

Taking off the thumb gore stitches

| At beg of rnd, k1MC, then put | | 13 sts | 15 sts | 13 sts | 17 sts | 17 sts | 19 sts | 19 sts | 19 sts |

on a piece of waste yarn. The first and last sts on the waste yarn should be CC sts.

| Using twisted M1 (p. 23) and maintaining color sequence (start with a CC st), cast on 5 sts over the gap. | Total: | 46 sts | 52 sts | 50 sts | 58 sts | 58 sts | 62 sts | 62 sts | 70 sts |

Working the hand

| Work even in pattern until hand above cuff measures about | (inches) | 5 | 5⅜ | 5⅞ | 6¼ | 6¾ | 6¼ | 6¾ | 7½ |
| | (cm) | 12.75 | 13.75 | 15 | 16 | 17 | 16 | 17 | 19 |

This will seem long, but the dec takes very little length, so keep with it to the end.

Closing the mitten tip

Nora Johnson, from whom I learned this pattern, has a pretty way of decreasing for this mitten that was included in *Fox & Geese & Fences* but was difficult to convey in writing. Some years ago, at the New Hampshire Farm Musem, I met a creative woman who had discovered another wonderfully effective decrease for stripes on a pair of gloves her grandmother had made that were found in the pockets of an old coat. Although I don't remember her name, I don't think she will mind if I pass it on to you.

Rearrange the sts so that Needle 1 has the 5 sts above the thumb gore in the middle, each needle has about one-third of the sts, and all needles begin with a CC st. (This will mean moving onto the left needles roughly then compensating so that each needle begins with a CC st).

	Child		Adult					
	2–4	6–8	WS	WM	WL	MM	ML	MXL
	5 sts	6 sts	6 sts	7 sts	7 sts	7 sts	7 sts	8 sts

Decs will be at the ends of all 3 needles. Rearranging sts in this way assures that whether the mitten is worn on the left or the right hand, the back of the hand will be attractive, with decs toward the outside, and the third dec will be roughly in the center of the palm side.

Knit or back up to the new beg of Needle 1.

Set-up rnd for dec:
Needle 1: K2tog MC (p. 24). Work even to end of needle, matching pattern to existing stripes.
Needle 2: Same as Needle 1.
Needle 3: K2tog MC, work to last 2 sts before end of needle and STOP.

At this point, all 3 needles begin and end with MC. Every dec rnd will begin and end here, before the last 2 sts on Needle 3. By decreasing at both ends of all needles every rnd, you will have matching stripes come together in a point, very smoothly, and the mittens will end quickly in a somewhat rounded point.

Total:	43 sts	49 sts	47 sts	55 sts	55 sts	59 sts	59 sts	67 sts

Dec Rnd:
End of Needle 3: SSK2tog (p. 24) in color of 2nd st from end of needle.
Needle 1: K2 sts tog in color of 2nd st. Work in pattern to last 2 sts on needle. SSK2tog in color of 2nd st from end of needle.
Needles 2 and 3: Same as Needle 1. The final dec ends 2 sts before the end of Needle 3.

Work Dec Rnd	5X	6X	6X	7X	7X	7X	7X	9X
Total remaining:	13 sts	13 sts	11 sts	13 sts	13 sts	17 sts	17 sts	13 sts

Check measurements against finished measurements at beg of directions. If you are satisfied, break yarn leaving two 6" (15 cm) tails. With yarn needle, thread one end through the remaining sts and draw up firmly. Draw other end to inside of mitten. Thread first end through drawn-up sts again, darn a few sts to secure it and draw to inside of mitten.

Working the thumb

Join MC and CC by sewing (p. 20), starting at right side of thumb hole.

	Child		Adult					
	2–4	6–8	WS	WM	WL	MM	ML	MXL
Needles 1 and 2: Pick up from waste yarn	13 sts	15 sts	13 sts	17 sts	17 sts	19 sts	19 sts	19 sts
From corners of thumb hole, pick up and twist onto needle a total of	2 sts	2 sts	2 sts	2 sts	2 sts	2 sts	2 sts	4 sts
Needle 3: Pick up 5 sts from top of thumb hole. Total:	20 sts	22 sts	20 sts	24 sts	24 sts	26 sts	26 sts	28 sts

Starting with Needle 1 at the right corner of thumb hole, k in pattern, matching colors to continue the stripes uninterrupted from both the thumb gore and the palm.

Work even until thumb is								
(inches)	1½	1¾	1⅝	2	2⅛	2	2⅛	1⅞
(cm)	*3.75*	*4.5*	*4.2*	*5*	*5.5*	*5*	*5.5*	*4.75*

Closing the tip of the thumb

Divide sts roughly evenly on 3 needles, each needle beginning with a CC st. Follow Set-up for Dec and Dec Rnd directions for hand.

Work Rnds 4–7	1X	2X	1X	2X	2X	3X	3X	3X
Remaining on 3 needles:	11 sts	7 sts	11 sts	9 sts	9 sts	5 sts	5 sts	7 sts

Check measurements against finished measurements at beg of directions before breaking yarn.

If you are satisfied, break yarn leaving two 6" (15cm) tails. With yarn needle, thread one end through the remaining sts and draw up firmly. Draw other end to inside of the thumb. Thread first end through drawn-up sts again, darn a few sts to secure it, and draw to inside of thumb.

Finishing the mitten

Turn mitten inside out and darn all ends into the back of the fabric. Repair any holes at corners of the thumb hole with nearby tails. On this mitten, you can hide the tails completely by sliding them under floats of the opposite color, moving vertically up or down the mitten. Trim ends closely.

Make another identical mitten. This mitten can be worn on either hand.

Salt and Pepper Mittens

Salt and Pepper, a simple one/one alternation of two colors, must be the granddaddy of all double-knitting patterns. It's definitely the most common double-knit in Maine, and in the whole Maine-Maritimes area, it is the most widespread.

In the Maritime Provinces, Salt and Pepper is rarely used for the whole mitten as it is in Maine, but when calculation of a pattern doesn't fit neatly into a space, as on the thumb or the tip of a mitten, the knitter often lapses into Salt and Pepper. In Maine, when such problems arise, the knitter usually knits plain, dropping the second color. Then again, it's colder in Newfoundland and Labrador than it is in Maine.

Called Salt and Pepper in Nova Scotia, it's properly called Snow-flake in Maine, when it's called anything, because in white and a darker color, it looks like snow falling heavily at night. Other knitters here have scoffed at my interest in named patterns. "I didn't do any-thing, just knit it double," they have said more than once of their Salt and Pepper mittens.

No double-knit pattern is simpler or more effective. The alterna-tion on an uneven number of stitches produces a fish-scale appearance and a dense, smooth fabric with easy mobility and no inside loops to catch fingers.

The mitten is usually knit with a dark or dull color emphasized (carried ahead) and a glowing, warm red or orange underneath. A friend of mine who saw such Salt and Pepper mittens for the first time, exclaimed, "It's like a hot coal!" This mitten is also traditionally knit in gray and white—more natural but also much less dramatic.

Salt and Pepper Mittens in two sizes

Salt and Pepper Mittens

Yarn Medium (worsted) weight yarn in two colors, either contrasting or close. I use Bartlettyarns Fisherman 2-ply yarn, a somewhat heavy medium weight yarn, or other similar yarns, but any worsted weight wool yarn that knits to the same gauge can be substituted.

Usually the darkest color (MC) is carried ahead (p. 16), with the lighter color (CC) appearing to show through the dark. Using variegated or ombre yarn for CC produces an interesting effect.

Equipment One set No. 4 double-pointed needles, or size needed to work correct gauge • One set No. 2 double-pointed knitting needles for optional ribbed cuff • 12" (30cm) waste yarn • Blunt-tipped yarn needle

Tension 6½ sts = 1 inch (2.5cm)

ABBREVIATIONS beg: beginning • CC: contrast color • dec(s): decrease(s) • inc(s): increase(s) • k: knit • k2tog: knit 2 together • M1: make 1 stitch • M1L: make 1 stitch left • M1R: make 1 stitch right • MC: main color • p: purl • rep: repeat • rnd(s): round(s) • SSK2tog: slip, slip, knit 2 sts together • st(s): stitch(es) • twisted M1: twisted make 1 cast-on

Pattern

A multiple of 2 sts and 2 rnds, knitted on an uneven number of sts. The uneven number of sts assures that a continuing alternation will form a tight check rather than stripes. The pattern wraps perfectly around the hand, and there is no visible joint in the pattern, hence no need to differentiate between right and left mittens. The mitten can be worn on either hand. Carry MC ahead at all times (p. 16).

This pattern can be knitted flat. If knitting the mitten flat, be sure to add 2 sts to allow for a seam, and to purl every second row.

Measurements—inches and *centimeters*

	Child Sizes			Adult Sizes					
	2–3	4–6	8–10	WS	WM	WL	MM	ML	XL
Hand length	4½	5½	6½	6½	7	7½	7	7½	8
	11.5	*14*	*16.5*	*16.5*	*18*	*19*	*18*	*19*	*20.25*
Hand circumference, incl. tip of thumb	6	7	8	7½	9	9	9½	9½	10
	15.25	*18*	*20.25*	*19*	*23*	*23*	*24.25*	*24.25*	*25.5*
Mitten hand length	4¾	6	7	7	7½	8	7½	8	9
	12	*15.25*	*18*	*18*	*19*	*20.25*	*19*	*20.25*	*23*
Mitten thumb (⅓ hand)	1⅛	2	2⅜	2⅜	2½	2⅝	2½	2⅝	3
	3	*5*	*6*	*6*	*6.5*	*6.75*	*6.5*	*6.75*	*7.5*
Mitten width	3	3½	4	3¾	4½	4½	4¾	4¾	5
	7.5	*9*	*10.25*	*9.5*	*11.5*	*11.5*	*12*	*12*	*12.75*

Off the Cuff

The cuff can be ribbed in one color (using smaller needles) *or* worked in stockinette with a 1-st wide vertical stripe (using larger needles). The vertical stripe pulls the knit up widthwise and makes a snug and warm double-knit cuff. Instructions for both styles follow on p. 96.

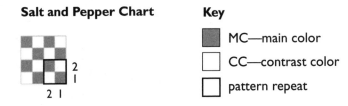

Salt and Pepper Chart

2
1
2 1

Key
- MC—main color
- CC—contrast color
- pattern repeat

Making a ribbed cuff

		Child			Adult					
		2–3	4–6	8–10	WS	WM	WL	MM	ML	XL

With MC, smaller needles, and using the Maine method (p. 13), cast on distributing sts on 3 needles:

		2–3	4–6	8–10	WS	WM	WL	MM	ML	XL
		39 sts	45 sts	51 sts	48 sts	57 sts	57 sts	60 sts	60 sts	63 sts
Needle 1:		12 sts	15 sts	15 sts	15 sts	18 sts	18 sts	18 sts	18 sts	21 sts
Needle 2:		15 sts	15 sts	18 sts	18 sts	21 sts	21 sts	21 sts	21 sts	21 sts
Needle 3:		12 sts	15 sts	18 sts	15 sts	18 sts	18 sts	21 sts	21 sts	21 sts

Join into triangle, being careful not to twist sts around the needles.

K2p1 in MC until cuff measures

		2–3	4–6	8–10	WS	WM	WL	MM	ML	XL
(inches)		1⅝	2	2⅓	2⅓	2½	2⅔	2½	2⅔	3
(cm)		*4*	*5*	*6*	*6*	*6.5*	*6.75*	*6.5*	*6.75*	*7.5*

—or longer, if you wish.

Set up for Salt and Pepper pattern: Change to larger needles and work 1 rnd MC, increasing by M1 (p. 20) to add (This will make an odd number of sts, so that the Salt and Pepper pattern will flow smoothly, without thought, from rnd to rnd.) Six sts from end of this rnd, join CC yarn (p. 18).

		2–3	4–6	8–10	WS	WM	WL	MM	ML	XL
		—	—	2 sts	1 st	2 sts	2 sts	1 st	1 st	2 sts
Total:		39 sts	45 sts	53 sts	49 sts	59 sts	59 sts	61 sts	61 sts	65 sts

Alternative: Making a Maine striped cuff

With a single strand of MC and larger needles, use the Maine method (p. 13) to cast on tightly

		2–3	4–6	8–10	WS	WM	WL	MM	ML	XL
		36 sts	42 sts	50 sts	46 sts	56 sts	56 sts	58 sts	58 sts	62 sts

Distribute sts on 3 needles, join into triangle and, carrying MC ahead, start striped pattern immediately: K1MC, k1CC for

		2–3	4–6	8–10	WS	WM	WL	MM	ML	XL
(inches)		1⅝	2	2⅓	2⅓	2½	2⅔	2½	2⅔	3
(cm)		*4*	*5*	*6*	*6*	*6.5*	*6.75*	*6.5*	*6.75*	*7.5*

Set up for Salt and Pepper: At beg of Needle 1, K both colors (CC then MC) into the front loop of St 1. You now have an uneven number of sts on your needles. Your next CC st will be above a MC st, and if you continue to alternate colors, you will be knitting Salt and Pepper.

Needle 2: Roughly opposite beg of rnd, k both colors into front loops of 2 adjoining sts in pattern sequence (thus adding 2 more sts for ease).

		2–3	4–6	8–10	WS	WM	WL	MM	ML	XL
Total:		39 sts	45 sts	53 sts	49 sts	59 sts	59 sts	61 sts	61 sts	65 sts

Starting the pattern and the thumb gore

	Child			Adult					
	2–3	4–6	8–10	WS	WM	WL	MM	ML	XL

Rnd 1: Work in pattern, starting at lower right corner of chart. Carry MC ahead throughout.

Note: Check after the first rnd that the rep comes out even. (The only place where 2 sts of the same color lie together is the first st on the left needle and the last st on the right needle—at the point where you are knitting.) A mistake here can throw everything else off and take the fun out of your project.

Rnd 2: Start thumb gore: K1CC. Inc 2 sts: K both colors (p. 21), in order, into the front loop of St 2. Rep in St 3. Lay a piece of contrasting waste yarn after the 2nd inc as a marker. (Lay this marker yarn back and forth between the same 2 sts after each inc to mark the outside of the thumb gore.) Complete rnd in pattern.
Total: 4 sts between St 1 and marker.

Rnds 3 through 5: Work even in pattern.

Rnd 6, Inc Rnd: K1 (in pattern). K both colors in pattern order into front loop of next st. Rep. K in pattern to 2 sts before marker. K both colors in pattern order into front loop of next 2 sts.

| Rep Rnds 3 through 6 | — | — | 1X | 1X | 1.5X** | 1.5X** | 2X | 2X | 2X |

**In WM/WL, inc only at beg of thumb gore the last time (thus adding only 2 more sts that rnd).

Total between St 1 and marker:	8 sts	8 sts	12 sts	12 sts	14 sts	14 sts	16 sts	16 sts	16 sts
Work even in pattern until thumb gore measures (inches)	1½	2	2⅓	2⅓	2½	2½	2½	2½	3½
(cm)	4	5	6	6	6.5	6.5	6.5	6.5	9

Taking off the thumb gore stitches

| Work 1 st. Remove waste yarn marker and with a yarn needle thread waste yarn through next | 11 sts | 11 sts | 15 sts | 15 sts | 17 sts | 17 sts | 19 sts | 19 sts | 19 sts |
| Using twisted M1 (p. 23), cast on 5 sts to bridge the gaping hole before the next st. Total: | 39 sts | 45 sts | 53 sts | 49 sts | 59 sts | 59 sts | 61 sts | 61 sts | 65 sts |

Working the hand

		Child			Adult					
		2–3	4–6	8–10	WS	WM	WL	MM	ML	XL
Work even in pattern until hand above cuff measures	(inches)	3¼	4¼	5	5¼	5½	6	5	6	6¾
	(cm)	*8.25*	*10.75*	*12.75*	*13.25*	*14*	*15.25*	*12.75*	*15.25*	*17*

Distribute sts as evenly as possible on 3 needles, keeping the beg/end of rnd in the same place.										
	Needle 1:	13 sts	15 sts	17 sts	17 sts	20 sts	20 sts	20 sts	20 sts	21 sts
	Needle 2:	13 sts	15 sts	18 sts	18 sts	20 sts	20 sts	20 sts	20 sts	22 sts
	Needle 3:	13 sts	15 sts	18 sts	18 sts	19 sts	19 sts	21 sts	21 sts	22 sts

Closing the mitten tip

Rnd 1: Starting at beg of rnd, dec:
Needle 1: K2tog (p. 24), in pattern, k in pattern to 2 sts from end of needle, SSK2tog (p. 24) in pattern.
Needles 2, 3: Same as Needle 1.

	Total:	33 sts	39 sts	47 sts	47 sts	53 sts	53 sts	55 sts	55 sts	59 sts

Rnd 2: Work even in pattern.

Rep Rnds 1 and 2		3 X	4 X	6 X	6 X	7 X	7 X	8 X	8 X	9 X
until there remain		15 sts	15 sts	11 sts	11 sts	11 sts	11 sts	13 sts	13 sts	11 sts

Check measurements against finished measurements at beg of directions. If you are satisfied, break yarn leaving a 6" (15cm) tail. With yarn needle, thread one end through the remaining sts and draw up firmly. Draw other end to inside of mitten. Thread first end through drawn-up sts again, darn a few sts to secure and draw it to inside of mitten.

Working the thumb

Needles 1 and 2: Pick up from waste yarn		11 sts	11 sts	15 sts	15 sts	17 sts	17 sts	19 sts	19 sts	19 sts
From corners of thumb hole, pick up and twist counterclockwise onto needles a total of		2 sts	3 sts	2 sts	2 sts	2 sts	2 sts	2 sts	2 sts	3 sts
Needle 3: Pick up 5 sts from top of thumb hole.	Total:	18 sts	19 sts	22 sts	22 sts	24 sts	24 sts	26 sts	26 sts	27 sts

Join MC and CC yarn by sewing (p. 20), starting at right corner of thumb hole. Work Salt and Pepper pattern, starting at right corner

		Child			Adult					
		2–3	4–6	8–10	WS	WM	WL	MM	ML	XL

(Needle 1), matching pattern to thumb gore.
In first rnd, k2tog at one corner, if necessary, to get a total of
Place this k2tog at the point where the pattern seems to go awry—
at the end of Needle 2 or the beg of Needle 3.

	2–3	4–6	8–10	WS	WM	WL	MM	ML	XL
	17 sts	19 sts	21 sts	21 sts	23 sts	23 sts	25 sts	25 sts	27 sts

Work even until, from base of thumb next to palm,
thumb measures

	2–3	4–6	8–10	WS	WM	WL	MM	ML	XL
(inches)	1¼	1½	1¾	2	2¼	2¼	2	2	2½
(cm)	3.25	4	4.5	5	5.75	5.75	5	5	6.5

Distribute sts on 3 needles

	2–3	4–6	8–10	WS	WM	WL	MM	ML	XL
Needle 1:	5 sts	6 sts	7 sts	7 sts	7 sts	7 sts	8 sts	8 sts	9 sts
Needle 2:	6 sts	6 sts	7 sts	7 sts	8 sts	8 sts	8 sts	8 sts	9 sts
Needle 3:	6 sts	7 sts	7 sts	7 sts	8 sts	8 sts	9 sts	9 sts	9 sts

Closing the tip of the thumb

Rnd 1: Dec:
Needle 1: In pattern, k2tog, work even to last 2 sts, SSK2tog.
Needles 2 and 3: Rep Needle 1.   Total remaining:

	2–3	4–6	8–10	WS	WM	WL	MM	ML	XL
	11 sts	13 sts	15 sts	15 sts	17 sts	17 sts	19 sts	19 sts	21 sts

Rnd 2: Work even in pattern.
Rep Rnd 1 once. (In the smallest size, don't dec on Needle 3.)
Total remaining:

	2–3	4–6	8–10	WS	WM	WL	MM	ML	XL
	7 sts	7 sts	9 sts	9 sts	11 sts	11 sts	13 sts	13 sts	15 sts

Rep Rnds 2 and 1 once more *in the 3 largest sizes only*.
Total remaining:

	2–3	4–6	8–10	WS	WM	WL	MM	ML	XL
							7 sts	7 sts	9 sts

Break both yarns leaving 6" (15cm) tails. With yarn needle, thread one
end through the remaining sts and draw up firmly. Draw other end to
inside of thumb. Thread first end through drawn-up sts again, darn a
few sts to secure it, and draw to inside of thumb.

Finishing the Mitten

Turn mitten inside out and darn all ends into the back of the fabric.
Repair any gaps at corners of the thumb hole with nearby tails.
Trim ends closely.
This mitten can be worn on either hand. Make another just like it.

Sawtooth Mittens

I first saw this pattern in a 1908 Priscilla Knitting Book published in Boston. It looked so in tune with Maine double-knit patterns that I took it for one.

I later learned that Sawtooth is knit throughout Nova Scotia and New Brunswick even today. My Maine informant, Nora Johnson, said her mother used to knit the pattern in the Farmington area, and a traditional craft writer in New Hampshire, Barbara Rogers, knows a woman who knits only this pattern, which she learned in her family.

The "teeth" of the Sawtooth pattern can be made in various sizes, from a multiple of five sts in width down to three sts in width for baby mittens. It's also fun to dec at the tip of the fingers and thumb by reducing the size of the sawteeth.

A vertical Sawtooth pattern is knitted on mittens in Quebec, where it is called *fleché*, or fletching, like the feathers on an arrow.

The traditional colors for this mitten in New England are bright red and gray. Every example I've seen by traditional knitters, even the 1908 picture, has been in these colors.

My pattern is loosely based on the Priscilla Knitting Book pattern and on examples lent by Janetta Dexter and the Nova Scotia Museum. Although the Priscilla Knitting Book version has a striped thumb, certain technicalities of the pattern make it easier to maintain the sawtooth throughout.

Sawtooth Mittens with ribbed cuff (underneath). Note the decorative circular decrease. Sawtooth Mittens with snug striped Maine cuff (on top).

Sawtooth Mittens

Yarn Bartlettyarns 2-ply Fisherman yarn or other medium weight wool yarn.

For a pair with a Maine snug cuff, you will need:
MC and CC, each

(oz)	1¾	2⅜	2⅜	2½	2½	3
(g)	50	67.75	67.75	71.25	71.25	85.5

For a pair with a ribbed cuff, you will need:
MC (including the cuff)

(oz)	2	3	3	3⅛	3⅛	3¾
(g)	57	85.5	85.5	89	89	107
CC (oz)	1½	1¾	1¾	1¾	1¾	2¼
(g)	42.75	50	50	50	50	64

Equipment 1 set Size 3 (3.25mm, Can. Size 10) double-pointed needles, or size you need to knit in pattern at correct tension • 1 set Size 1 (2.25mm, Can. Size 13) double-pointed needles for optional ribbed cuff • 6" (15cm) length of contrasting waste yarn • Blunt-tipped yarn needle

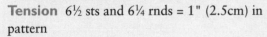

Tension 6½ sts and 6¼ rnds = 1" (2.5cm) in pattern

Measurements—inches and *centimeters*

	Child 8–10	WM	WL	MM	ML	XL
			Adult			
Hand length	6½	7	7½	7	7½	8½
	16.5	18	19	18	19	21.5
Hand circumference, incl. tip of thumb	8	9	9	9½	9½	10
	20.25	23	23	24.25	24.25	25.5
Mitten hand length	7	7½	8	7½	8	9
	18	19	20.25	19	20.25	23
Mitten thumb (⅓ hand)	2⅜	2½	2⅝	2½	2⅝	3
	6	6.5	6.75	6.5	6.75	7.5
Mitten width	4	4⅜	4⅜	4⅝	4⅝	5
	10.25	11.25	11.25	11.75	11.75	12.75

As with any mitten in which the width is limited by the number of sts in the pattern rep, Sawtooth, with a 5-stitch rep, may be slightly narrower or wider than the standard measurements. The Adult Medium and Large sizes will fit closely, but not uncomfortably.

ABBREVIATIONS beg: beginning • CC: contrast color • dec(s): decrease(s) • inc(s): increase(s) • k: knit • k2tog: knit 2 together • M1: make 1 stitch • M1L: make 1 stitch left • M1R: make 1 stitch right • MC: main color • p: purl • rep: repeat • rnd(s): round(s) • SSK2tog: slip, slip, knit 2 sts together • st(s): stitch(es) • twisted M1: twisted make 1 cast-on

Pattern

Although the appearance of the pattern is of perfectly square blocks sliced diagonally, the block is actually 6 rnds and 5 sts, with two rnds worked in solid colors. This can be knitted flat with double-pointed needles. All incs are in Rnd 2 of the chart.

Some knitters like to reverse the slant of the sawteeth for the left mitten—perhaps to show that the mittens are handmade. If you don't, you can knit two left or two rights, because the pattern wraps perfectly around the hand and the decs are made around the entire hand. You will find people, kids or adults, do wear them on either hand anyhow.

Off the Cuff

I've provided directions for a traditional Maine snug cuff with 2-st-wide vertical stripes in stockinette and for a stretchier ribbed cuff in one color.

Sawtooth

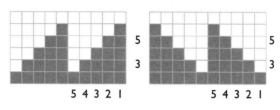

Pattern for left hand   Pattern for right hand

Sawtooth—final decreases

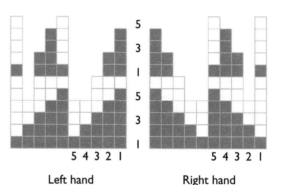

Left hand   Right hand

Key

☐ MC–main color

■ CC–contrast color

Making the striped cuff

		Child	Adult				
		8–10	WM	WL	MM	ML	XL
With MC, larger needles, and using the Maine method (p. 13), cast on		48 sts	52 sts	52 sts	60 sts	60 sts	64 sts
Distribute sts on 3 needles:	Needle 1:	12 sts	12 sts	12 sts	12 sts	12 sts	16 sts
	Needle 2:	24 sts	28 sts	28 sts	32 sts	32 sts	32 sts
	Needle 3:	12 sts	12 sts	12 sts	16 sts	16 sts	16 sts
Join into a triangle, being careful not to twist sts around needles. Join CC by sewing (p. 20).							
Work k2 MC, k2 CC for	(inches)	2⅛	2½	2⅝	2½	2⅝	3
	(cm)	5.5	6.5	6.75	6.5	6.75	7.5
Work 1 rnd MC and inc, evenly spaced,		2 sts	3 sts	3 sts	—	—	1 st
	Total (a multiple of 5 sts):	50 sts	55 sts	55 sts	60 sts	60 sts	65 sts

Alternative: Making a ribbed cuff

		Child	Adult				
		8–10	WM	WL	MM	ML	XL
With MC, smaller needles, and using the Maine method (p. 13), cast on		48 sts	54 sts	54 sts	60 sts	60 sts	63 sts
Distribute sts so that each needle begins with the first k st of a rib:	Needle 1:	12 sts	12 sts	12 sts	12 sts	12 sts	15 sts
	Needle 2:	24 sts	27 sts	27 sts	33 sts	33 sts	33 sts
	Needle 3:	12 sts	15 sts	15 sts	15 sts	15 sts	15 sts
Work k2, p1 ribbing for	(inches)	2⅛	2½	25/8	2½	2⅝	3
	(cm)	5.5	6.5	6.75	6.5	6.75	7.5
Change to larger needles and stockinette. Work Rnd 1 MC and inc on Needle 2		2 sts	1 st	1 st	—	—	2 sts.
Six sts before end of rnd, join CC (p. 18) and work to end of rnd.							
	Total (multiple of 5):	50 sts	55 sts	55 sts	60 sts	60 sts	65 sts

Starting the pattern and the thumb gore

Start Sawtooth Chart, Left or Right, at lower right.

Begin thumb gore in Rnd 2 of chart. You will inc 5 sts every 6th rnd, laying in a complete new pattern rep each time. This placement of the inc will locate the joint in the pattern out of sight on the palm.

Mark sides of thumb gore with short pieces of waste yarn, as it's easy to lose track in the radial symmetry of Sawtooth. Every couple of rnds, lay the waste yarn back or forth between the same two sts to have a moving marker that you will be in no danger of knitting.

Right mitten: Work Rnd 2 of chart to 2 blocks before end of rnd. In next 5 sts, inc 5 sts above 5 sts: Place marker, k both strands (MC then CC) into the front of St 1, M1CC (p. 20), k1CC into St 2. K both strands (CC then MC) into St 3, M1 CC, k1 CC into St 4, M1CC, k1CC into St 5.

You have just completed two blocks of pattern above 5 sts and should be about to work St 1 of Line 2 of the chart. Lay a second piece of waste yarn here and knit even in pattern to end of rnd.

Left mitten: (The beg of the rnd marks this side of the thumb gore.) K1CC into St 1, M1CC, k1CC into St 2, k both colors (CC then MC) into St 3, M1CC; k1CC into St 4, M1CC, k both colors (CC then MC) into St 5.

You have just completed two blocks of pattern above 5 sts and are about to work St 1 of the second block of Line 2 on the chart. Lay a second piece of waste yarn here and knit even in pattern.

	Child 8–10	Adult				
		WM	WL	MM	ML	XL
Both mittens: Inc in this way a total of	3 X	4 X	4 X	4 X	4 X	5 X
Total between waste-yarn markers:	20 sts	25 sts	25 sts	25 sts	25 sts	30 sts
Work even in pattern until thumb gore measures (inches)	2⅛	2⅜	2½	23/8	2½	2⅞
(cm)	5.5	6	6.5	6	6.5	7.25
and put onto the waste yarn the center pattern reps, that is:	15 sts	20 sts	20 sts	20 sts	20 sts	25 sts

Both mittens: Inc in this way a total of Each time, place the inc toward the center of the thumb gore. The second inc will be slightly off center toward the beginning of the thumb gore. The third can be placed dead center, the fourth again will be slightly offset, but the offset in both cases will not be obvious.

Complete band of pattern.

Taking off the thumb gore stitches

Pattern Rnd 1: Before knitting the thumb gore sts, remove waste yarn markers and put onto the waste yarn the center pattern reps, that is:

With twisted M1 (p. 23), cast on 5 sts in CC over the gap.
Finish the rnd.

Finish band of pattern and work Rnd 1 of next band—OR, go back
one or two rnds to be at the end of Rnd 1, whichever is closer.

Closing the mitten tip

You will begin decreasing by k2tog 5 times next in 5 adjacent st pairs
to eliminate one or more whole blocks of pattern at once. When it
comes down to the last two bands of decs, you will use a technically
and artistically sweet final dec devised by Nora Johnson particularly for
this mitten. The result is a mitten or thumb tip that looks like a little
MC flower or pinwheel. Cute!

		Child 8–10	Adult				
			WM	WL	MM	ML	XL
With twisted M1 (p. 23), cast on 5 sts in CC over the gap. Finish the rnd.	Total:	55 sts	60 sts	60 sts	65 sts	65 sts	70 sts
Work even in pattern until hand above cuff measures	(inches)	5	5½	6	5½	6	7
	(cm)	12.75	14	15.25	14	15.25	18
or 2" (5cm) less than the desired final length.							
Initial dec: Pattern Line 2: Dec by k2tog in pattern 5 times, starting at the beg of a block in the middle of needle(s)		2	2	2	2 & 3	2 & 3	All
	Total remaining:	50 sts	55 sts	55 sts	55 sts	55 sts	55 sts
Complete Lines 2 through 4 of pattern band.							
Final dec: Follow Final Dec chart, choosing right or left according to the slant of the sawteeth on your mitten. After Rnd 5, there will be		40 sts	44 sts	44 sts	44 sts	44 sts	44 sts
After second Rnd 1, there will be		30 sts	33 sts	33 sts	33 sts	33 sts	33 sts
After second Rnd 3, there will be		20 sts	22 sts	22 sts	22 sts	22 sts	22 sts
After second Rnd 5, there will be		10 sts	11 sts	11 sts	11 sts	11 sts	11 sts

Check measurements against finished measurements at beg of directions. If
you are satisfied, break yarn leaving two 6" (15cm) tails. With yarn needle,
thread one end through the remaining sts and draw up firmly. Draw other
end to inside of the thumb. Thread end through drawn-up sts again,
darn a few sts to secure it, and draw it to inside of thumb.

Working the thumb

		Child	Adult				
		8–10	WM	WL	MM	ML	XL
On Needle 1, pick up 5 sts from top of thumb hole. On Needles 2 and 3, pick up from waste yarn		15 sts	20 sts	20 sts	20 sts	20 sts	25 sts
On the same 2 needles, pick up and twist 1 st onto needles from each corner of thumb hole.	Total:	22 sts	27 sts	27 sts	27 sts	27 sts	32 sts
Work even in pattern until, measuring from the base of thumb by the palm, the thumb measures	(inches)	1⅝	1¾	1⅞	1¾	1⅞	2¼
	(cm)	*4.25*	*4.5*	*4.75*	*4.5*	*4.75*	*5.75*

Finish band of pattern or rip back to Rnd 1 of pattern, whichever is closer. (Remember that it's better for the thumb to be a tad too long than a tad too short!)

Closing the tip of the thumb

Work Final Dec chart for left or right mitten, omitting first Lines 5 and 6 in chart.		Child	Adult				
	After Rnd 1, there will be	16 sts	20 sts	20 sts	20 sts	20 sts	24 sts
	After Rnd 3, there will be	12 sts	15 sts	15 sts	15 sts	15 sts	18 sts
	After Rnd 5, there will be	8 sts	10 sts	10 sts	10 sts	10 sts	12 sts

Check measurements against finished measurements at beg of directions. If they satisfy you, break yarn leaving a 6" (15cm) tail. With yarn needle, thread one end through the remaining sts and draw up firmly. Draw other end to inside of the thumb. Thread first end through drawn-up sts again, darn a few sts to secure it, and draw to inside of thumb.

Finishing the mitten

Turn mitten inside out and darn all ends into the back of the fabric. Repair possible holes at corners of the thumb hole with nearby tails. Trim ends closely.

This mitten is a right- or a left-handed mitten. Knit another, being careful that it is for the opposite hand. Practically speaking, however, this mitten can be worn on either hand.

Incredible Checkerboard Mittens

For those who tire of Salt and Pepper knitting, a one-one alternation of two colors that makes a smooth, thick mitten fabric, there's Checkerboard, also called Block or Two-Two, but having nothing to do with trains.

Checkerboard is an alternation of colors in a two-two sequence—two rounds of 2 MC, 2 CC followed by two rnds of the opposite. It shouldn't be very different from Salt and Pepper, but it is. For a reason known only to yarn engineers, this particular alternation pulls the fabric up into ridges like cornrows, thickening the mitten fabric greatly. It looks like a fancy stitch, but it isn't. It's plain old stockinette.

Checkerboard can be knit with 3 sts and 3 rnds per check, or even with 3 sts and rnds, but the most common pattern has 2 of each.

Checkerboard is knit in central (Farmington) and northern (Aroostook County) Maine, as well as New Brunswick and Nova Scotia. I've never seen a Checkerboard Mitten from southern Maine, but that doesn't mean there aren't any. The entire mitten pattern must have come from Scandinavia—I discovered one identical to it in a collection of Norwegian mittens in *Annie Blatt*, a German women's magazine—same rounded tips, same pull-up effect, even the same unusual increase all at the bottom of the thumb gore

Two versions are presented in this book, one taken intact from a mitten in New Sweden, Maine, and a very light version in sport weight yarn for babies and young children (p. 189).

The heavy weight mittens are super—super thick, super warm, super solid, super flexible. They were originally knitted for woodsmen, who wore them as liners under leather mittens.

The woman who gave me the pattern, Beda Spooner, of New Sweden, told me she is Swedish. Both her mother and father were Swedish, she said. Mrs. Spooner is the only woman I interviewed who still sends fleeces to Bartlett Mills to exchange for yarn. Her son keeps and shears the sheep and takes the fleeces to Harmony, Maine, where he gets her gray and white natural yarn.

She washes the heavy 3-ply yarn in hot water in the skein, and then winds it for her winter knitting. Mrs. Spooner has a local reputation for her mittens and was afraid that publishing her instructions might damage her business. I hope it didn't.

I tried knitting these mittens without shrinking the yarn ahead and found that they turned out wishy-washy—flaccid and easy to stretch out of shape. The next time, I simmered the yarn, in the skein, for 20 to 30 minutes with water and a little Orvus animal shampoo (from the feed store, but any fine soap would work), and then rinsed it thoroughly in cold water. The yarn became thicker, ropier, *softer*, and quite interesting to work with—but harder to knit at 6 sts per inch. The mittens neither stretched nor shrank afterward. I wore them to Reid State Park one sunny spring day, dropped them, and never found them again.

In spite of the simple and curious manner of putting on the thumb gore (all at once at the bottom), this is not an easy mitten to knit because of the thickness of the yarn and the tightness of the knit. Nonetheless, it's well worth the effort to knit a pair, though only in Bartlettyarns 3-ply Homespun Yarn, prewashed in boiling water! They are warm, soft, flexible, and—unless you lose them—will last for years.

Checkerboard Mitten by Beda Spooner of New Sweden, Maine. Note the sudden increase at the thumb just above the cuff.

Incredible Checkerboard Mittens

Yarn MC: 3 oz (85g) dark color 3-ply Homespun from Bartlettyarns • CC: 3 oz (85g) light color 3-ply Homespun from Bartlettyarns. This yarn is about twice as heavy as ordinary medium weight yarn. Remember that, for best results, this yarn should be boiled as described in the introduction. After the yarn has cooled, put it in the washing machine on the spin cycle (only!), then hang or lay to dry thoroughly before you start to knit. Do not use synthetics or Superwash™-treated wool yarns as they will not respond to boiling.

Equipment 1 set Size 8 (5mm, Can. Size 6) double-pointed needles, or size you need to knit in pattern at correct tension • 1 set Size 5 (3.75mm, Can. Size 9) double-pointed needles for ribbing • 12" (30cm) length of contrasting waste yarn • Blunt-tipped yarn needle

Tension 6 sts and 5½ rnds = 1" (2.5cm) in pattern

ABBREVIATIONS beg: beginning • CC: contrast color • dec(s): decrease(s) • inc(s): increase(s) • k: knit • k2tog: knit 2 together • M1: make 1 stitch • M1L: make 1 stitch left • M1R: make 1 stitch right • MC: main color • p: purl • rep: repeat • rnd(s): round(s) • SSK2tog: slip, slip, knit 2 sts together • st(s): stitch(es) • twisted M1: twisted make 1 cast-on

---

Measurements—inches and *centimeters*

	WM	WL	MM	ML
Hand length	7	7½	7	7½
	18	*19*	*18*	*19*
Hand circumference, incl. tip of thumb	9	9	9½	9½
	23	*23*	*24.25*	*24.25*
Mitten hand length	7½	8	7½	8
	19	*20.25*	*19*	*20.25*
Mitten thumb length (⅓ hand)	2½	25/8	2½	25/8
	6.5	*6.75*	*6.5*	*6.75*
Mitten width*	4	4	4½	4½
	10.25	*10.25*	*11.5*	*11.5*

* Checkerboard Mittens are quite flexible, and although this measurement seems scant for the measurement around the hand, it is comfortable and adequate. The mitten tends to stretch somewhat widthwise over time, and it is easy to make it too wide.

Pattern

The pattern is a 4-st, 4-rnd rep. Its tendency to pull up sharply in wide ridges is a desirable feature of the pattern and should not be discouraged.

Key

■ MC–main color

□ CC–contrast color

Checkerboard Chart

Checkerboard Thumb Gore

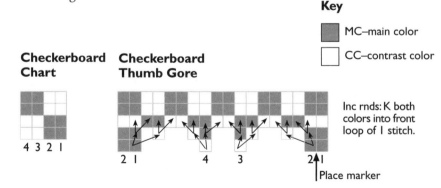

Inc rnds: K both colors into front loop of 1 stitch.

4 3 2 1

2 1   4   3   2 1

Place marker

Making the cuff

	WM	WL	MM	ML
With MC, smaller needles, and using the Maine method (p. 13), cast on	36 sts	36 sts	42 sts	42 sts

Divide sts equally between 3 needles, starting each needle with the beg of a k rib. Join into a triangle, being careful not to twist sts around the needles. Work k2, p1 ribbing in MC for 6 rnds. Join CC (p. 18) in last 8 sts. Continue ribbing CC for 3 rnds, MC for 4 rnds, CC for 3 rnds, MC for 4 rnds, and CC for 3 rnds. (Don't break the yarn at the end of a stripe, but carry it up to its next appearance.)

	WM	WL	MM	ML
Change to larger needles and stockinette. K1 rnd CC, picking up the little loop between every pair of k sts, thus increasing	12 sts	36 sts	14 sts	14 sts
Total:	48 sts	48 sts	56 sts	56 sts
Distribute sts among 3 needles: Needle 1:	16 sts	16 sts	16 sts	16 sts
Needle 2:	16 sts	16 sts	20 sts	20 sts
Needle 3:	16 sts	16 sts	20 sts	20 sts

Starting the pattern and thumb gore

Start Checkerboard chart at lower right. Carry MC ahead throughout (p. 16).

Start thumb gore immediately: Thumb gore incs will be above the first 2 ribs on Needle 2. In the first 2 pattern rnds, you will inc 12 sts just above 4 sts of these 2 ribs. This will be the only thumb gore inc. See Checkerboard Thumb Gore chart for a graphic representation of the incs.

Rnd 1, Needle 1: *K2 MC, k2 CC; rep from * to end of needle.

Needle 2: Lay in the waste yarn at beg of this needle to mark the beg of thumb gore. K1 MC; k both colors into St 2 (p. 21)—first MC then CC; k both colors into St 3—first CC then MC; k both colors into St 4—MC then CC; k both colors into St 5—CC then MC; k1 MC into St 6. This adds 4 new sts. Lay waste yarn after St 6 from the preceding rnd, to mark the end of thumb gore. Continue in pattern to end of the rnd.

	WM	WL	MM	ML

Note: Check after the first rnd that the rep comes out even. A mistake here can throw everything off and take the fun out of the project.

Rnd 2 of the pattern is identical to Rnd 1, but when you reach the marker, k1 MC, work the same pattern of incs across next 8 sts, then k1 MC. You will have 18 sts between markers. 12 of these sts are incs. Total:

	WM	WL	MM	ML
Total:	60 sts	60 sts	68 sts	68 sts

When thumb gore incs are complete, work even in pattern for a total of 14 rnds (7 two-rnd bands) above the cuff.

Taking off the thumb gore stitches

Place the 18 thumb gore sts between the marking lines onto waste yarn, starting with first st of a pair. Remove waste yarn markers. Using twisted M1 (p. 23), cast on 2 sts in pattern over the gap.

	WM	WL	MM	ML
Total:	44 sts	44 sts	52 sts	52 sts

Inc 4 sts above thumb hole in the next rnd: Knit both colors, in order, into the st before thumb hole; knit both colors into both sts over thumb hole; knit both colors into st after thumb hole always maintaining the color sequence to match the rest of the rnd.

	WM	WL	MM	ML
Total:	48 sts	48 sts	56 sts	56 sts

Distribute sts among 3 needles:

	WM	WL	MM	ML
Needle 1:	16 sts	16 sts	18 sts	18 sts
Needle 2:	16 sts	16 sts	18 sts	18 sts
Needle 3:	16 sts	16 sts	20 sts	20 sts

Work even in pattern until work above cuff measures

	WM	WL	MM	ML
(inches)	6	6½	6	6½
(cm)	*15.25*	*16.5*	*15.25*	*16.5*

This is 10 to 12 two-rnd bands of pattern.

Closing the mitten tip

On this fairly narrow mitten, the fit works best if the dec area is brief, producing a short, rounded tip. The decs are thus 6 decs to a rnd, every rnd, with a final 9- or 10-st dec. While Mrs. Spooner uses only k2tog

	WM	WL	MM	ML
(p. 24) on her mittens, I have combined k2tog with SSK2tog (p. 24), which seems to preserve the pattern better.				
Dec Rnd: Needle 1: K2 tog in pattern, k to 2 sts from end of needle, SSK2tog in pattern. Needles 2 and 3: Same as Needle 1. **Note:** The pattern of the dec sts is the pattern on the needle you are working on. It's easy to be tempted to continue the pattern on, for example, the last or first st on the needle.				
Rep Dec Rnd every rnd until there remain	18 sts	18 sts	20 sts	20 sts.
Last rnd: Alternate colors while you k2tog, k2tog, SSK2tog. (In the larger size, where there are 8 sts on one needle, k2tog 3 times, then SSK2tog, still alternating colors.)				

Check measurements against finished measurements at beg of directions. If you are satisfied, break yarn, leaving a 6" (15cm) tail. With a yarn needle, thread one end through the remaining sts and draw up firmly. Draw other end to inside of mitten. Thread first end through drawn-up sts once more, darn a few sts to secure end and draw end to inside of mitten.

Working the thumb

The thumb is the same width in all four sizes but a tad longer in the two Large sizes.

Join both yarns by sewing (p. 20) into back of fabric starting at the right side of the thumb hole.
Needles 1 and 2: Pick up 18 sts from waste yarn.
Needle 3: Pick up and twist 2 sts onto needle in each corner of thumb hole. Pick up 2 sts at top of thumb hole. Total: 24 sts.

Starting at right corner, work in pattern, matching pattern to that on thumb gore.

		WM	WL	MM	ML
Work even until thumb next to palm measures	(inches)	1⅞	2⅛	1⅞	2⅛
	(cm)	*4.75*	*5.25*	*4.75*	*5.25*

Closing the tip of the thumb

Dec as on hand: In pattern, k2tog, work to 2 sts from end of needle, SSK2tog. Do this on all needles, once, then k2tog, k2tog, SSK2tog on all needles. 9 sts remain.

Break yarns, leaving 6" (15cm) tails. With a yarn needle, thread one end through the remaining sts and draw up firmly. Draw other end to inside of thumb. Thread first end through drawn-up sts again, darn a few sts to secure it, and draw to inside of thumb.

Finishing the mitten

Turn mitten inside out and darn all ends into the back of the fabric. Repair possible holes at corners of the thumb hole with nearby tails. Trim ends closely.

Make another identical mitten. This mitten can be worn on either hand.

Chebeague Island Fishermen's Wet Mittens (p. 28), one pair knitted by Minnie Doughty and treasured as keepsakes by her daughters, the other pair, shrunk and well used, knitted by Chebeague Island Methodist Church Ladies' Aid

Left: Fleece-Stuffed Mittens (p. 54) and cap (p. 113).
Right: Sawtooth Mittens (p. 100) and
Sawtooth-patterned watch cap (p. 113)

Fox and Geese Mittens and toque (pps. 77 and 149)

Shag on the Inside Mitten (p. 62), Flying Geese Glove (p. 120)

Striped Mittens (p. 87). On bottom mitten, white was carried ahead halfway up the hand, then blue was carried ahead. On middle mitten, red was carried ahead. Mitten in background was knitted by Nora Johnson.

Incredible Checkerboard Mittens (p. 107) in gray and white, Salt and Pepper Mittens (p. 94) in red and black

Left to right: Mrs. Martin's Finger Mitt (p. 164) with Waves pattern, Labrador Diamonds Mitten (p. 156), Mrs. Martin's Finger Mitt (p. 164) with Diamond Stripes pattern, Big Waves Mitten (p. 174)

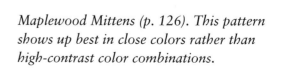

Maplewood Mittens (p. 126). This pattern shows up best in close colors rather than high-contrast color combinations.

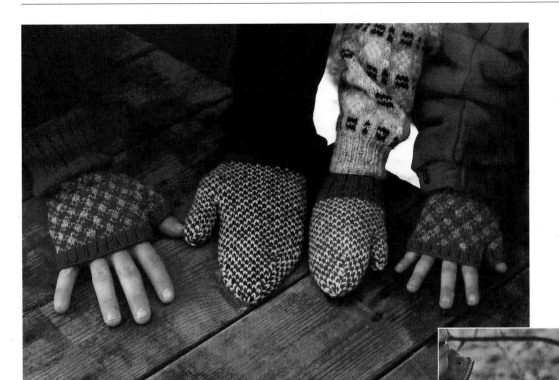

Outside: Two sizes of Chipman's Check Wristers (p. 142). Inside: Two sizes of Salt and Pepper Mittens (p. 94).

Two versions of Mittens Hooked on a Dowel (p. 47): green mittens hooked in acrylic yarn by Albert Miller, blue and white mitten hooked by the author in wool yarn

Left to right: Wee Checkerboard Mitten (p. 189), child's Sawtooth Mitten (p. 100), Baby Foxes and Goslings Mitten (p. 184)

Left to right: Spruce Mittens (p. 134) and Spruce-patterned watch cap (p. 113), Baby Foxes and Goslings Mittens (p. 184), baby helmet (p. 207) with Fox and Geese pattern

Compass Mittens for Small Mariners (p. 194)
in two sizes

Double-Rolled Mittens (p. 36). Edna Mower made the
larger pair with ribbed cuffs. Smaller mitten with shagged
(and ribbed) cuff was copied from a mitten at the Maine
State Museum made by Hattie Stover Brown.

Petites Mitaines en Fleur-de-lis (p. 200):
Size 0–6 months with no thumb and a ribbed cuff,
Size 0–6 months with no thumb and a wide patterned
cuff and tie, Size 6–12 months with ribbed cuff

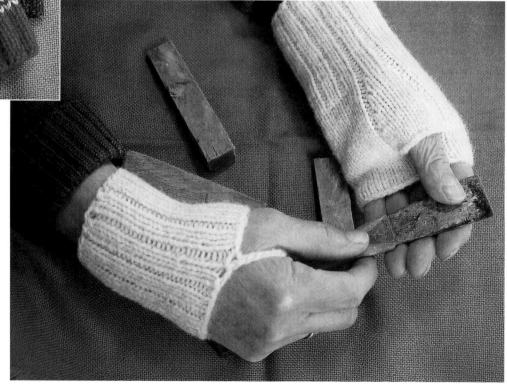

Left: Mitten with Double Irish Chain pattern (p. 180) made from Labrador Diamonds Mittens directions (p. 157). A narrow strip of Newfoundland Palm Stitch is visible on left edge of mitten. Right: Newfoundland palm stitch (p. 181) on a small mitten

Left to right: Laura Ridgewell's Wrister (p. 70) and Phyllis Wharton's Wrister (p. 72)

A Patterned Watch Cap
to Match Your Mittens

If you have traditional double-knit mittens, it's nice to have at least a hat to go with them. Some people also like to knit socks and sweaters to match, but we will leave that to traditional knitters making clothes for their grandchildren. This cap is a design I've seen in Newfoundland and Maine.

There are two reasonable places to put a double-knit design on a cap—on the crown and on the stockinette turn-up of a toque. You can apply any of the small geometric patterns to either of these caps, but think a little about the pattern first. Very small patterns look better on the crown, while big, blocky patterns look good in both places, but great on the turn-up.

For a toque with a patterned turn-up, see p. 149.

The pattern on this cap is on the crown. It's a cap seen often in Newfoundland, but rarely in other parts of the area, where handmade caps are usually knitted in one-color ribbing or in Norwegian color patterns.

Watch cap and mitten in spruce pattern

Patterned Watch Cap

Yarn This cap is knitted in medium weight yarn. We have used Bartlettyarns 2-ply Fisherman yarn, Rauma Istra, and McAusland's 2-ply Medium with equal success, but you can use any medium-weight wool or synthetic yarn that knits in pattern to the correct tension.

MC	(oz)	2	2¼	2½	3
	(g)	*57*	*64*	*71.25*	*85.5*
CC	(oz)	1	1¼	1½	2
	(g)	*28.5*	*35.5*	*42.75*	*57*

Equipment 1 set (5) Size 6 (4mm, Can. size 8) 10" (25.5cm) long, double-pointed needles, or size you need to knit in pattern at correct tension • 1 set (5) Size 4 (3.5mm, Can. Size 9 or 10) 10" (25.5cm) long, double-pointed (or straight) needles for ribbing • Blunt-tipped yarn needle

Tension 6 sts = 1" (2.5cm) in pattern.

Note: Knitting tension is looser on caps than on mittens. Soft and fluffy is good, as there is no call for dense and durable caps. No one wears out the top of their hat, except possibly jugglers who balance unicycles on their heads. The difference in tension doesn't affect the appearance of the color patterns much.

Pay special attention to your tension if you use Stripes or Checkerboard, as the fabric has a tendency to pull up in ridges (thus tightening the tension) in these patterns. Check it after about 10 rnds of pattern. Or, make a test swatch ahead of time: Cast on 24 sts in the yarn and needles of your choice and knit circularly for 3" to 4" (7.5–10.25cm). Bind off, and flatten the piece on a work surface. Measure sts per inch at several points. If you have more sts per inch than called for, move to a larger size needle. If you have fewer than called for, use a smaller size needle. I generally find that I gain or lose about one-half st per inch per American needle size.

Measurements—inches and *centimeters*

	Child Sizes		Adult Sizes	
	S	M	M	L
Around the head	16	18	20	22
	40.5	*45.75*	*50.75*	*56*
Over the head— earlobe to earlobe	14	15	16	17
	35.5	*38*	*40.5*	*43.25*
Width of cap, just above turn-up	8	9	10	11
	20.25	*23*	*25.5*	*28*
Height from turn-up to tip of cap	7	7½	8	8½
	18	*19*	*20.25*	*21.5*

For a good fit, the cap should be about the same size as the head measurement, taken around the head about where a normal hat (baseball cap, cowboy hat, etc.) rests.

Pattern

The edge of the cap is worked in ribbing, which can be turned up on the outside of the cap and pulled down over the neck and ears in extreme winter weather. Or turn half the ribbing under and hem it to form a warm inside band, which will also warm the ears.

The crown can be worked either by continuing the ribbing or by knitting one of the charted patterns in this book.

To wrap a pattern around a cap—or a mitten—the total number of sts must be a multiple of the pattern rep. You may have to add or subtract up to 4 sts fom the number given here to accommodate the

---

ABBREVIATIONS beg: beginning • CC: contrast color • dec(s): decrease(s) • inc(s): increase(s) • k: knit • k2tog: knit 2 together • MI: make I stitch • MIL: make I stitch left • MIR: make I stitch right • MC: main color • p: purl • rep: repeat • rnd(s): round(s) • SSK2tog: slip, slip, knit 2 sts together • st(s): stitch(es) • twisted MI: twisted make I cast-on

pattern rep. Add or subract the least number of sts necessary in order to match the pattern rep. If there is a question of the cap being too large or too small by more than an inch, consider knitting a different pattern from that on the mittens, but using the same colors. Color can make dissimilar patterns "match" perfectly!

If knitting flat, p every second row of the color pattern and read the chart from left to right on p rows. Add one more st to each end for the seam. (Neither Fox and Geese nor Compass patterns work well in flat knitting.)

Making the ribbed edge

	Child		Adult	
	S	M	M	L
With MC, smaller needles, and using the Maine method (p. 13), cast on on 4 needles, distributing sts more or less evenly, with an even number on each needle, so that each needle begins the first st of a k rib. Join, being careful not to twist sts around the needles.	96 sts	108 sts	120 sts	132 sts
Work k1, p1 ribbing for (inches)	3	3½	4	4
(cm)	*7.5*	*9*	*10.25*	*10.25*

Note: Here's the math for figuring out whether to add or subtract to match the charted pattern you choose. The number of sts on your needles—96, 108, 120 or 132—is divisible by 2, 3, 4, 6, and 12, so any pattern with a rep of those numbers can be knitted on the cap without adding or subtracting sts. Stripes, Salt and Pepper, Chipman's Check, Checkerboard, Fox and Geese, and Vertical Waves fall into this category. For other patterns, you need to adjust:

To work a 5-st rep, (Sawtooth)	–1 st	+2 sts	—	–2 sts
To work a 7-st rep, (Maplewood, Diamond Checks, Waves)	+2 sts	–3 or +4 sts	–1 st	+1 st
To work an 8-st rep, (Compass, Double Irish Chain, Labrador Diamonds)	—	–4 or +4 sts	—	–4 or +4 sts
To work a 10-st rep, (Flying Geese, Diving Geese)	+4 sts	+2 sts	—	–2 sts

Starting the pattern

Change to larger needles and stockinette. Work 1 rnd in MC, adding sts by M1 (p. 20) or decreasing by k2tog (p. 24), evenly distributed, if necessary to make your chosen color pattern come out even. Six sts before end of rnd, join CC (p. 18).

Start pattern of your choice, reading chart from lower right. Carry MC ahead throughout. Check after the first rnd that the rep comes out even. A mistake here can throw everything else off and take the fun out of the project.

Note: After 10 rnds, check to be sure your tension is correct, and rip back if it is off by more than one-half st per inch. (If you are knitting a large cap, with 132 sts at 6 sts = 1" or 2.5cm (the correct tension), the cap will measure 22" or 56cm around when you are finished. If you knit 1 st per inch more tightly, 7 sts = 1 inch or 2.5cm, the same cap will measure only 18" or 45.75cm—about the size for a ten-year-old!)

	Child		Adult	
	S	M	M	L
Work even in pattern until crown measures (inches)	3¾	4½	5	5
(cm)	9.5	11.5	12.75	12.75

from top of ribbing.

Closing the top of the cap

Some of the color patterns have an attractive dec built into the pattern—Fox and Geese, Chipman's Check, and Sawtooth, among others. You can use these decs at the top of your cap as well as at the ends of mittens by working the dec as described for the mitten to the top of the pattern rep, then starting a new pattern rep and repeating the dec on the new band of pattern until 12–18 sts remain.

Other patterns, such as Stripes, Checkerboard, or Salt and Pepper can be decreased at 3 points, all the way to the top of the cap.

To make a 3-point dec, adjust sts onto 3 needles, with about same number of sts on each needle, approximately:	32 sts	36 sts	40 sts	44 sts

then follow the dec directions for the mittens, repeating until 12 to 18 sts remain.

Measure the cap and compare with the measurements at the beg of directions—OR, ideally, try the hat on the recipient at this point. If you are both satisfied with the fit, break yarn leaving two 6" (15cm) tails. With yarn needle, thread one end through the remaining sts and draw up firmly. Draw other end to inside of cap. Thread first end through drawn-up sts again, darn a few sts to secure it and draw to inside of cap.

Finishing the cap

Turn the cap inside out and darn all ends into the back of fabric. Trim ends closely.

PART THREE

Double-Knit Patterns from Atlantic Canada

Most of the double-knit mittens in Maine, Nova Scotia, and New Brunswick are worked in small allover geometric patterns that come from families of primarily Yankee/Scots-Irish/Scottish/English descent. They have been on this continent a long time. No one knows for sure where the patterns came from. Some are knitted in the North Atlantic islands today in much the same way they are knitted here. Some are knitted in parts of Scandinavia as well and certainly in the Swedish northern Aroostook County of Maine.

Some Mainers attribute certain patterns to acquaintances from the Maritime Provinces or Nova Scotia. Some Canadians are sure the patterns came to them from the States with the Loyalists and other immigrants. In fact, there has been so much backing and forthing between the Maritimes and New England and there are so many shared attributes between the two areas that the mingled traditions will probably never be sorted out. And it probably doesn't matter.

Janetta Dexter has written much of this section because she collected double-knit patterns in Nova Scotia and New Brunswick before it ever occurred to me. She knows more about the knitting in those two provinces than I ever will. Of the patterns here, graphs of Flying Geese, Maplewood, and Mattie Owl's Patch (Compass) first appeared in her book *Nova Scotian Double-Knitting Patterns*. (See "Read More about Traditional Mittens" on p. 213.) I've put in a word or two concerning those of her patterns which also occur in Maine or which I know something about, but really, this section belongs to Janetta.

Janetta Dexter, retired school teacher, sheep farmer, spinner, dyer, and knitter, who collected traditional double-knitting patterns in Nova Scotia and New Brunswick and self-published a booklet of patterns that sold out in three days.

Flying Geese Gloves

Anyone who lives along the flight routes of the wild geese knows the thrill of hearing their honking in the fall and the early spring as they pass overhead in long V-formations. Besides knitting patterns, there are quilt patterns, Pueblo Indian pottery designs, and Navaho rug designs named Flying Geese, reflecting the empathy that we earthbound feel for the large birds in their cooperative flights north and south. — *Robin Hansen*

Flying Geese Gloves, knitted by Janetta Dexter based on oral descriptions

To make Flying Geese Mittens, substitute the charted Flying Geese pattern on the Labrador Diamonds Mittens (p. 157). You may wish to adapt the Labrador Diamonds thumb pattern to show the Flying Geese design, as on the Flying Geese Gloves.

This pattern was shown to me by Mrs. Murdock Hollingsworth, of Truro, Nova Scotia, in 1974. She told me that it was traditionally used for gloves, with four bands of pattern on the back of the hand and carried up to the ends of the fingers. A fifth band is carried the length of the thumb.

With the medium-weight yarn ordinarily used for double knitting in Nova Scotia, this made much too large a glove. I could reproduce it only by using a very fine yarn (Lady Galt Kroy) and Canadian Number 14 (US Size 0) needles. I have so far knit them only in one width, although the length of the fingers can easily be adjusted. One way to widen the pattern would be to add more stitches between pattern elements: rather than a single-stitch white line separating the "geese" (column 1 on the chart), knit *two* one-stitch lines of white separated by a single-stitch dark line.

This glove pattern is certainly not for beginners, but a careful, experienced knitter can create a masterpiece.

The pattern itself is simple to knit and can be used with coarser, worsted (medium) weight yarn for mittens or hunter's mitts, with three bands of pattern each on the back and the palm.

I usually use white or light gray for the geese against a navy blue, black, or dark gray background. —*Janetta Dexter*

Flying Geese Gloves

Yarn: 2 oz (60g) each of 2 colors fingering or sport weight yarn. The samples were made in Lady Galt Kroy by Paton and Baldwin. Another elegant yarn for this project would be Rauma Finullgarn, but any wool sport- or fingering-weight yarn will work.

Equipment 1 set Size 2 (2.75mm, Can. size 12) double-pointed needles, or size you need to knit in pattern at correct tension • 1 set Size 0 (2mm, Can. Size 14) double-pointed needles for the ribbed cuff • 6" (15cm) length of contrasting waste yarn • Blunt-tipped yarn needle

Tension 9 sts = 1"(2.5cm). Check your tension for this project before you start by knitting a little tubular swatch, or check it after you've knitted about an inch in pattern. But be sure to check it, and don't cheat, or your Flying Geese Gloves won't be what they should be—a masterpiece of needlecraft. It's easier to rip out an inch than to fall into despondency when the first glove comes out too large or too small.

Measurements—inches and *centimeters*

	Man's M	Man's L
Hand length	7	7½
	17.75	*19*
Hand circumference, incl. tip of thumb	9½	9½
	24	*24*
Mitten hand length	7½	8
	19	*20.25*
Mitten thumb (⅓ hand)	2½	2⅝
	6.5	*6.75*
Mitten width	4¾	4¾
	12	*12*

Patterns

Flying Geese (or its variant, Diving Geese) on the back of the hand and the thumb gore. Salt and Pepper on the palms. Both variants of the Flying Geese pattern are a multiple of 10 sts plus 1. (Because the geese are knitted only on the back of the gloves, you must add one more contrasting st in each rnd to finish the design.) Flying Geese has a 4-rnd rep; Diving Geese, a 6-rnd rep.

Salt and Pepper, used for the palm side of the gloves, is a multiple of 2 stitches and 2 rnds. In Atlantic Canada, Salt and Pepper is used as a filling pattern where a large pattern is difficult to fit into a space.

Ideally, carry MC ahead (p. 16) in Salt and Pepper, CC ahead in the Flying Geese pattern. This is difficult to remember, but will make the proper color stand out in each pattern.

Flying Geese Thumb Gore Increase Chart

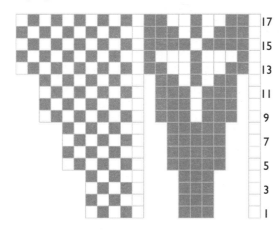

17
15
13
11
9
7
5
3
1

Flying Geese Chart

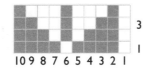

3

1

10 9 8 7 6 5 4 3 2 1

Diving Geese Chart

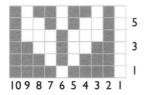

5

3

1

10 9 8 7 6 5 4 3 2 1

Key

MC–main color

CC–contrast color

ABBREVIATIONS beg: beginning • CC: contrast color • dec(s): decrease(s) • inc(s): increase(s) • k: knit • k2tog: knit 2 together • M1: make 1 stitch • M1L: make 1 stitch left • M1R: make 1 stitch right • MC: main color • p: purl • rep: repeat • rnd(s): round(s) • SSK2tog: slip, slip, knit 2 sts together • st(s): stitch(es) • twisted M1: twisted make 1 cast-on

	Man's M	Man's L

Making the cuff

With MC, larger needles, and using the Maine method (p. 13), cast on 72 sts, 24 sts to a needle. Join into a triangle, being careful not to twist sts around the needles. Knit off onto smaller needles using a k2, p1 ribbing. Continue ribbing for 3" (7.5cm).

Change to larger needles and stockinette stitch and work 1 rnd in MC, increasing 4 sts on each needle by M1 (p. 20) between knit sts of the ribbing. Six sts before end of Needle 3, join CC (p. 18) and complete needle in MC.   Total: 84 sts   84 sts

Starting the patterns and thumb gore

The thumb gore of this glove is unique in that it has two portions, a back portion matching the Flying Geese pattern on the back of the hand and a palm portion matching the Salt and Pepper pattern on the palm of the hand. This begins in the very first rnd of pattern.

Right glove: The first 8 sts on Needle 1 form the beginning of the thumb gore.
Needle 1: K3 MC, k1 CC. Work 4 sts Salt and Pepper. Place marker. Continue Salt and Pepper to end of needle.
Needle 2: Place a marker between Sts 14 and 15. Work Salt and Pepper up to the marker, slip the marker and begin Flying (or Diving) Geese pattern with a CC st. Follow chart, starting at lower right. Repeat Flying Geese to end of needle.
Needle 3: Continue Flying Geese pattern, ending with k1 CC st at end of needle. Transfer this last CC st to Needle 1. Work 3 more rnds even in pattern.

Left glove: The last 8 sts on Needle 3 form the beginning of the thumb gore.
Needle 1: Begin working Flying Geese (or Diving Geese) pattern.
Needle 2: Continue Flying Geese pattern to the middle of the needle, ending the fourth block of pattern with the extra CC stitch. Work the remaining sts on this needle in Salt and Pepper pattern.
Needle 3: Work Salt and Pepper pattern up to 8th st from end of needle. Place a marker and continue to work Salt and Pepper pattern for 4 more sts. (This is the palm side of the base of the thumb gore.) Now knit the base of the *back* of the thumb gore: K1 CC, k3 MC. The last CC st needed to close the Flying Geese portion of the thumb gore is located at the beg of Needle 1. Knit it and transfer it to Needle 3.

	Man's M	Man's L

Increasing on the thumb gore is a little tricky, as Salt and Pepper and the Flying Geese patterns have different methods of increasing. You will inc 2 sts in each portion of the thumb gore in each inc rnd.

Inc Rnd:
Flying Geese portion: Work 1 CC st, M1L (p. 20) in MC, knit MC to CC st, M1R, k1 CC.
Salt and Pepper portion: between the marker and the Flying Geese portion, k both colors, in correct pattern order (p. 21), into a MC st then into a CC st. This can be anywhere within the Salt and Pepper part of the thumb gore.

When you have increased in both portions of the thumb gore, you will have 4 more sts (total 13 sts) between marker and end of rnd.

Follow the inc chart, adding the goose pattern as shown starting at the second inc. You will inc a total of 3 times. There will be 21 sts between the marker and the end of the needle.

		Man's M	Man's L
Work even in patterns until hand above cuff measures	(inches)	2¼	2½
	(cm)	*5.75*	*6.4*

Taking off the thumb gore stitches

Work next rnd in pattern, but before knitting them, put the 21 thumb gusset sts on a piece of waste yarn for the thumb. Using twisted M1 (p. 23), cast on 9 sts over the gap.

		Man's M	Man's L
Work even until hand above cuff measures	(inches)	3¾	4
	(cm)	*9.5*	*10.25*

Take off stitches for the fingers

Take off sts for the *little finger:* Work up to 11 sts before the center of the second needle. Place 22 sts—11 Salt and Pepper, 11 Flying Geese—on a piece of waste yarn for the little finger. Cast on 6 sts over the gap in pattern(s) and k 2 rnds in pattern.

Take off sts for the *ring finger:* K up to 12 sts from the center of the second needle: Place 24 sts on a string for the ring finger. Cast on 6 sts in patterns(s) between fingers and work 1 rnd.

Take off sts for the *middle finger:* K up to 13 sts from center of Needle 2 and put 26 sts on a piece of waste yarn for the middle finger. Cast on 6 sts over the gap.

		Man's M	Man's L
Work index finger: Arrange remaining 30 sts on 3 needles, with all Flying Geese sts on Needle 1. Work index finger with one Flying Geese block on the back and the remainder in Salt and Pepper. Be careful that the 2 white lines continue unbroken from the back of the hand. Work even until finger measures	(inches)	2¾	3¼
	(cm)	7	*8.25*

Decrease for all fingers and the thumb

At the beg of each needle, SSK2 tog in pattern (p. 24), work in pattern to 2 sts from end of needle, k2 tog in pattern (p. 24). This leans the decreases away from the "seams" but maintains the white line on each side of the Flying Geese pattern. Do this every needle, every rnd, until 6 sts remain. Break yarn and use a yarn needle to pull up these 6 sts on both strands.

		Man's M	Man's L
Work middle finger: Join both yarns by sewing (p. 20) into back of fabric near the base of the index finger. Pick up 6 sts along lower edge of index finger, being careful not to leave holes in the corners. Place these and the stitches from the waste yarn on 3 needles. Total 32 sts. K middle finger like index finger, until it is	(inches)	3	3½
	(cm)	7.5	9

Finish like the index finger.

		Man's M	Man's L
Work ring finger and little finger the same way, picking up all sts from the waste yarn and 6 sts from the base of the preceding finger. Work ring finger for	(inches)	2¾	3¼
	(cm)	7	*8.25*

then dec, close, and finish.

		Man's M	Man's L
Work little finger for	(inches)	2½	2¾
	(cm)	6.4	7

then dec, close, and finish.

Working the thumb

Join yarn by sewing into back of fabric starting at the right side of the thumb hole.

With Needle 1, pick up 11 sts at corners and the top of thumb hole. Put the 21 sts from the waste yarn on the other 2 needles.

		Man's M	Man's L
Work even in patterns until thumb measures	(inches)	2½	2¾
	(cm)	6.5	7

Check measurements against finished measurements at beg of directions before breaking yarn. If you are satisfied, break yarn leaving a 6" (15cm) tail. With a yarn needle, thread one end through the remaining sts and draw up firmly. Draw other end to inside of thumb and each finger. Thread first end through drawn-up sts again, darn a few sts to secure end and draw end to inside of thumb and each finger.

Finishing the glove

Turn glove inside out and darn all ends into the back of the fabric. Repair possible holes at corners of the thumb hole and between fingers with nearby tails. Trim ends closely.

This glove is a right- or a left-handed glove. Knit another, being very careful that it is for the opposite hand!

Maplewood Mittens

I found this old pattern framed in the small museum at Maplewood, Lunenburg County, Nova Scotia. I later learned that it was a piece of a Larrigan sock, the huge, double-knit socks men used to wear under their moccasin-like Larrigan boots and over their heavy wool work pants.

I called the pattern by its place of origin for some time before I found out that its rightful name is Northern Star. If you look at the pattern, you can see two stars—a dark one with a light rectangle and a dark diamond in the center, and a light one with a dark rectangle and a light diamond in the center. It's an optical illusion of the sort craftswomen love to play with. —*Janetta Dexter*

Quilters who see this pattern always exclaim, "Rob Peter to pay Paul!" Any patchwork pattern that seems to use the leftover parts of one square to make up its opposite in the next square is named with this colorful expression, which sprang up when a church tax in the Middle Ages was diverted from the building of St. Peter's Cathedral to the building of St. Paul's. It's almost a pity we can't apply the name to this pattern, but although it seems to burst forth spontaneously from the lips of quilters, it really has nothing to do with knitting.

I first saw this pattern at Janetta's house, where she had knitted it into a mitten, dark blue and bright blue, as in the color photo. I loved it immediately, but when I asked her to knit a sample for this book, she knitted it in light sheep's gray and navy. Although easier to see in

Maplewood Mitten in close colors, showing split block on thumb gore and index-finger line.

the black and white photo, the pattern was completely changed by the sharp color contrast, which emphasized all its little bits and pieces. It was hard to see the design at all. Because Northern Star is a fairly busy pattern, it looks best knitted in two fairly close colors like dark and light gray, dark navy and medium blue, or maybe maroon and a heathery red.

These directions are for the experienced knitter—kind of a double-black-diamond of knitting. Good luck! —*Robin Hansen*

Maplewood Mittens

Yarn Use DK or medium-weight yarn in two close colors. For the sample we used a Canadian 2-ply yarn from Cottage Craft (Sources, p. 215). Bartlettyarns 2-ply Fisherman or other medium weight yarn will work too.

MC	(oz)	1½	2	2	3	3	3½
	(g)	42.75	57	57	85.5	85.5	100
CC	(oz)	1	1½	1½	2	2	2½
	(g)	28.5	42.75	42.75	57	57	71.25

Equipment 1 set Size 4 (3.5mm, Can. Size 9) double-pointed needles, or size you need to knit in pattern at correct tension • 1 set Size 2 (2.75mm, Can. Size 12) double-pointed needles for ribbed cuff • 12" (30cm) length of contrasting waste yarn • Blunt-tipped yarn needle

Tension 6 sts oand 7 rnds = 1" (2.5cm)

ABBREVIATIONS beg: beginning • CC: contrast color • dec(s): decrease(s) • inc(s): increase(s) • k: knit • k2tog: knit 2 together • M1: make 1 stitch • M1L: make 1 stitch left • M1R: make 1 stitch right • MC: main color • p: purl • rep: repeat • rnd(s): round(s) • SSK2tog: slip, slip, knit 2 sts together • st(s): stitch(es) • twisted M1: twisted make 1 cast-on

Measurements—inches and *centimeters*

	Child Sizes			Adult Sizes		
	2–4	4–6	8–10	M	L	XL
Hand length	4½	5½	6½	7	7½	8½
	11.5	*14*	*16.5*	*17.75*	*19*	*21.5*
Hand circumference, incl. tip of thumb	6	7	8	9	9½	10–10½
	15.25	*17.75*	*20.25*	*22.75*	*24*	*26.75*
Mitten hand length	4¾	6	7	7½	8	9
	12	*15.25*	*17.75*	*19*	*20.25*	*22.75*
Mitten thumb (⅓ hand)	1⅝	2	2⅜	2½	2⅝	3
	4	*5*	*6*	*6.5*	*6.75*	*7.5*
Finished width	3	3½	4	4⅝	4⅝	5¼
	7.5	*9*	*10.25*	*11.75*	*11.75*	*13.25*

Note: Maplewood Adult M/L sizes are slightly narrower than this book's standard men's size and a tad wider than our woman's size, but should comfortably fit the size hand indicated because of the ease allowed in the hand measurement.

Pattern

With a rep of 5 rnds and14 sts (two 7-st blocks), Maplewood is awkward in some sizes and impossible in others. Janetta and I have devised two ways to wrap the pattern around the hand successfully.

When there is an even number of pattern blocks that wraps perfectly around the hand, I've called that an "even wrap." On sizes where there's an odd number of 7-st blocks (Child's 4–6 and Adult M/L), the extra block would ordinarily adjoin an identical pattern block, which would look funny and possibly make for annoying knitting. This situation also comes up each time a 7-st-rep is added at the thumb gusset.

Janetta arranges the pattern so that the joint between these two blocks is on the little finger edge of the hand, with one on the palm, the other on the back, of the hand. Robin splits the odd block in two and runs this split block up the center of the thumb gore, then up the palm to the index finger. This makes the pattern work and looks intriguing if anyone happens to notice it. We've included a chart of a split block to help you out. Please note that it has 8 rather than 7 sts.

Carry the darker color ahead (p. 16) throughout. On Chart Lines 3 and 8, weave in (p. 18) the color not in use on the 2nd and 3rd sts of each diamond.

Off the Cuff

This pattern from New Brunswick has a k2, p1 ribbed cuff with a simple stripe pattern.

Key

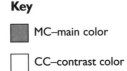

MC—main color

CC—contrast color

Maplewood Chart

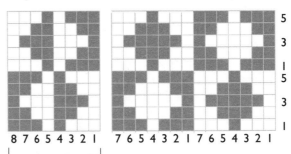

Split pattern block for fitting an odd number of blocks into a perfect wrap

Maplewood Increase Chart A

Going from split block to even wrap

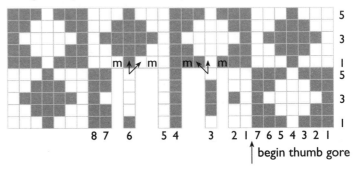

begin thumb gore

Maplewood Increase Chart B

Going from even wrap to split block

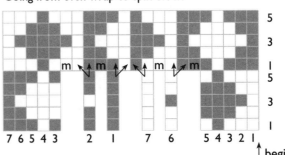

begin thumb gore

Making the cuff

		Child			Adult		
		2–4	4–6	8–10	M	L	XL
With MC, larger needles, and using the Maine method, cast on		36 sts	39 sts	45 sts	51 sts	51 sts	57 sts

Join into a triangle, being careful not to twist sts around needles.

Knit off onto smaller needles in k2, p1 ribbing. Distribute sts:							
	Needle 1:	12 sts	12 sts	15 sts	18 sts	18 sts	18 sts
	Needle 2:	12 sts	15 sts	15 sts	15 sts	15 sts	21 sts
	Needle 3:	12 sts	12 sts	15 sts	18 sts	18 sts	18 sts
Work k2, p1 ribbing in MC for		4 rnds	6 rnds	8 rnds	8 rnds	8 rnds	10 rnds

Stripes: In ribbing work 1 rnd CC then1 rnd MC, 5 times.							
Continue ribbing in MC until work measures	(inches)	2	2	2½	2½	2¾	3
	(cm)	5	5	6.5	6.5	7	7.5

Don't break CC after the stripes. Carry it up to use in the pattern, catching it around the working yarn every 3rd or 4th rnd.

Change to larger needles and stockinette. Work 1 rnd in MC and inc		—	3 sts	5 sts	5 sts	5 sts	7 sts
evenly spaced on 3 needles. Total:		36 sts	42 sts	50 sts	56 sts	56 sts	64 sts

(This will start you with a multiple of 14 sts in Child sizes 4–6
and Adult M and L. In all the sizes, you will alternate between a
multiple of 7 sts and a multiple of 7 sts + 1 as you inc for the thumb.
Use one of the ruses above under "Pattern" to handle the discrepancy.)

This allows for a		split block	even wrap	split block	even wrap	even wrap	split block

Starting the pattern and thumb gore

Note: Carry MC ahead throughout (p. 16). Check after the first rnd
that the rep comes out even. A mistake here can throw everything else
off and take the fun out of the project.

Right mitten: Begin chart at lower right on Line 1, starting with the
split block in the sizes indicated. The first 7 (8) sts are the base of the
thumb gore. The beg of the rnd is also the beg of the thumb gore and
needs no marker.

Left mitten: Begin chart at lower right on Line 1, and rep around, ending with an 8-st split block in the sizes indicated. Lay a piece of waste yarn before the first st of this 8-st block to mark the beg of the thumb gore.

Both left and right mittens: Work 5 rnds even in pattern, laying the waste yarn back and forth between the same sts every few rnds.

Inc on Line 1 of next 5-rnd band of pattern.
Inc rnd: At the thumb gore you will inc
and at the same time go from an even wrap to a split block (or vice versa):

Follow the thumb gore inc charts religiously, choosing A (split block to even wrap) or B (even wrap to split block) according to where you are.

Work Lines 2 through 5 of the chart even.
In Rnd 6,
using Chart
centering the inc on the second block of the thumb gore.
The pattern colors will match the chart.

Work even until thumb gore measures

and you have completed
5-rnd bands of pattern above the cuff.

		Child			Adult		
		2–4	4–6	8–10	M	L	XL
Inc rnd: At the thumb gore you will inc		6 sts	8 sts	6 sts	8 sts	8 sts	6 sts
go to		even wrap	split block	even wrap	split block	split block	even wrap
	Total:	42 sts	50 sts	56 sts	64 sts	64 sts	70 sts
In Rnd 6,		—	—	—	inc again	inc again	inc again
using Chart		—	—	—	A (6 sts)	A (6 sts)	B (8 sts)
	Total:	42 sts	50 sts	56 sts	70 sts	70 sts	78 sts
Work even until thumb gore measures (inches)		1½	2	2	2⅜	2½	2⅞
(cm)		3.75	5	5	6	6.5	7.25
		2	3	3	3½	3½	4

Taking off the thumb gore stitches

Starting at beg of rnd (right mitten) or marker (left mitten), place on waste yarn the next

Using twisted M1 (p. 23), cast on
in pattern over the gap, allowing for a

Work even until pattern above cuff measures about

		Child			Adult		
		2–4	4–6	8–10	M	L	XL
place on waste yarn the next		10 sts	14 sts	14 sts	20 sts	20 sts	20 sts
Using twisted M1 (p. 23), cast on		4 sts	6 sts	8 sts	6 sts	6 sts	6 sts
		split block	even wrap	split block	even wrap	even wrap	split block
	Total:	36 sts	42 sts	50 sts	56 sts	56 sts	64 sts
Work even until pattern above cuff measures about (inches)		3¾	4¾	5½	6	6½	7½
(cm)		9.5	12	14	15.25	16.5	19

Decreasing—right mitten

These mittens are decreased on both thumb and little finger sides of the hand, ending with a squared-off tip.

		Child			Adult		
		2–4	4–6	8–10	M	L	XL
Without moving beg of rnd, redistribute sts:	Needle 1:	9 sts	11 sts	13 sts	14 sts	14 sts	16 sts
	Needle 2:	9 sts	10 sts	12 sts	14 sts	14 sts	16 sts
	Needle 3:	18 sts	21 sts	25 sts	28 sts	28 sts	32 sts

Dec Rnd 1:
Needle 1: K2tog (p. 24), matching pattern to following sts. Work to end of needle.
Needle 2: Work to 2 sts from end of needle, SSK2tog (p. 24), matching pattern to preceding sts.
Needle 3: K2tog in pattern, work to 2 sts from end of needle, SSK2tog.

Rnd 2: Work even in pattern.

Rep dec Rnds 1 and 2 until there are		16 sts	18 sts	22 sts	24 sts	24 sts	32 sts

Ideally, end at Line 5 or 10 of the charted pattern.

Decreasing—left mitten

Move beg of rnd 7 sts to the left (to the opposite side of the thumb gore). Undo your knitting to that point.

Then without moving beg of rnd again, redistribute sts:	Needle 1:	18 sts	21 sts	25 sts	28 sts	28 sts	32 sts
	Needle 2:	9 sts	10 sts	12 sts	14 sts	14 sts	16 sts
	Needle 3:	9 sts	11 sts	13 sts	14 sts	14 sts	16 sts

Dec Rnd 1:
Needle 1: K2tog in pattern (p. 24), work to 2 sts from end of needle, SSK2tog (p. 24).
Needle 2: K2tog, matching pattern to following sts, work to end of needle.
Needle 3: Work to 2 sts from end of needle, SSK2tog, matching pattern to preceding sts.

Rnd 2: Work even in pattern.

Rep dec Rnds 1 and 2 until there are		16 sts	18 sts	22 sts	24 sts	24 sts	32 sts

Ideally, end at Line 5 or 10 of the charted pattern.

Closing the mitten tip—both mittens

Place remaining sts on 2 needles, the palm sts on one, the back sts on the other. Break yarn, leaving two 18" (45cm) tails. Lay needles side by side.

Sew tip together using Kitchener st: Thread tail onto yarn needle and sew back and forth between needles in pattern, so the resultant sts look like a row of stockinette holding the 2 sides together. Slip the sts off the needles as they are secured. Work above the yarn not in use, which will then be carried inside the mitten. When all remaining sts are sewn together, darn down the last half st at the end of the seam and draw the tail to the inside of the mitten.

Working the thumb

Join both yarns by sewing into back of fabric starting at the right side of the thumb hole.

	Child			Adult		
	2–4	4–6	8–10	M	L	XL
Needles 1 and 2: pick up from waste yarn	10 sts	14 sts	14 sts	20 sts	20 sts	20 sts
Pick up and twist onto Needle 1 st in each corner of thumb hole. Needle 3: At top of thumb hole, pick up	4 sts	6 sts	8 sts	6 sts	6 sts	6 sts
Total:	16 sts	22 sts	24 sts	28 sts	28 sts	28 sts
In first rnd, SSK2tog at left corner	yes	—	yes	—	—	—
Allow for Place the split block on Needle 3, out of sight.	even wrap	split block	split block	even wrap	even wrap	even wrap
At end of rnd, k first and last st tog	yes	—	yes	—	—	—
You will have	14 sts	22 sts	22 sts	28 sts	28 sts	28 sts
Work even in pattern for (inches)	1	1⅜	1¾	1⅞	2	2⅜
(cm)	2.5	3.5	4.5	4.75	5	6

Closing the tip of the thumb

Dec at both edges of every 7-st pattern block. Maintain both the outer edge of the block and the center of the diamond to the tip of the thumb.

	Child			Adult		
	2–4	4–6	8–10	M	L	XL
Rnd 1. At beg of pattern block, SSK2tog, work to 2 sts before end of pattern block, k2tog. Total remaining:	6 sts	10 sts	10 sts	12 sts	12 sts	12 sts

Break yarn, leaving a 6" (15cm) tail. With a yarn needle, thread one end through the remaining sts and draw up firmly. Draw other end to inside of the thumb. Thread first end through drawn-up sts again, darn a few sts to secure it, and draw to inside of thumb.

Finishing the mitten

Turn mitten inside out and darn all ends into the back of fabric. Repair possible holes at corners of the thumb hole with nearby tails. Trim ends closely.

This mitten is a right- or a left-handed mitten. Make another, being careful that it is for the opposite hand!

Spruce Mittens

Spruce Mitten with patterned cuff

This pattern appeared in an old Bartlettyarns catalog, nameless except for the designation "Patterned Mitten." The instructions didn't include a thumb gore or a double-knit thumb. When I began to knit the pattern in green on a white background, it looked like a spruce or fir twig, so I decided to call it that.

When I showed the finished mitten to Janetta Dexter, who collected many Nova Scotia double-knitting patterns, she said it is also knitted there and called Jacob's Ladder.

Call it what you like, it's a striking pattern. It also shows up on mittens and gloves from the Middle East, often as 12 (or so)-rnd bands on cuffs or palms.

The inc for the thumb is in the middle of the thumb gore rather than at the sides, based on Nora Johnson's Fox and Geese pattern and Bida Spooner's Checkerboard pattern.

Spruce Mittens

Yarn For one pair of mittens with patterned cuff you will need about:

MC	(oz)	1¼	1½	1¾	1¾	2	2	2¼	2¼
	(g)	35.5	42.75	50	50	57	57	64	64
CC	(oz)	1¼	1½	1¾	1¾	2	2	2¼	2¼
	(g)	35.5	42.75	50	50	57	57	64	64

For one pair of mittens with ribbed cuff, you will need about:

MC (including cuff)

(oz)	1½	1¾	2	2	2¼	2¼	2½	2½
(g)	42.75	50	57	57	64	64	71.25	71.25

CC (oz)	1	1¼	1½	1½	1¾	1¾	2	2
(g)	28.5	35.5	42.75	42.75	50	50	57	57

The sample is worked in Rauma 3-ply Strikkegarn, a DK weight wool yarn, creating a light but durable mitten. The directions will work with any DK to medium-weight yarn that knits comfortably at the recommended tension.

Equipment 1 set Size 4 (3.5mm, Can. Size 9 or 10) double-pointed needles, or size you need to knit in pattern at correct tension • 1 set Size 2 (2.75mm, Can. Size 12) double-pointed needles for alternative ribbed cuff • 6" (15cm) length of contrasting waste yarn • Blunt-pointed yarn needle.

Tension 7 sts and 7½ rnds = 1" (2.5cm) in pattern

Measurements—inches and *centimeters*

	Child Sizes			Adult Sizes				
	2–4	4–6	8–10	WS	WM	WL	MM	ML
Length of hand	4½	5½	6½	6½	7	7½	7	7½
	11.5	*14*	*16.5*	*16.5*	*17.75*	*19*	*17.75*	*19*
Hand circumference incl. tip of thumb	6	7	8	7½	9	9	9½	9½
	15.25	*17.75*	*20.25*	*19*	*22.75*	*22.75*	*24*	*24*
Length of mitten hand	4¾	6	7	7	7½	8	7½	8
	12	*15.25*	*17.75*	*17.75*	*19*	*20.25*	*19*	*20.25*
Mitten thumb (⅓ hand)	1⅝	2	2⅜	2⅜	2½	2⅝	2½	2⅝
	4	*5*	*6*	*6*	*6.5*	*6.75*	*6.5*	*6.75*
Mitten width	3	3½	4	3¾	4½	4½	4¾	4¾
	7.5	*9*	*10.25*	*9.5*	*11.5*	*11.5*	*12*	*12*

ABBREVIATIONS beg: beginning • CC: contrast color • dec(s): decrease(s) • inc(s): increase(s) • k: knit • k2tog: knit 2 together • M1: make 1 stitch • M1L: make 1 stitch left • M1R: make 1 stitch right • MC: main color • p: purl • rep: repeat • rnd(s): round(s) • SSK2tog: slip, slip, knit 2 sts together • st(s): stitch(es) • twisted M1: twisted make 1 cast-on

Pattern

The 2-color pattern is a 4-st, 2-rnd rep. The pattern itself can be knitted flat, but an extra st should be added at each end for a seam. The directions are for a circularly knit mitten.

Off the Cuff

The cuff is in pattern and stockinette, but I give an alternative ribbed cuff, which I find more congenial to young children. Your choice.

Spruce

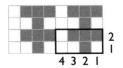

4 3 2 1

Spruce
First and Second Thumb Gore Increases

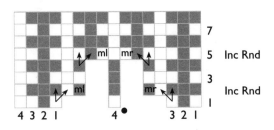

4 3 2 1   4 •   3 2 1

Key

☐ MC–main color

■ CC–contrast color

mr Make 1 right

ml Make 1 left

↗ k both colors into 1 st

• place marker

☐ pattern repeat

Spruce Mitten Hand Decrease

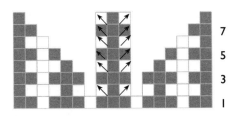

Making the cuff

Patterned cuff

	Child			Adult				
	2–4	4–6	8–10	WS	WM	WL	MM	ML

With MC, larger needles, and using the Maine method (p. 13), cast on quite firmly

| | 40 sts | 48 sts | 56 sts | 52 sts | 60 sts | 60 sts | 64 sts | 64 sts |

Distribute the sts about equally on 3 needles. Join CC by sewing (p. 20). Join into a triangle, being careful not to twist sts around the needles.

Start charted pattern at lower right, Line 1 and work to end of rnd. Check at end of first rnd that the rep comes out even. A mistake here can throw everything else off and take the fun out of the project.

| Work even for (inches) | 1⅝ | 2 | 2⅜ | 2⅜ | 2½ | 2⅝ | 2½ | 2⅝ |
| *(cm)* | *4* | *5* | *6* | *6* | *6.5* | *6.75* | *6.5* | *6.75* |

Alternative ribbed cuff

With MC, smaller needles, using the Maine method (p. 13), cast on	39 sts	48 sts	54 sts	51 sts	60 sts	60 sts	63 sts	63 sts
Distribute sts on 3 needles. Needle 1:	12 sts	15 sts	18 sts	15 sts	18 sts	18 sts	21 sts	21 sts
Needle 2:	15 sts	18 sts	18 sts	18 sts	24 sts	24 sts	21 sts	21 sts
Needle 3:	12 sts	15 sts	18 sts	18 sts	18 sts	18 sts	21 sts	21 sts

With this distribution, each needle starts a new k rib, and you can rib without looking constantly at your hands.

Join into a triangle, being careful not to twist sts on the needles.

| Work k2, p1 ribbing until work measures (inches) | 1⅝ | 2 | 2⅜ | 2⅜ | 2½ | 2⅝ | 2½ | 2⅝ |
| *(cm)* | *4* | *5* | *6* | *6* | *6.5* | *6.75* | *6.5* | *6.75* |

Change to larger needles and stockinette. K 1 rnd in MC and, on Needle 2, inc by M1 (p. 20) a total of

| | 1 st | — | 2 sts | 1 st | — | — | 1 st | 1 st |
| Total: | 40 sts | 48 sts | 56 sts | 52 sts | 60 sts | 60 sts | 64 sts | 64 sts |

Both versions of cuff

Redistribute sts so that half are on Needle 1 (back of hand) and one quarter each on Needles 2 and 3.

Needle 1:	20 sts	24 sts	28 sts	26 sts	30 sts	30 sts	32 sts	32 sts
Needle 2:	10 sts	12 sts	14 sts	13 sts	15 sts	15 sts	16 sts	16 sts
Needle 3:	10 sts	12 sts	14 sts	13 sts	15 sts	15 sts	16 sts	16 sts

Centered increases of the
Spruce Mitten thumb gore

	Child				Adult			
	2–4	4–6	8–10	WS	WM	WL	MM	ML

Starting the hand and the thumb gore

Spruce Mittens have the thumb gore inc in the center of the thumb
gore, with incs branching off on both sides of a single line of sts.
The thumb gore for the right mitten will be on Sts 2–5 of Needle 2.
The thumb gore for the left mitten will be on the last 6 sts of Needle 3.
Set up this location in the first rnd:

Rnd 1, Needle 1: Work Line 1 of charted pattern. Needles 2 and 3: Insert
marker for thumb gore as follows:

Right mitten: Continue charted pattern, laying a piece of waste yarn as
a marker between Sts 3 and 4 of Needle 2. St 4 of needle 2 will be the
centerline for all incs. Work to end of rnd in pattern.

Left mitten: On Needle 2, continue charted pattern. Needle 3: Work up to
5 sts from end of needle (Line 1, St 4, of Chart). Lay a piece of waste yarn
between sts as a marker before knitting St 4, which will be the centerline
for all incs. Work to end of rnd in pattern.

Note: If you made a ribbed cuff and are just starting the charted pattern,
check after this rnd that the rep comes out even. A mistake here can throw
everything else off and ruin your fun.

Rnd 2: Start thumb gore inc in Line 2 of charted pattern. Thumb gores
for both left and right mittens are worked the same way, as follows:

Work to 1 st before marker in pattern. K both colors—CC then MC—
into one st (p. 21.), M1R CC (p. 21), K1 CC, M1L CC, k both
colors—MC then CC—into one st. You should now have 4 new sts

	Child 2–4	Child 4–6	Child 8–10	Adult WS	Adult WM	Adult WL	Adult MM	Adult ML
grouped around a St 4 of the previous rnd. This center st should now be CC. Complete rnd in pattern.								
Inc this way, every 4th rnd, as shown on thumb gore chart, a total of	2X	1X	2X	2X	2X	2X	3X	3X
Total inc:	8 sts	4 sts	8 sts	8 sts	8 sts	8 sts	12 sts	12 sts
Altogether you will have :	48 sts	52 sts	64 sts	60 sts	72 sts	72 sts	80 sts	80 sts
When thumb gore incs are complete, work even until thumb gore measures (inches)	1⅝	2	2⅜	2⅜	2½	2⅝	2½	2⅝
(cm)	*4*	*5*	*6*	*6*	*6.5*	*6.75*	*6.5*	*6.75*

Taking off the thumb gore stitches

	Child 2–4	Child 4–6	Child 8–10	Adult WS	Adult WM	Adult WL	Adult MM	Adult ML
Needle 1: Locate the st following the marker (the center st of the incs). On each side of this st count off	5 sts	5 sts	7 sts	7 sts	7 sts	7 sts	9 sts	9 sts
Work in pattern up to the first of these sts. Thread onto waste yarn:	11 sts	11 sts	15 sts	15 sts	15 sts	15 sts	19 sts	19 sts
Using twisted M1 (p. 23), cast on 7 sts in pattern over the gap. Total:	44 sts	48 sts	56 sts	52 sts	64 sts	64 sts	68 sts	68 sts
Work even in pattern until work above cuff measures (inches)	3½	4½	5½	5¼	6¼	6¾	6	6½
(cm)	*9*	*11.5*	*14*	*13.25*	*16*	*17*	*15.25*	*16.5*

Closing the mitten tip

Overview: This mitten looks best with a continuous pattern strip up the sides, with the decs appearing to feed into it. The dec band will consist of Sts 1, 2, and 3 of the charted pattern—one complete "spruce twig" without its MC edging.

	Child 2–4	Child 4–6	Child 8–10	Adult WS	Adult WM	Adult WL	Adult MM	Adult ML
Where you place the dec strips depends on whether you have an odd or even number of pattern reps around the hand. There are 4-st reps, making your size	11 odd	12 even	14 even	13 odd	16 even	16 even	17 odd	17 odd

On both mittens, the "twig" closest to the thumb and toward the back of the hand will be one dec strip. The other dec strip will be the "twig" (Sts 1, 2, and 3) exactly opposite this first twig in sizes 4–6, 8–10, and

	Child			Adult				
	2–4	4–6	8–10	WS	WM	WL	MM	ML

WM and ML, which all have an even number of reps. In sizes Child 2–4, WS, and MM and ML, there are an odd number of reps, so there won't be a CC twig directly opposite. Choose the "twig" closest to opposite, but toward the back of the hand. The spruce twig on each dec strip will continue to the mitten tip.

Redistribute 1 st of each dec strip so that each band has 1 st on Needle 1 and 2 sts on either Needle 2 or 3.

Rnd 1, Dec. Needle 1: In pattern, SSK2tog (p. 24), work in pattern to next to last st, k2tog (p. 24), matching pattern to following 2 sts. Needle 2: K1, SSK2tog, work in pattern to end of needle. Needle 3: Work in pattern to 3rd to last st, k2tog, k1.

Rnd 2: Work even in pattern.

Work Rnds 1 and 2 once, then work Rnd 1 every rnd until 16 sts remain.	6X	7X	9X	8X	11X	11X	12X	12X

Check measurements against finished measurements at beg of directions. If you are satisfied, break yarn leaving two 6" (15cm) tails. With yarn needle, thread one end through the remaining sts and draw up firmly. Draw other end to inside of the mitten. Thread first end through drawn-up sts again, darn a few sts to secure it, and draw it to inside of mitten.

Working the thumb

Join both yarns by sewing into back of fabric starting at the right side of the thumb hole. Pick up sts for the thumb:

Needles 1 and 2: Pick up from waste yarn Pick up and twist 1 st in each corner of thumb hole. Needle 3: Pick up 7 sts at top of thumb hole.	11 sts	11 sts	15 sts	15 sts	15 sts	15 sts	19 sts	19 sts
Total	20 sts	20 sts	24 sts	24 sts	24 sts	24 sts	28 sts	28 sts

Start knitting at right corner, continuing pattern from thumb gore. The pattern should match perfectly on all sides, although the sts on the inside of the thumb will be in the opposite direction from those on the palm.

Work even in pattern until thumb measures	(inches)	1¼	1½	2	2	2¼	2½	2¼	2½
	(cm)	*3.25*	*3.75*	*5*	*5*	*5.75*	*6.5*	*5.75*	*6.5*

Closing the tip of the thumb

Starting in 2nd pattern rnd, dec sharply:
Rnd 1: * K1 MC, k1 CC, SSK2tog CC and rep from * to end of rnd.
There are

Rnd 2: * K1 MC, k2tog CC and rep from * to end of rnd.

Total remaining:

Rnd 3: in MC, K2 together around.

Total remaining:

	Child			Adult				
	2–4	4–6	8–10	WS	WM	WL	MM	ML
There are	15 sts	15 sts	18 sts	18 sts	18 sts	18 sts	21 sts	21 sts
Total remaining (Rnd 2):	10 sts	10 sts	12 sts	12 sts	12 sts	12 sts	14 sts	14 sts
Total remaining (Rnd 3):	5 sts	5 sts	6 sts	6 sts	6 sts	6 sts	7 sts	7 sts

Check measurements against finished measurements at beg of directions before breaking yarn. If you are satisfied, break yarn leaving two 6" (15cm) tails. With a yarn needle, thread one end through the remaining sts and draw up firmly. Draw other end to inside of the thumb. Thread end through drawn-up sts again, darn a few sts to secure, and draw it to inside of thumb.

Finishing the mitten

Turn mitten inside out and darn all ends into the back of fabric. Repair any holes at corners of the thumb hole with nearby tails. Trim ends closely.

This is a right- or a left-handed mitten. Make another, being careful that it is for the opposite hand!

Chipman's Check Wristers

Chipman's Check is a bit of feminine deception. At first glance it appears to be a check—little bands of dark and light interwoven diagonally—and maybe tricky to knit.

Look more closely. It's two rows of three light/three dark alternated with two rows of one light/one dark (otherwise known as Salt and Pepper). No little squares on the diagonal. In fact, no diagonals at all.

Chipman's Check was sent to Janetta Dexter by an acquaintance in New Brunswick, where Chipman has long been a common family name. The roots of this pattern seem to be British, and even today similar checks are knitted into mittens and gloves in England (McGregor, 1983) and Scotland, but to our knowledge, they lack the clever *trompe l'oeil* of this pattern.

Janetta provided a mitten pattern in Chipman's Check in *Flying Geese & Partridge Feet*. Here is a wrister instead. It is a fun pattern to knit, mainly because it looks like something it isn't.

Chipman's Check Wristers with 2-color Maine cast-on on cuffs

Chipman's Check Wristers

Yarn Any DK or medium weight wool yarn will do, if it knits to the correct tension. We used McAusland's 2-ply Medium for these pairs in Child's 4–6 and Woman's Large, but also recommend Rauma Hifa or Rauma 3-ply Strikkegarn, or Halcyon Yarns Victorian.

The cuffs—the emphasis of these wristers—are a half-inch longer than the usual ⅓ hand length and so absorb a larger percentage of the yarn. To make one pair you will need:

MC (with solid color cuff)

(oz)	1½	1¾	2	2¼	2¼	2½	2½	2¾
(g)	42	50	58	64.5	64.5	71.5	71.5	78.5

CC

(oz)	½	⅔	¾	⅞	⅞	⅞	⅞	⅞
(g)	14	19	21.5	25	25	25	25	25

Equipment 1 set Size 3 (3.25mm, Can. Size 11) double-pointed needles, or size you need to knit in pattern at correct tension • 1 set Size 1 (2.25mm, Can. Size 13) double-pointed needles for ribbed cuff • 6" (15cm) contrasting waste yarn • Blunt-tipped yarn needle

Tension 7½ sts = 1" (2.5cm)

ABBREVIATIONS beg: beginning • CC: contrast color • dec(s): decrease(s) • inc(s): increase(s) • k: knit • k2tog: knit 2 together • M1: make 1 stitch • M1L: make 1 stitch left • M1R: make 1 stitch right • MC: main color • p: purl • rep: repeat • rnd(s): round(s) • SSK2tog: slip, slip, knit 2 sts together • st(s): stitch(es) • twisted M1: twisted make 1 cast-on

Measurements—inches and *centimeters*

	Child Sizes		Adult Sizes					
	4–6	6–8	WS	WM	WL	MM	ML	XL
Hand length	5½	6½	6½	7	7½	7	7½	8½
	14	16.5	16.5	17.75	19	17.75	19	21.5
Hand circumference, incl. tip of thumb	7	8	7½	9	9	9½	9½	10
	17.75	20.25	19	22.75	22.75	24	24	25.5
Length of wrister hand	3¼	3¾	3¾	4	4¼	4	4¼	5
	8.25	9.5	9.5	10.25	10.75	10.25	10.75	12.75
Wrister width	3½	4	3¾	4½	4½	4¾	4¾	5
	9	10.25	9.5	11.5	11.5	12	12	12.75

Pattern

Chipman's Check is a 6-st rep and wraps seamlessly around the mitten. Incs are worked in the rnds with 1 MC, 1 CC by adding 6 sts close together in 2 rnds to insert an entire 6-st element at once without an obvious break in the pattern.

I was confused when 2 sts of the same color came together at the end/beg of Lines 1 and 2 of the chart. This never happens in real Salt and Pepper, which is worked on an uneven number of stitches. Chipman's Check *must* have an even number of stitches because the overall pattern is a 6-st rep. Don't try to make Salt and Pepper work there, or your checked pattern won't come out even.

Because the pattern wraps around the hand, both wristers are the same and gain right- and left-handedness in use.

Other 6-st patterns can be substituted on these wristers, but use the thumb gore incs for that pattern.

Chipman's Check

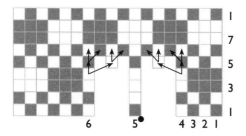

Key

■ MC—main color

□ CC—contrast color

● place marker

◸ k both colors into 1 st

Chipman's Check Thumb Increase

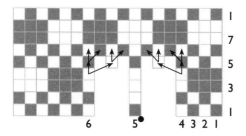

Off the Cuff

The cuff is worked in MC and k2, p1 ribbing, with a narrow edging of CC. This edging is the sort of touch that identifies the work of individual knitters, who often tag their work with distinctive striping. One knitter I interviewed briefly was carrying on her grandmother's trademark of knitting a half-inch (1cm) of the mitten's color pattern in the middle of the cuff.

Here's how to make this simple edging. Instead of measuring a long tail of the main color for the cast-on, use a slipknot to tie both colors around one needle, about 6" (15cm) from the end of both yarns. Make the slipknot so that it can be released from the 6" (15cm) end. Cast on using the Maine method (p. 13), but hold CC in the left hand and MC in the right hand. At the end of the rnd, break CC, leaving a 6" (15cm) tail and release the knot.

Later, either work all 3 ends into the back of the fabric or use them to crochet a little button loop on one wrister and attach a toggle on the other. OR, sew the edge together at the joint between rnds and braid the tails together so the mittens can be tied in a pair. Scandinavian and Middle Eastern mittens often have such ties.

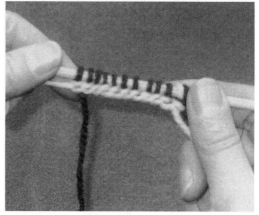

This is how the 2-color Maine cast-on will look.

Making the cuff

With MC, 3 smaller needles, and using the Maine method (p. 13),
cast on tightly
making edging as described in "Off the Cuff" above.
Distribute sts among needles:

	Child		Adult					
	4–6	6–8	WS	WM	WL	MM	ML	MXL
	42 sts	48 sts	54 sts	60 sts	60 sts	66sts	66 sts	72sts
Needle 1:	12 sts	12 sts	15 sts	18 sts	18 sts	18 sts	18 sts	21 sts
Needle 2:	18 sts	18 sts	18 sts	21 sts	21 sts	24 sts	24 sts	24 sts
Needle 3:	12 sts	18 sts	21 sts	21 sts	21 sts	24 sts	24 sts	27 sts

Every needle will begin with a k st and end with a p st.

Join into a triangle, being careful not to twist sts around the needles.
K2, p1 to end of rnd.

Work even until ribbing measures (inches)	1½	2	2¼	2½	3	2½	3	3½
(cm)	3.75	5	5.75	6.5	7.5	6.5	7.5	9

Next rnd: Change to larger needles and stockinette and work
1 rnd MC, while increasing 2 sts every needle. Inc by M1 (p. 20)
between k sts of ribbing. K to 6 sts before end of rnd. Join CC
(p. 18) and finish rnd in MC.

Total:	48 sts	54 sts	60 sts	66 sts	66 sts	72 sts	72 sts	78 sts
On Needle 1 you will have	14 sts	14 sts	17 sts	20 sts	20 sts	20 sts	20 sts	23 sts

Starting the pattern and thumb gore

Note: Carry MC ahead throughout (p. 16). Check after the first rnd
that the rep comes out even. A mistake here can throw everything else
off and take the fun out of the project.

Start chart at lower right. Work Lines 1 through 4 of chart
without increasing.

Overview of inc. On this mitten, you inc an entire 6-st pattern rep at a
time so that the pattern seems to remain undisturbed. Incs are all worked
by knitting both colors into 1 st (p. 21). When knitting these sts, keep
the colors in the correct sequence for the pattern.

Incs are worked in the thumb gore area in 2 rnds, on Lines 5 and 6 or
Lines 1 and 2 of the chart and are centered on the points of one "diamond."

If you work incs consistently on Lines 1 and 2, there will be a line of CC chevrons up the center of the thumb with single MC sts separating them vertically. If you work them consistently on Lines 5 and 6, there will be a line of MC chevrons up the center of the thumb with single CC sts separating them vertically. I opted to alternate between 5 and 6 and 1 and 2, which gave me a pair of chevrons in each color, but nothing strong enough to detract from the checked pattern.

Inc Rnd 1 (Line 1 or 5 of chart): Start thumb gore on Needle 1, St 4 of chart: K both colors into this st (always in pattern order). Lay waste yarn between inc and next st, k1 st even, then k both colors into next st, k to end of rnd in pattern. You have added 2 sts in this rnd.

Inc Rnd 2 (Line 2 or 6 of chart): Work up to 2 sts before waste yarn marker. K both colors into next 2 sts, k1, k both colors into next 2 sts. Work in pattern to end of rnd. You have added 4 sts in this rnd, making a total of 6 sts inc in 2 rnds.

	Child		Adult					
	4–6	6–8	WS	WM	WL	MM	ML	MXL
Total on Needle 1	20 sts	20 sts	23 sts	26 sts	26 sts	26 sts	26 sts	29 sts
Continue to work pattern and incs a total of	1X	1X	2X	2X	2X	3X	3X	3X
Total on Needle 1	20 sts	20 sts	29 sts	32 sts	32 sts	38 sts	38 sts	41 sts
Work even until wrister above cuff measures (inches)	2	2⅜	2⅜	2½	2⅝	2½	2⅝	3
(cm)	*5*	*6*	*6*	*6.5*	*6.75*	*6.5*	*6.75*	*7.5*

Taking off the thumb gore stitches

For the best-looking finished wrister, take off the thumb sts on chart Lines 2, 4, 6, or 8, so that when you pick up sts for the thumb later, the pattern on the thumb will match that on the hand perfectly. Work to one of those lines now, then take off the thumb sts.

	Child		Adult					
K2 sts in pattern, place the next on waste yarn. The sts should be centered on the un-increased st after the marker.	11 sts	11 sts	17 sts	17 sts	17 sts	23 sts	23 sts	23 sts

Remove marker. Using twisted M1 (p. 23), cast on 5 sts over gap.

		Child		Adult					
		4–6	6–8	WS	WM	WL	MM	ML	MXL

Work even in pattern on
until pattern above cuff measures *(inches)*
(cm)

	Child		Adult					
	4–6	6–8	WS	WM	WL	MM	ML	MXL
Work even in pattern on until pattern above cuff measures	48 sts	54 sts	60 sts	66 sts	66 sts	72 sts	72 sts	78 sts
(inches)	2¾	3¼	3¼	3½	3¾	3½	3¾	4¼
(cm)	7	8.25	8.25	9	9.5	9	9.5	10.75

(This is half the length of the hand, about where the fingers begin.) End with Lines 1 and 2 (or 5 and 6) of the chart to close the checked pattern.

Finishing the top edge

Work 1 rnd in MC. Change to smaller needles and work 4 rnds in k2, p1 ribbing.

To avoid a flaccid top edge that turns over easily, bind off this way: SSK2tog (p. 24), *p1, pass first st over second st, SSK2tog, pass first st over second st; rep from * to end of rnd. For a slightly looser edge, SSK2tog only every 2nd pair of k sts.

Break yarn, leaving a 6" (15cm) tail, and pull tail through the last st.

Working the thumb

Join both yarns by sewing (p. 20) into back of fabric starting at the right side of thumb hole.

	Child		Adult					
	4–6	6–8	WS	WM	WL	MM	ML	MXL
Pick up from waste yarn Pick up 5 sts from cast-on sts at top of thumb hole.	11 sts	11 sts	17 sts	17 sts	17 sts	23 sts	23 sts	23 sts
Pick up and twist onto needle in each corner of thumb hole	1 st	2, 3 sts	1 st	1 st	1 st	1 st	1 st	1 st
Total sts:	18	21**	24	24	24	30	30	30

Alternatively, pick up the same number of sts, but work 6 rnds of k2, p1 ribbing without working pattern at all. For Child's 6–8, only this thumb treatment will work.

Work around in pattern, matching pattern on thumb gore.
Complete 1 band of pattern, then work 1 rnd MC.
Change to smaller needles and k 3 to 4 rnds k2, p1 ribbing.
Bind off as on hand.

Finishing the wrister

Turn wrister inside out and darn all ends into the back of the fabric.
Repair possible holes at corners of the thumb hole with nearby tails.
Trim ends closely.

Make another identical wrister. This wrister can be worn on either hand.

Chipman's Check Mittens. To make these, use the wristers pattern, but continue up
the hand following *hand length* (only) measurements for Sawtooth Mittens on p. 100.
Decreases will be in Lines 1 and 2 of the chart—four in Line 1, two in Line 2, directly
above the first decrease.

	Child		Adult					
	2–4	6–8	WS	WM	WL	MM	ML	MXL

A French-Canadian Toque to Match Your Mittens

The pattern on this cap is on the turned-up edge, which is worked in stockinette. While this *could* mean you will have to purl either the entire cuff or the entire crown of the toque, it doesn't. You will turn the work inside out at the top of the cuff and reverse direction, so that you are knitting on the other side of your work.

You can work the crown in plain stockinette, you can cover the crown with a tiny pattern like Salt and Pepper or Stripes, or you can rep the pattern used on the turn-up in a little pinwheel of pattern just before the last decs, as in the Fox and Geese version photographed.

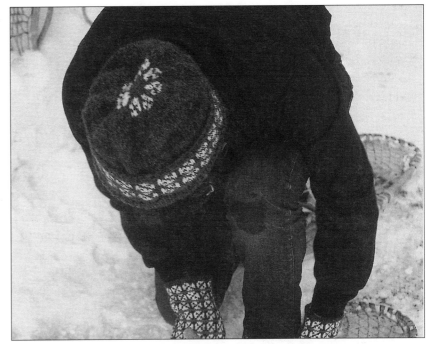

Toque with three-color Fox and Geese pattern on turned-up edge. The center of the Fox and Geese pattern has been repeated at the top, minus the third color.

Yarn This cap is knitted in medium weight yarn. We have used Bartlettyarns 2-ply Fisherman, Rauma Istra, and McAusland's 2-ply Medium with equal success, but you can use any medium weight wool or synthetic yarn that knits in pattern to the correct tension.

MC	(oz)	2	2¼	2½	3
	(g)	57	64	64	85.5
CC	(oz)	1	1¼	1½	2
	(g)	28.5	35.5	42.75	57

Equipment 1 set (5) Size 8 (5 mm, Can. size 6) 10" (25.5cm) long, double-pointed needles, or size you need to knit in pattern at correct tension • 1 set (5) Size 5(3.75mm, Can. Size 9) 10" (25.5cm) long, double-pointed needles for ribbing • blunt tipped yarn needle

Tension 5½ sts = 1" (2.5cm) in pattern. **Note:** The knitting tension is looser on caps than on mittens. Soft and fluffy is good, as there is no need for densely knitted, durable caps unless you spend a lot of time standing on your head outdoors in winter. The difference in tension does not affect the appearance of the color patterns much.

Pay special attention to your tension if you use Stripes or Checkerboard, as the fabric has a tendency to pull up in ridges (thus increasing the tension) in these patterns. Check it after about 10 rnds of pattern. Or, make a test swatch ahead of time: Cast on 24 sts in the yarn and needles of your choice and knit circularly for 3–4" (7.5–10.25cm). Measure sts-per-inch at several points. If you have more sts per inch than called for, move to a larger size needle. If you have fewer sts than called for, use a smaller size needle. I generally find that I gain or lose about a half st per inch per American needle size.

ABBREVIATIONS beg: beginning • CC: contrast color • dec(s): decrease(s) • inc(s): increase(s) • k: knit • k2tog: knit 2 together • M1: make 1 stitch • M1L: make 1 stitch left • M1R: make 1 stitch right • MC: main color • p: purl • rep: repeat • rnd(s): round(s) • SSK2tog: slip, slip, knit 2 sts together • st(s): stitch(es) • twisted M1: twisted make 1 cast-on

Measurements—inches and *centimeters*

	Child Sizes		Adult Sizes	
	S	M	M	L
Around the head	16	18	20	22
	40.75	*45.75*	*50.75*	*56*
Width of hat	8	9	10	11
	20.25	*22.75*	*25.5*	*28*
Height from turn-up to tip of cap*	7	7½	8	8½
	17.75	*19*	*20.25*	*21.5*

*For the height above the turn-up, measure from earlobe to earlobe and divide by 2. When measuring the cap itself, flatten the curve of the cap outward to measure the full height. To find the head measurement (the circumference), measure around the head about where the band of a hat (baseball cap, cowboy hat) would rest.

Pattern

The turned-up edge is worked in a charted pattern—your choice from those in this book. To wrap a pattern around a cap—or a mitten—the total number of sts must be a multiple of the pattern rep. You may have to add or subtract up to 4 sts to fit the pattern in correctly. Go whichever way (more or fewer sts) is the least. If there is a question of making the hat too large or too small by more than an inch, consider using a different color pattern from the mittens, but the same colors. Color can make dissimilar patterns look fine together!

The crown of the toque is worked in plain stockinette in MC. Alternatively, work the crown in Salt and Pepper or narrow Stripes, using the dec methods for those patterns. OR, put a little pinwheel of pattern at the top of the crown. Fox and Geese or Sawtooth work well.

If knitting flat, p every second row of the color pattern and read the chart from left to right on p rows. Add one more stitch to each end for the seam. (Fox and Geese and Compass do not work well in flat knitting.)

Making the band

	Child		Adult	
	S	M	M	L
With MC, smaller needles, and using the Maine method (p. 13), cast on on 4 needles, distributing sts more or less evenly. Each needle should have an even number of sts, beginning with a k st and ending with a p st. Join, being careful not to twist sts around the needles.	90 sts	102 sts	108 sts	120 sts

Work k1, p1 ribbing for 4 rnds.

You will be changing to larger needles and stockinette for the patterned portion, but there is figuring to do first.

Starting the pattern

Note: The number of sts on your needles—90, 102, 108, or 120—is divisible by 2, 3, and 6, which means that any pattern with a rep of those numbers can be knitted on the cap without adding or subtracting sts. Stripes, Salt and Pepper, Chipman's Check, Checkerboard, Fox and Geese, and Mrs. Martin's Waves #2 fall into this category. For other patterns, you will first have to adjust the number of sts:

	S	M	M	L
To work a 4-st rep (Checkerboard, Fleur-de-lis)	+2 sts	−2 sts	—	—
To work a 5-st rep (Sawtooth)	—	+3 sts	+2 sts	—
To work a 7-st rep (Maplewood, Mrs. Martin's Diamonds, Mrs. Martin's Waves #1)	+1 sts	+3 sts	+4 sts	+6 sts
To work an 8-st rep (Compass, Flying Geese, Double Irish Chain, Labrador Diamonds)	+6 sts	+2 sts	+4 sts	—
To work a 10-st rep (Flying Geese, Diving Geese)	—	−2 sts	+2 sts	—

Change to larger needles and stockinette. Work 1 rnd in MC, adding sts by M1 (p. 20) or decreasing by k2tog (p. 24), evenly distributed, if necessary to make your chosen color pattern come out even. Check after the first rnd that the rep comes out even. A mistake here can throw everything else off and take the fun out of the project.

	Child		Adult	
	S	M	M	L

Note: Check after 10 rnds to be sure your tension is correct, and rip back if your tension is off by more than a half stitch per inch. If you are knitting a large cap, with 120 sts at 5½ sts = 1 inch (the correct tension for this pattern), the cap will measure 22" (56cm) around when you are finished. If you knit 1 st per inch more tightly, at 6½ sts = 1 inch (2.5cm), the same cap will measure only 18½" (47cm)—about the size for a ten-year-old!

Work even in pattern for 12–16 rnds, whatever works for your charted pattern. Break CC.

K 1 rnd MC, weaving in CC tail in the first six sts (p. 18) and dec exactly the number of sts you added to make the pattern fit, spacing the decs evenly around.   Total:

	90 sts	102 sts	108 sts	120 sts

Change to smaller needles, and in MC, work k1, p1 ribbing for 9 rnds.

Working the crown

Now, *turn your knitting inside out.* You will knit the crown from this side, knitting into the last stitch you just purled and continuing in that direction—in other words, knitting on the former back side of your work. This will leave a little hole at the break of the rnd, which you can repair later if it troubles you.

If you want a color pattern on the crown, join CC in the last 6 sts of the rnd.

Work even in MC or your chosen pattern for   (inches)

(cm)

	4	4¼	4½	4½
	10.25	*10.75*	*11.5*	*11.5*

Closing the top of the cap

You have several choices for repeating your selected pattern as you decrease for the top of the cap.

If working in MC only or in a simple 2-st pattern, use this dec for an effective spiral finish:
Rnd 1: *K 10 sts, K2tog, and rep from * to end of rnd.
Rnds 2 and 3: Work even.

Rnd 4: *K 9 sts, K2tog. Rep from * to end of rnd.
Rnds 5 and 6: Work even.
Rnd 7: *K 8 sts, K2tog. Rep from * to end of rnd.
Rnds 8 and 9: Work even.
Rnd 10: *K 7 sts, K2tog. Rep from * to end of rnd.
Rnd 11: Work even.
Rep Rnds 10 and 11, *but k 1 st fewer* in each unit of Rnd 10 until
you reach k1, K2tog. Then work k1, K2tog every rnd until about
32 sts remain.

Alternative treatment for an all-MC crown: Reflect the pattern on the
brim in the dec sts at the very top, when there are just enough sts between
dec points to allow a pattern rep plus 2 or 3 sts between. This works
best with block patterns like Fox and Geese, Maplewood, or one of
the Diamonds patterns. Continue the dec rnds as above, decreasing only
between blocks of pattern.

Alternative if you have used Sawtooth pattern on the brim: Start Sawtooth
on the work-even rnd when the next dec rnd will be k3, K2tog. Use Nora
Johnson's pinwheel dec (p. 105).

Alternative if you have covered the crown with an allover pattern: Use the
dec for that pattern from the mitten directions. Be creative.

Finishing the cap

Turn up the brim and, ideally, try the toque on the recipient at this
point, or check measurements against finished measurements at beg of
directions. If you—and the mitten recipient—are satisfied, break yarn(s)
leaving 6" (15cm) tail(s). With yarn needle, thread one end through the
remaining sts and draw up firmly. Draw other end to inside of cap.
Thread first end through drawn up sts again, darn a few sts to
secure it, and draw to inside of cap.

Turn the cap inside out and darn all ends into the back of fabric.
Trim ends closely.

	Child		Adult	
S		M	M	L

PART FOUR

Diamonds and Waves from Newfoundland and Labrador

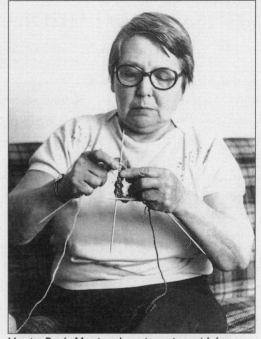

Harriet Pardy Martin, whose interview with her daughter Doris Saunders in *Them Days* magazine is the basis for most of the mittens in this section.
PHOTOGRAPH COURTESY OF *THEM DAYS* MAGAZINE

In Newfoundland and Labrador, the style of mittens changes radically from the allover patterns knit in Maine, New Brunswick, and Nova Scotia. A blending of traditions—Norwegian, Channel and Shetland Islands, Irish and Scottish—results in something different and special.

Knitting in two colors is not called double-knitting here, but two-ball knitting, or double-ball knitting. The pattern doesn't wrap around the mitten but is confined to the back of the mitten or glove, with the rest usually knitted in Salt and Pepper pattern.

In Newfoundland, mittens are called cuffs, mitts, or sometimes thumbies (Pocius, *Textile Traditions of Eastern Newfoundland,* 1979) and knitting needles are called skivvies.

Sometimes the pattern is markedly Scandinavian. The Selby Star that one sees everywhere on Norwegian mittens shows up here too—apparently lifted intact from a Norwegian knitting book and dropped into the folk medium in Newfoundland—and a reindeer pattern from the same book is commonly knitted throughout the area and known as Deer or Caribou.

Then again, a mitten may have one of many patterns of checks or diamonds that knitters seem fond of here, or waves, running either lengthwise or across the hand. Sometimes it is a combination—a Norwegian eight-pointed star with diamonds as the fill between the points of the star, or a checked pattern with a striped thumb and fleur-de-lis on the palm. The wave and diamond patterns are featured on the mittens in the following pages.

In this region, more often than anywhere else in Maine and Atlantic Canada, the index finger will be separated or the hand covering will be a complete glove with all the fingers separate. Sometimes the ends of the mitten are rounded, as they are farther south; other mittens, the ones with a strong Norwegian look, have the pointed Norwegian hand and thumb tips.

Knitting mitts and socks and hand spinning the wool of one's own sheep are still viable home crafts in Newfoundland and Labrador, and many families maintain traditional patterns. Knitters also play with patterns, changing a stitch here or there, taking a little of the drudgery out of necessary, constant knitting. Every pair of Diamond mitts seems to be different.

Although Newfoundland folklorist Jerry Pocius wrote that knitting in Newfoundland is now mainly recreational—a hobby—the fact that almost everyone owns a pair of two-ball mittens or gloves shows the importance of handknitting here in contrast to New England, New Brunswick, and Nova Scotia, where whole communities have forgotten the skill of double-knitting wool mittens or turning the heel of a sock.

Labrador Diamonds Mittens

This design was taken from a child's mitt knitted in the Saint Anthony's area of Newfoundland, but all the families I met in Happy Valley, Labrador, had similar mittens, so the name is not far off base.

Usually the design is knitted only to the base of the fingers, with a modified Salt and Pepper pattern from there to the tip of the mitten. On this mitten, I've carried the design all the way up the fingers because it looks smashing that way. I hope that's an adequate excuse for changing someone's traditional design slightly.

Since learning this pattern, I saw in Ann Feitelson's *The Art of Fair Isle Knitting* (Interweave, 1996) that similarly shaped mittens have been handed down in families on the Shetland mainland, "made by households for their own use, for wear and warmth, and not for sale." On the Shetland mittens, the back pattern was carried all the way to the fingertips.

Double Irish Chain (p. 181), also an 8-st pattern, can be substituted for Labrador Diamonds on this mitten without any other changes. If you wish to substitute any of the 7-st patterns from the other Newfoundland-Labrador patterns (e.g., one of the Diamond Checks on p. 167), adjust the number of sts on the back of the mitten by taking sts from the palm on the little-finger side.

The decs are worked on both edges and in every rnd.

This pattern was first published in *Needlecraft for Today*, 1985.

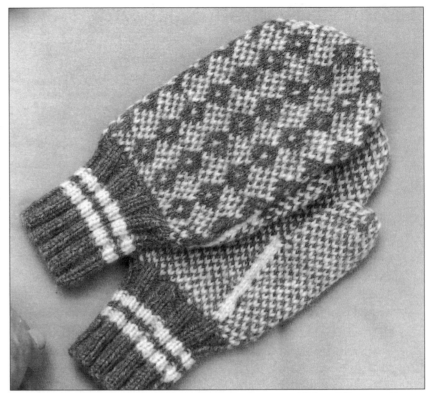

Labrador Diamonds Mittens with an outlined thumb gore and Salt and Pepper pattern on palm and thumb

Labrador Diamonds Mittens

Yarn For a lightweight mitten, use Briggs & Little 2/12, McAusland's 2-ply Fine, or other DK or medium weight yarn. For a heavier mitten with the same tension, I use Bartlettyarns 2-ply Fisherman or Rangeley. Briggs & Little 2/8 also works well. For 1 pair you will need about

MC	(oz)	2	2¼	2½	2½	2¾	2¾	3
	(g)	57	64	71.25	71.25	78.5	78.5	85.5
CC	(oz)	1½	2	2¼	2¼	2¼	2¼	2¾
	(g)	42.75	57	64	64	64	64	78.5

Equipment 1 set Size 4 (3.5mm, Can. Size 9) double-pointed needles, or size you need to knit in Salt and Pepper pattern at correct tension • 12" (30cm) length of contrasting waste yarn • Blunt-tipped yarn needle

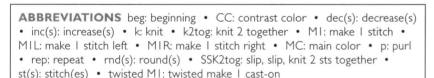

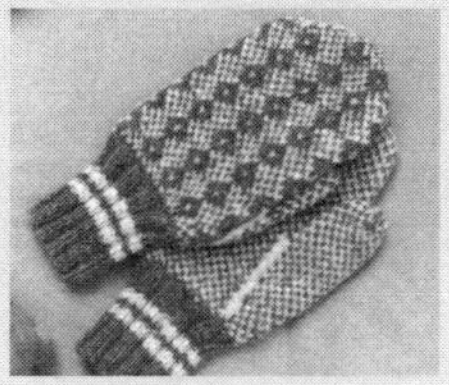

Tension 6½ sts and 7 rnds = 1" (2.5cm) in Salt and Pepper pattern

ABBREVIATIONS beg: beginning • CC: contrast color • dec(s): decrease(s) • inc(s): increase(s) • k: knit • k2tog: knit 2 together • M1: make 1 stitch • M1L: make 1 stitch left • M1R: make 1 stitch right • MC: main color • p: purl • rep: repeat • rnd(s): round(s) • SSK2tog: slip, slip, knit 2 sts together • st(s): stitch(es) • twisted M1: twisted make 1 cast-on

Measurements—inches and *centimeters*

	Child Sizes		Adult Sizes				
	4–6	8–10	WM	WL	MM	ML	XL
Length of hand	5½	6½	7	7½	7	7½	8½
	14	*16.5*	*17.75*	*19*	*17.75*	*19*	*21.5*
Hand circumference, incl. tip of thumb	7	8	9	9	9½	9½	10
	17.75	*20.25*	*22.75*	*22.75*	*24*	*24*	*25.5*
Length of mitten hand	6	7	7½	8	7½	8	9
	15.25	*17.75*	*19*	*20.25*	*19*	*20.25*	*22.75*
Mitten thumb (⅓ hand)	2	2⅜	2½	2⅝	2½	2⅝	3
	5	*6*	*6.5*	*6.75*	*6.5*	*6.75*	*7.5*
Mitten width	3½	4	4½	4½	4¾	4¾	5
	9	*10.25*	*11.5*	*11.5*	*12*	*12*	*12.75*

Pattern

   Newfoundland/Labrador mittens have a distinct front and back and are right or left mittens. Because it's desirable to have the pattern on the back very flat with no sign of needle changes, I have followed Harriet Pardy Martin's suggestion to put all the back sts on Needle 1 and the palm sts on Needles 2 and 3. The end of the rnd will fall on a pattern change at the edge of the hand, and there is no obvious joint at the end of the rnd. Give the two yarns a half twist together at the beginning of Needles 1 and 2 to emphasize the turn to the other side of the mitt. Carry the darker color ahead at all times (p. 16).

   Use Salt and Pepper pattern for the palm and the thumb, but you are free to use either Labrador Diamonds or Double Irish Chain charts (p. 180) or any other 8-st + 1 rep without changes. I have provided adjustments in the directions to use the 7-st Diamond or Waves charts

Labrador Diamonds Chart

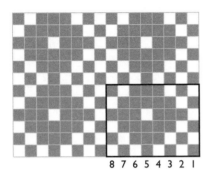

8 7 6 5 4 3 2 1

Key

■ MC—main color

□ CC—contrast color

□ one pattern repeat

Labrador Diamonds Thumb increase

(This number of incs is for Medium sizes)

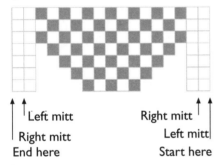

↑ ↑Left mitt   Right mitt ↑ ↑

|Right mitt   Left mitt|

End here   Start here

(under "Mrs. Martin's Finger Mitts," p. 167) for the back of the mitten. (It's all right if the pattern on the back of the hand runs over slightly at the little finger edge of the hand but it should be knitted on Needle 1 only.)

Although many Newfoundland and Labrador mitts have only as much large pattern as would normally be found on the back of a glove, with the whole finger area in Salt and Pepper, I have continued the pattern to the fingertip. You are, of course, free to knit the finger area in Salt and Pepper. Some knitters find a four-by-four square of diamonds more balanced and appealing than a pattern covering the entire back of the mitten.

Off the Cuff

The cuff is worked in k3, p1 ribbing, a traditional ribbing for Newfoundland and Labrador. It is worked on the same size needles as the rest of the mitt, with sts added at the base of the hand to accommodate the different tensions of ribbing and stockinette.

The striped pattern on this cuff is typical but not universal. Optionally, knit the cuff plain or use another of the Newfoundland striping patterns. Cuffs on Newfoundland/Labrador mittens fit closely. I have loosened them up a little for ease in taking them on and off.

		Child Sizes		Adult Sizes				
		4–6	8–10	WM	WL	MM	ML	XL

Making the cuff

	4–6	8–10	WM	WL	MM	ML	XL
With MC, and using the Maine method (p. 13), cast on	36 sts	40 sts	44 sts	44 sts	48 sts	48 sts	52 sts

K3, p1 for 10 rnds in MC. Six sts before end of last rnd, join CC (p. 18). Alternate 1 rnd CC, 1 rnd MC until there are 5 rnds CC. Work 7 rnds MC. (Knitters in this part of Canada are partial to having 26 rnds in their mitten cuffs. Although the stripes vary in number and width, the cuffs all seem to have 26 rnds.)

Starting the hand

		4–6	8–10	WM	WL	MM	ML	XL
Now, without moving the beg of the rnd, distribute sts:	Needle 1:	18 sts	20 sts	22 sts	22 sts	24 sts	24 sts	26 sts
	Needle 2:	9 sts	10 sts	11 sts	11 sts	12 sts	12 sts	13 sts
	Needle 3:	9 sts	10 sts	11 sts	11 sts	12 sts	12 sts	13 sts

		4–6	8–10	WM	WL	MM	ML	XL
Change to stockinette and work 1 rnd MC, increasing by M1 (p.20) between k sts of the ribs.	On Needle 1, inc:	6 sts	6 sts	8 sts	8 sts	8 sts	8 sts	6 sts
	On Needle 2, inc:	3 sts	3 sts	3 sts	3 sts	3 sts	3 sts	4 sts
	On Needle 3, inc:	3 sts	3 sts	3 sts	3 sts	3 sts	3 sts	4 sts
	Total with incs:	48 sts	52 sts	58 sts	58 sts	62 sts	62 sts	66 sts

Setting up the hand

Needle 1 will hold all the sts for the back of the hand.

	4–6	8–10	WM	WL	MM	ML	XL
If you are using Labrador Diamonds or Double Irish Chain or other 8 sts +1 rep, transfer sts to or from the little-finger side of the palm to get on Needle 1, then even up the sts on the palm needles for ease in knitting.	25 sts	25 sts	33 sts	33 std	33 sts	33 sts	33 sts
If you re using any of the 7-st rep charts, transfer sts to or from the little finger side of the palm to get on Needle 1. Then even up the sts on the palm needles for ease in knitting.	28 sts	28 sts	35 sts	35 sts	35 sts	35 sts	35 sts

Starting the pattern and the thumb gore

Rnd 1: Needle 1, back of hand: Work 7- or 8-st pattern chart of your choice, starting at lower right. In all cases, carry the darker color ahead throughout (p. 16).

Needles 2 and 3, palm and thumb gore: Work Salt and Pepper, *starting thumb gore marking sts immediately:*

Right mitten:
Needle 2: The thumb gore starts on the first 8 sts. K1 MC (marking st), work 5 sts Salt and Pepper, k2 MC (marking sts), finish needle in Salt and Pepper. The first MC st marks the entrance to the thumb gore. The last 2 MC sts mark the exit from the thumb gore. Maintain these marking sts to the top of the thumb gore.
Needle 3: Continue Salt and Pepper pattern to end of needle.

Left mitten:
Needle 2: Work Salt and Pepper pattern.
Needle 3: The thumb gore starts on the last 8 sts of this needle. Continue Salt and Pepper to last 8 sts, then k2 MC (marking sts), work 5 sts in Salt and Pepper, work 1 MC (marking st). The 2 MC sts mark the beg of the thumb gore. The last k1 MC marks the end of the thumb gore sts. Maintain these marking sts to the top of the thumb gore.

Note: Check after the first rnd that the rep comes out even. A mistake here can throw everything else off and take the fun out of the project. Also, if this is your second mitt, be sure it's for the other hand!

Rnd 2, *both left and right:*
Needle 1: Work next line of diamonds (or other) chart.

Right mitten:
Needle 2: Follow thumb inc chart, increasing on both sides, just inside the marking sts, by knitting both colors, in correct order, into one st (p. 21). Work to end of rnd in Salt and Pepper.

Left mitten:
Needle 2: Work even in pattern. Needle 3: Work in pattern to marking sts, Follow thumb inc chart, increasing on both sides, just inside the marking sts, by knitting both colors, in correct order, into one st (p. 21).

Child Sizes		Adult Sizes				
4–6	8–10	WM	WL	MM	ML	XL

		Child Sizes		Adult Sizes				
		4–6	8–10	WM	WL	MM	ML	XL
Continue to work Diamonds (or other) chart on Needle 1 and to inc 2 sts in thumb gore every rnd until there are within the two MC marking lines.		11 sts	13 sts	15 sts	15 sts	17 sts	17 sts	19 sts
Work even in pattern until thumb gore measures	(inches)	2	2⅜	2½	2⅝	2½	2⅝	3
	(cm)	5	6	6.5	6.75	6.5	6.75	7.5

Taking off the thumb gore stitches

Place all the thumb gore sts between (but not including) the marking lines onto waste yarn. Using twisted M1 (p. 23), cast on 5 sts in pattern over the gap. Discontinue the two marking lines, working them into the Salt and Pepper pattern.	Total is again:	48 sts	52 sts	58 sts	58 sts	62 sts	62 sts	66 sts
Work even until mitt above cuff measures	(inches)	4¾	5¾	6	6½	6	6½	7⅛
	(cm)	12	14.5	15.25	16.5	15.25	16.5	18

Closing the mitten tip

Dec every other rnd once, then every rnd:

Needle 1: K2tog (p. 24), work in pattern to 2 sts from end of needle, SSK2tog (p. 24).

Needle 2: K2tog, work in pattern to end of needle.

Needle 3: Work in pattern to 2 sts from end of needle, SSK2tog.

Repeat every rnd until there remain:	12 sts	12 sts	14 sts	14 sts	14 sts	14 sts	14 sts.

Check measurements against finished measurements at beg of directions before breaking yarn. If you are satisfied, break yarn leaving two 6" (15cm) tails. With yarn needle, thread one end through the remaining sts and draw up firmly. Draw other end to inside of mitten. Thread first end through drawn-up sts again, darn a few sts to secure and draw it to inside of mitten.

Working the thumb

Join both yarns by sewing (p. 20) into back of fabric starting at right side of the thumb hole.

		Child Sizes		Adult Sizes				
		4–6	8–10	WM	WL	MM	ML	XL
Pick up from waste yarn:	Needle 1:	5 sts	6 sts	7 sts	7 sts	8sts	8 sts	9 sts
	Needle 2:	6 sts	7 sts	8 sts	8 sts	9sts	9 sts	10 sts
Needle 3: Pick up 6 sts at top of thumb hole. In each corner of thumb hole, pick up and twist 1 st onto needle.	Total:	19 sts	21 sts	23 sts	23 sts	25 sts	25 sts	27 sts
Distribute sts:	Needle 1:	6 sts	7 sts	7 sts	7 sts	8 sts	8 sts	9 sts
	Needle 2:	6 sts	7 sts	8 sts	8 sts	8 sts	8 sts	9 sts
	Needle 3:	7 sts	7 sts	8 sts	8 sts	9 sts	9 sts	9 sts
Work even, matching pattern to Salt and Pepper pattern on the thumb gore until thumb measures	(inches)	1½	1⅞	1⅞	2	1⅞	2	2⅜
	(cm)	3.75	4.75	4.75	5	4.75	5	6

or work reaches just to the end of the thumb nail.

Closing the tip of the thumb

Rnd 1, all needles: K2tog, work in pattern to 2 sts from end of needle, SSK2tog.

Rnd 2: Work even.

	4–6	8–10	WM	WL	MM	ML	XL
Work Rnd 1 altogether	2X	2X	3X	3X	3X	3X	3X
Total remaining:	7 sts	9 sts	5 sts	5 sts	7 sts	7 sts	9 sts

Break yarn, leaving two 6" (15cm) tails. With yarn needle, thread one end through the remaining sts and draw up firmly. Draw other end to inside of thumb. Thread first end through drawn-up sts again, darn a few sts to secure it, and draw to inside of thumb.

Finishing the mitten

Turn mitten inside out and darn all ends into the back of the fabric. Repair possible holes at corners of the thumb hole with nearby tails. Trim ends closely.

This mitten is a right- or a left-handed mitten. Make another, being careful that it is for the opposite hand!

Child Sizes		Adult Sizes				
4–6	8–10	WM	WL	MM	ML	XL

Labrador Diamonds Mittens with the Diamond Check #1 pattern from from Mrs. Martin's Finger Mitts (p. 167) on the back

Mrs. Martin's Finger Mitts

Them Days: Stories of Early Labrador is a quarterly devoted to interviews with local people about "them days" past, much like the *Salt* and *Foxfire* books in the United States. In 1981, *Them Days* researcher Doris Saunders recorded her mother Harriet Pardy Martin telling how to knit a finger mitt (or hunter's mitt), one with the index finger separate.

Mrs. Martin's account is so to-the-point and so complete that I am reproducing it here* as the basic set of instructions for the Labrador Diamonds and Waves patterns. (Directions for making these finger mitts in 7 different sizes follow, on p. 166.) Most of the mitts and finger mitts in Part 4 of this book are knit using her instructions, which make it easier to knit the palm and back in different patterns.

Mrs. Martin's Diamonds pattern is the first chart on p. 167. Four variations on the Diamonds and the two Waves designs are also charted. All but Waves Pattern 2 have a multiple of 7 sts and can be substituted for one other on the backs of mittens. (Waves 2 has a 6-st repeat.) All the Diamond patterns can be arranged either as checkerboards or, as Mrs. Martin has done, in broad vertical stripes. Each pattern and each arrangement has its own dynamic and speaks highly of the design sense of these knitters of the subarctic.

Here, now, Mrs. Martin:

I learned to knit when I was a very small girl. I used to make doll's clothes. Sometimes 'twould come out good, other times 'twould be really funny. I knits like Aunt Mary Lamare—holds my needles like she used to. Aunt Mary was the one who taught me how to knit mitts. I was sixteen then. Mary is a few years younger than me.

The first pair of finger mitts that I made was a woman's pair. I makes them for men, women, children, and babies now. I mostly used the Diamond pattern when I started makin' mitts at first. After I got married, Ethel Coombs showed me how to do the deer and snowflake pattern. I likes white and black best, and I likes three-ply wool, kind of soft.

When I'm makin' finger mitts for a woman, I take four Size 10 [US Size 3] and cast on 40 sts, 12 on 1 needle, 16 on the other, and 12 on the third needle. On the band I knit 10 rows of main color [MC], 3 rows of contrast color [CC], 1 MC, 3 CC, and 9 MC. Now rearrange the sts so's there will be 10 on 1 needle, 20 on the second needle, and 10 on the third. The 20 will be the back of the mitt. I adds sts now according to the size I wants, for this pair, I'll add 4, 8, 4.

On the first needle I'll k 6, add 1, k 1, add 1, k 1, add 1,

Mrs. Martin's Finger Mitt

*Used by permission of Doris Saunders.

k 1, add 1, k 1; that's 14 sts. Now on the back, I'll k 6, and k the same as on the first needle to the last 6 sts, knit them. The last needle is done opposite to the first one. Now I have 14, 28, and 14 sts.

Now for the pattern, on the front needles, you k 1 MC, 1 CC, 1 MC and so on, and change each row to get the checkered pattern [Salt and Pepper]. Now for the back, you start off, 3 MC, 1 CC, 3 MC; 3 CC, 1 MC, 3 CC; 3 MC, 1 CC, 3 MC; 3 CC, 1 MC, 3 CC. When I starts up the thumb [immediately], I k 1 CC, 5 sts [MC, CC, MC, CC, MC], and 2 CC. Each following row I adds 2 more sts 'til I gets to 14 sts between the 2 solid lines of CC. Some people don't add sts for the thumb part. I likes the shape you gets when you adds on. When you gets up to where you wants your thumb, leave 14 sts on a st holder. [Cast on 5 sts over the gap.]

Now you continue knitting on the main part of the mitt to where you wants the finger [at the top of a column of 4 diamonds]. Take 7 sts from the first needle, and pick up 7 [2 from the first needle, 3 cast on between fingers and 2 from the third needle] on the second and take 7 sts from the last needle. K up 21 rows.

To cast off, k 3 sts together. This keeps the checkered pattern even. Cast off [decrease] until there is only 1 st left on each of the 3 needles. Break both pieces of wool and thread it [either, or both] on a darning needle and finish off the finger.

The main part of the mitt is 10, 21, and 10. K up 22 rows and cast off as you did the finger. The thumb is 7, 7, 7, and 18 rows. Cast off again as with the finger.

Do the same things for the other mitt, rememberin' to put the thumb on the opposite side. You wouldn't want two mitts for one hand.

There is one thing to remember: you hold the main color ahead of the contrast color. If you hold the contrast color ahead of the main color, you'll get a ridge in your knitting. The main color has to be ahead *all* the time.*

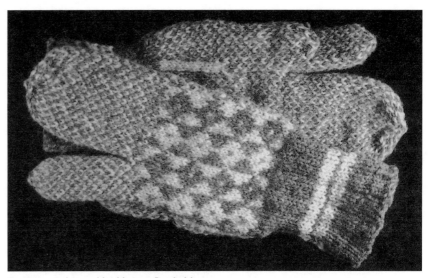

Finger mitts knitted by Harriet Pardy Martin. COURTESY OF *THEM DAYS* MAGAZINE

*In my experience, it doesn't matter too much which color you carry ahead in this pattern as long as you're consistent. Both colors are emphasized equally in this case. Should one of your colors be white, carry the darker color ahead. —*R.H.*

Mrs. Martin's Finger Mitts with More Sizes

Yarn Medium weight wool yarn. For a lightweight finger mitt, use Briggs & Little 2/12, McAusland's 2-ply, or other medium weight wool yarn. Mrs. Martin probably uses one of these. For a heavier finger mitt with the same gauge, I used Bartlettyarns 2-ply Fisherman or Rangeley. Briggs & Little 2/8 also works well. For a pair you will need about

MC (includes cuff)

(oz)	2	2¼	2½	2½	2¾	2¾	3
(g)	57	64	71.25	71.25	78.5	78.5	85.5

CC	(oz)	1½	2	2¼	2¼	2¼	2¼	2¾
	(g)	42.75	57	64	64	64	64	78.5

Equipment 1 set Size 4 (3.5mm, Can. Size 9) double-pointed needles, or size you need to knit in pattern at correct tension • 18" (45cm) length of contrasting waste yarn • Blunt-tipped yarn needle

Tension 6½ sts = 1" (2.5cm) in Salt & Pepper pattern

ABBREVIATIONS beg: beginning • CC: contrast color • dec(s): decrease(s) • inc(s): increase(s) • k: knit • k2tog: knit 2 together • M1: make 1 stitch • M1L: make 1 stitch left • M1R: make 1 stitch right • MC: main color • p: purl • rep: repeat • rnd(s): round(s) • SSK2tog: slip, slip, knit 2 sts together • st(s): stitch(es) • twisted M1: twisted make 1 cast-on

---

Measurements—inches and *centimeters*

	Child Sizes		Adult Sizes				
	4–6	8–10	WM	WL	MM	ML	XL
Length of hand	5½	6½	7	7½	7	7½	8½
	14	16.5	17.75	19	17.75	19	21.5
Hand circumference, incl. tip of thumb	7	8	9	9	9½	9½	10
	17.75	20.25	22.75	22.75	24	24	25.5
Length of mitten hand	6	7	7½	8	7½	8	9
	15.25	17.75	19	20.25	19	20.25	22.75
Mitten thumb (⅓ hand)	2	2⅜	2½	2⅝	2½	2⅝	3
	5	6	6.5	6.75	6.5	6.75	7.5
Mitten width	3½	4	4½	4½	4¾	4¾	5
	9	10.25	11.5	11.5	12	12	12.75

These finger mitts fit closely, like gloves.

Pattern

All of the charted Diamonds patterns have a 7-stitch block which can be assembled into vertical stripes, 2 blocks wide, or checks, 4 blocks square. The functional unit here is the 7-st 7-row block. Waves pattern No. 1 is 7 sts wide by 6 rows high; Waves No. 2 is 6 sts by 7 rows. Salt and Pepper, used on the palm and the thumb, is 2 sts by 2 rows.

Although Mrs. Martin arranges her stitches on the needles so that the end of the rnd falls in the center of the palm, I have shifted them, giving Needle 1 all the back stitches and Needles 2 and 3 the palm stitches. The end of the rnd then falls on the edge of the hand where the pattern changes, and there is no obvious joint in the pattern at the end of the rnd.

Diamond Stripes

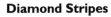
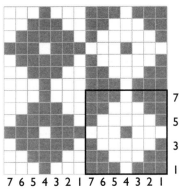

Diamond Check 1

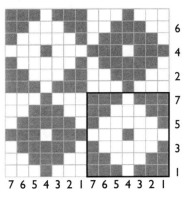

Diamond Check 2

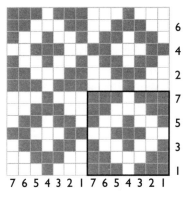

Diamond Check 3

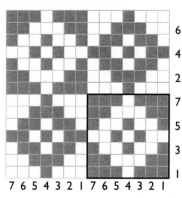

Diamond Check 4

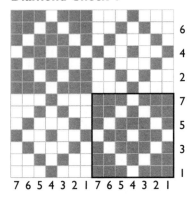

Waves 1

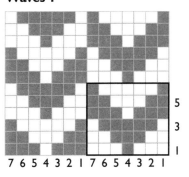

Waves 2

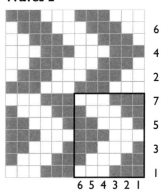

Thumb Gore Technique

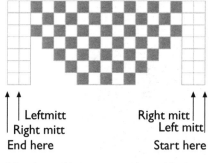

Leftmitt
Right mitt
End here

Right mitt
Left mitt
Start here

Number of increases varies with size.
Follow directions.

Salt and Pepper

2
1
2 1

Key

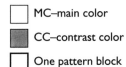

☐ MC–main color

■ CC–contrast color

☐ One pattern block

Off the Cuff

The cuff is worked in k3, p1 ribbing, a traditional ribbing for Newfoundland and Labrador. It is worked on the same size needles as the rest of the finger mitt, with stitches added at the base of the hand. Knitters in this part of Canada are partial to having 26 rnds in their mitten cuffs. Although the stripes vary in number and width, the cuffs all seem to have 26 rnds.

		Child Sizes		Adult Sizes				
		4–6	8–10	WM	WL	MM	ML	XL

Making the cuff

In MC and using the Maine method (p. 13), cast on — 32 sts / 36 sts / 40 sts / 40 sts / 44 sts / 44 sts / 48 sts

K3, p1 for 10 rnds in MC. Six sts before end of last rnd, join CC (p. 18). Work 3 rnds CC, 1 rnd MC, 3 rnds CC, then 9 rnds MC. Catch up CC with a half twist, about at the beg of Rnd 5 and Rnd 9.

Now, without moving the beg of the rnd, distribute the stitches so that half are on Needle 1 and a quarter each on Needles 2 and 3.

	4–6	8–10	WM	WL	MM	ML	XL
Needle 1:	16 sts	18 sts	20 sts	20 sts	22 sts	22 sts	24 sts
Needle 2:	8 sts	9 sts	10 sts	10 sts	11 sts	11 sts	12 sts
Needle 3:	8 sts	9 sts	10 sts	10 sts	11 sts	11 sts	12 sts

Change to stockinette and work 1 rnd MC, increasing by M1 (p. 20) between k sts of the ribs and spacing the incs evenly in the rnd.

	4–6	8–10	WM	WL	MM	ML	XL
On Needle 1, inc	6 sts	6 sts	8 sts	8 sts	10 sts	10 sts	12 sts
On Needle 2, inc	3 sts	3 sts	4 sts	4 sts	5 sts	5 sts	6 sts
On Needle 3, inc	3 sts	3 sts	4 sts	4 sts	5 sts	5 sts	6 sts
Total:	44 sts	48 sts	56 sts	56 sts	64 sts	64 sts	72 sts

Starting the pattern and the thumb gore

Needle 1 will hold all the sts for the back of the hand and will be worked in one of the charted Diamonds patterns or Waves 1 pattern. For any of these patterns, you need a multiple of 7 sts on Needle 1. Transfer stitches to or from Needle 2 or 3 (the little-finger side) so that Needle 1 has — 21 sts / 28 sts / 28 sts / 28 sts / 35 sts / 35 sts / 35 sts

Rnd 1. Work chart of your choice on Needle 1. Carry one color ahead consistently throughout (p. 16). If one of the colors is white, carry the dark color ahead.

Needles 2 and 3—palm and thumb gore—are worked in in Salt and Pepper pattern. You will also begin the lines of MC marking sts for the thumb gore in this rnd.

Right mitten, Needle 2: K1 MC, work Salt and Pepper for 5 sts, k2 MC. The first MC st marks the entrance to the thumb gore. The last 2 MC sts mark the exit from the thumb gore. Maintain these as marking sts in every rnd. (See thumb gore chart.) Needle 3: Continue Salt and Pepper pattern to end of rnd.

Left mitten, Needle 2: Work Salt and Pepper pattern. Needle 3: Continue Salt and Pepper to last 8 sts of the needle, then k2 MC, work 5 sts in Salt and Pepper, work 1 MC. The 2 MC sts mark the entrance to the thumb gore. The last MC st marks the exit from the thumb gore. Maintain these as marking sts in every rnd.

Rnd 2: Work Line 2 of Diamonds chart on Needle 1.

Right mitten, Needle 2: K1 MC, M1L (p. 20), work Salt and Pepper up to marking sts. M1R (p. 21), k2 MC. Complete rnd in Salt and Pepper.

Left mitten, Needle 2: Work even in Salt and Pepper pattern. Needle 3: Work Salt and Pepper to marking sts, k2 MC, M1L, work Salt and Pepper up to last st, M1R, k1 MC.

	Child Sizes		Adult Sizes				
	4–6	8–10	WM	WL	MM	ML	XL
Both mittens: Continue pattern on Needle 1 and increasing 2 sts in thumb gore every rnd until there are within the 2 MC marking lines.	11 sts	13 sts	15 sts	15 sts	19 sts	19 sts	21 sts
Work even in pattern until thumb gore measures (inches)	2	2⅜	2½	2⅝	2½	2⅝	3
(cm)	5	6	6.5	6.75	6.5	6.75	7.5

Taking off the thumb gore stitches

Place all thumb gore sts between (but not including) the marking lines onto waste yarn. Using twisted M1 (p. 23), cast on 5 sts in pattern over the gap. Discontinue the two marking lines, working them into the Salt and Pepper pattern.

Total is again	44 sts	48 sts	56 sts	56 sts	64 sts	64 sts	72 sts

Working the hand

		Child Sizes		Adult Sizes				
		4–6	8–10	WM	WL	MM	ML	XL
Work even in pattern until hand above cuff measures	(inches)	3	3½	3¾	4	3¾	4	4½
	(cm)	7.5	9	9.5	10.25	9.5	10.25	11.5

For ML and WL sizes, you will probably have completed four bands of Diamonds or Waves pattern. In the other sizes, complete the band of pattern on the back of the hand and the index finger *after* you have taken off stitches for the finger hole.

If you have the hand you're knitting for available, try on the finger mitt at this point. You have reached the separation point for the index finger if you can comfortably slide the free knitting needle through the knitting on the needles and the "crotch" of the index and middle fingers.

Take off index finger stitches when work reaches the crotch of the index and middle fingers.
COURTESY OF *THEM DAYS* MAGAZINE

Separate index finger

Place on waste yarn half from Needle 1 and half from above the thumb on Needle 2 or 3.		14 sts	16 sts	18 sts	18sts	20 sts	20 sts	22 sts,
Using twisted M1 (p. 23), cast on over the gap continuing Salt and Pepper pattern from the palm.		1 st	1 st	3 sts	3 sts	5 sts	5 sts	5 sts
	Total:	31 sts	33 sts	41 sts	41 sts	49 sts	49 sts	55 sts
Work even in patterns until hand above cuff measures	(inches)	5⅜	5⅞	6⅜	6½	6⅜	6½	7⅜
	(cm)	13.75	15	16.25	16.5	16.25	16.5	18.75

or until just above the nail of the ring finger.

Closing the mitten tip

		Child Sizes		Adult Sizes				
		4–6	8–10	WM	WL	MM	ML	XL
Redistribute sts:	Needle 1:	10 sts	11 sts	14 sts	14 sts	16 sts	16 sts	18 sts
	Needle 2:	10 sts	11 sts	14 sts	14 sts	16 sts	16 sts	18 sts
	Needle 3:	11 sts	11 sts	13 sts	13 sts	17 sts	17 sts	19 sts

Dec both ends of all needles every other rnd: K2tog, k in pattern to last 2 sts, SSK2tog. (Notice that I didn't suggest knitting 3 sts together, as Mrs. Martin did. I feel that it weakens the knit.)

	4–6	8–10	WM	WL	MM	ML	XL
Continue working decs every other rnd until you have only	6 sts	8 sts	8 sts	8 sts	8 sts	8 sts	8 sts

Check length against measurements at beg of this pattern, p. 166.

If you are satisfied, break yarn, leaving a 6" (15cm) tail. With a yarn needle, thread one end through the remaining sts and draw up firmly. Draw other ends to inside of mitten. Thread first end through drawn-up sts once more, darn a few sts to secure it, and draw to inside of mitten.

Working the index finger

Join both yarns by sewing (p. 20) into back of fabric, starting at the side of finger hole between fingers.

	4–6	8–10	WM	WL	MM	ML	XL
On Needle 1 (between the fingers), pick up 2 sts from one end of index-finger waste yarn, pick up between the fingers and 2 sts from opposite end of index-finger waste yarn:	1 st	1 st	3 sts	3 sts	5 sts	5 sts	5 sts
On Needle 2, pick up from waste yarn	5 sts	6 sts	7 sts	7 sts	8 sts	8 sts	9 sts
On Needle 3, pick up from waste yarn	5 sts	6 sts	7 sts	7 sts	8 sts	8 sts	9 sts
Total:	15 sts	17 sts	21 sts	21 sts	25 sts	25 sts	27 sts

Optionally, to minimize small holes at the base of the finger, pick up an additional st in each of the two corners of the finger hole and k them tog with the adjacent sts in the first rnd.

On the palm sts, work Salt and Pepper, continuing pattern from the palm. On the back of the hand, finish any incomplete band of Diamonds or

		Child		Adult					
		2–4	6–8	WS	WM	WL	MM	ML	MXL

Waves pattern, then continue in Salt and Pepper, matching the rest of the finger. Tucking the finished portion of the hand into the mitten makes working the finger easier.

		Child		Adult					
		2–4	6–8	WS	WM	WL	MM	ML	MXL
Work even in pattern until hand and finger above cuff measure	(inches)	5⅜	6	6½	7¼	6½	7¼	8	
	(cm)	13.75	15.25	16.5	18.5	16.5	18.5	20.25	

or you reach just to the tip of the index fingernail.

Dec:
Rnd 1: On all needles, k2tog, work even to last 2 sts, SSK2tog. Match pattern to the rest of each needle.
Rnd 2: Work even in pattern.

		Child		Adult					
Work Rnd 1 altogether		1X	2X	2X	2X	3X	3X	3X	
Total remaining:		9 sts	5 sts	9 sts	9 sts	7 sts	7 sts	9 sts	

Break yarn with a 6" (15cm) tail. With a yarn needle, thread one end through the remaining sts and draw up firmly. Draw other end to inside of mitten. Thread first end through drawn-up sts once more, darn a few sts to secure end, and draw end to inside of mitten.

Working the thumb

Join both yarns by sewing (p. 20) into back of fabric starting at the right side of thumb hole.

		Child		Adult					
On Needles 1 and 2, pick up from waste yarn		11 sts	13sts	15 sts	15 sts	17 sts	17 sts	21 sts	

On Needle 3, pick up 6 sts from the cast-on sts above thumb hole.
Pick up and twist 1 st onto needle in each corner of thumb hole.

		Child		Adult					
Total:		19 sts	21 sts	23 sts	23 sts	25 sts	25 sts	29 sts	
Work even, matching pattern to Salt and Pepper pattern on the thumb gore until thumb measures	(inches)	1¾	2	2	2¼	2	2¼	2⅞	
	(cm)	4.5	5	5	5.75	5	5.75	7.25	

or you reach just to the tip of the thumbnail.

Closing the tip of the thumb

Dec:

Rnd 1: On all needles, K2tog, work in pattern to 2 sts from end of needle, SSK2tog.

Rnd 2. Work even.

Work Rnd 1 altogether

	Child		Adult					
	2–4	6–8	WS	WM	WL	MM	ML	MXL
Work Rnd 1 altogether	2X	2X	3X	3X		3X	3X	3X
Total remaining:	7 sts	9 sts	5 sts	5 sts		7 sts	7 sts	9 sts

Break yarn with a 6" (15cm) tail. With a yarn needle, thread one end through the remaining sts and draw up firmly. Draw other end to inside of mitten. Thread first end through drawn-up sts once more, darn a few sts to secure end and draw end to inside of mitten.

Finishing the Mitten

Turn mitten inside out and darn all tails into the back of fabric. Repair possible holes at corners of the thumb hole with nearby tails. Trim ends closely.

And don't forget: "Do the same things for the other mitt, rememberin' to put the thumb on the opposite side. You wouldn't want two mitts for one hand!"

Finger Mitts in Waves design purchased in St. John's, Newfoundland. Note that the knitter was not careful about which color she carried ahead on the palms and fingers. While this pair was not made from the directions here, you can make a similar pair by using Waves Pattern 2 on p. 167.

Big Waves for Big Mittens

Big Waves Mitten (left) copied from a mitten in the pattern bag of Phyllis Montague in Northwest River, Labrador.

Waves are a recurring theme in Newfoundland and Labrador mittens, and all the waves are pointed. Two smaller Waves patterns are included in the charts on p. 167. Another Waves pattern is presented here with all the peculiarities of traditional knitting. This pattern, as is, makes only a man's large mitten, but was so spectacular that I couldn't leave it out.

Phyllis Montague, of Northwest River, Labrador, had this mitten in a bag of patterns her mother (from St. Anthony's, Newfoundland) had made her, which also included a Caribou design and one I call Shining Star (at right in photo). This Waves Mitten was huge but grand. I photographed it and reconstructed the knitting by counting stitches in the photograph. Mrs. Montague herself didn't knit many of these. She felt that mittens with caribou sold more readily.

Big Waves has many long floats between color changes, which necessitate catching up the other color behind the work, a process that invariably causes some lumps. If you don't want to catch up the other color and can keep the floats fairly relaxed, you could make a pair, then wash them in cool water, scrubbing and rubbing them to encourage the loops to adhere to the inside surface. But you would have to exercise care in putting them on until they became somewhat matted together.

If you are inventive and like this pattern, maybe you can figure out how to make it smaller—either by using a finer yarn and needles, or by cutting down the design itself. A fingering yarn at 9 sts = 1 inch (2.5cm) will bring it down to a woman's Medium without altering the pattern.

Big Waves Mittens

Yarn MC 3 oz (light color) medium-weight yarn • CC 3 oz (dark color) medium-weight yarn. I used Bartlettyarns 2-ply Fisherman Yarn, which is a little lighter than Briggs & Little 2/8, and a little heavier than commercial medium weight yarns.

Equipment 1 set Size 3 (3.25mm, Can. Size 10) double-pointed needles, or size you need to knit in Fleur-de-lis pattern at correct tension • 6" (15cm) length of contrasting waste yarn • Blunt-tipped yarn needle

Tension 7 sts and 7½ rnds = 1" (2.5cm) in pattern

Measurements—inches and *centimeters*

	XL only
Hand Length	8½ *(21.5)*
Hand circumference, including tip of thumb	10 *(25.5)*
Mitten hand length	9 *(22.75)*
Mitten thumb (⅓ hand)	3 *(7.5)*
Mitten width	5 *(12.75)*

ABBREVIATIONS beg: beginning • CC: contrast color • dec(s): decrease(s) • inc(s): increase(s) • k: knit • k2tog: knit 2 together • M1: make 1 stitch • M1L: make 1 stitch left • M1R: make 1 stitch right • MC: main color • p: purl • rep: repeat • rnd(s): round(s) • SSK2tog: slip, slip, knit 2 sts together • st(s): stitch(es) • twisted M1: twisted make 1 cast-on

Pattern

In order to knit the same tension in Big Waves pattern, *do not* weave in the unused strand on floats of only 4 sts. The knitting may be a little ridgey, but not in a bad way. You can steam the mitten lightly with an iron and a damp cloth afterward.

Do be sure to weave in the second strand (p. 18) behind your work when color changes are *more* than 4 sts apart.

Follow the charts on pps. 176–77 exactly. Fleur-de-lis (the palm-side pattern) is a multiple of 4 sts and 6 rnds. Big Waves is a multiple of 12 sts and 24 rnds. Carry the darker color ahead throughout.

Off the Cuff

The cuff is a traditional Newfoundland/Labrador k3, p1 ribbing. Occasionally, one sees mittens from this region with k4, p1 cuffs, which almost cease to have any elastic function at all. It is also traditional to use one size needle for both stockinette and ribbing and to inc at the top of the cuff to accommodate the difference in tension.

Making the cuff

With MC, and using the Maine method (p. 13), cast on 44 sts. Join, being careful not to twist sts. Distribute sts: Needle 1—16 sts; Needle 2—12 sts; Needle 3—16 sts.

K3, p1 for 26 rnds.

Starting the pattern and thumb gore

Note: Carry CC (the darker color) ahead (p. 16). Check after the first rnd of pattern that the rep comes out even. A mistake here can throw everything else off and take the fun out of the project.

Work 1 rnd plain stockinette, adding 2 sts between the 3 k sts of every rib by M1 (p. 20) or by knitting into the loop between sts. Total 66 sts.

Arrange sts: Needle 1—35 sts; Needle 2—17 sts; Needle 3—14 sts. Needle 1 will be the back of the hand; Needles 2 and 3 will be the palm. The beg/end of the rnd will be between Needles 3 and 1.

Begin Chart A at lower right on Needle 1 (the back), move to palm Chart B and insert the thumb gore Chart C in the hole of Chart B.

Note: Palm Chart B shows the right mitten. For the left mitten, read Chart B from bottom left to right (while knitting from right to left, of course).

Right mitten: The first 5 sts of Needle 2 form the base of the thumb gore, including an outline (in Chart B) of a single CC marking st on each side.

Left mitten: The last 5 sts of Needle 3 form the base of the thumb gore, including an outline (in Chart B) of a single CC marking st on each side.

Increase for the thumb gore

Both mittens: Every third rnd, inc within the 2 CC marking lines: K1CC; M1L (p. 20) MC; work up to second CC marking st; M1R, (p. 21) MC. See Chart C for a visual representation of this. In Rnd 6, begin color pattern on thumb gore, following Chart C.

Key

☐ MC–main color

■ CC–contrast color

mr make 1 right

ml make 1 left

Big Waves Chart A

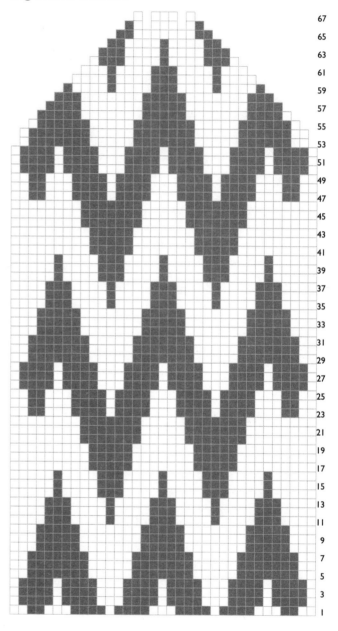

Big Waves Chart B

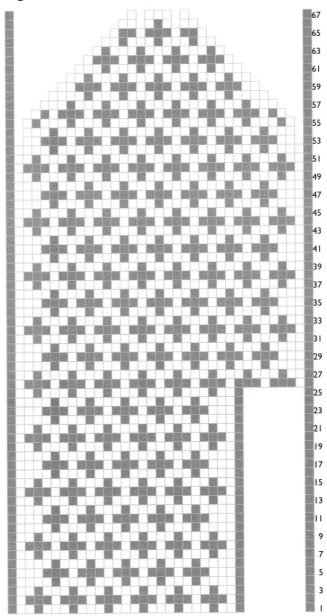

Right mitten: Work Chart B from right to left.
Left mitten: Work Chart B from left to right.

Big Waves Chart C

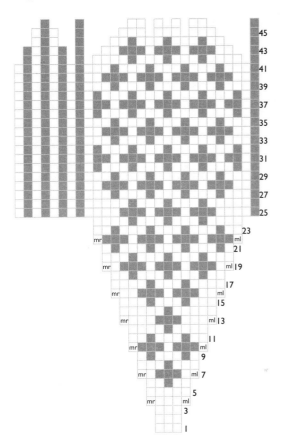

Taking off the thumb gore stitches

When there are 17 sts between (but not including) the CC marking sts, work even in pattern until thumb gore above cuff measures 3"(7.5cm).

Put 17 thumb gore sts on waste yarn.

Using twisted M1 (p. 23), cast on 7 sts in pattern over the gap. Discontinue marking sts on palm (include them in the palm pattern), but not on index finger edge. Total: 70 sts.

Following charts, work even until pattern above cuff measures 7⅜" (18.75cm).

Closing the mitten tip

Needle 1: SSK2tog MC (p. 24). Work in pattern to last 2 sts of needle, k2tog MC (p. 24).

Needles 2 and 3: K1 CC, SSK2tog MC; work in pattern to last 3 sts of Needle 3, k2tog MC, k1 CC.

This creates a 3-st dec strip along both edges of the mitten (1 MC, 1 CC, 1 MC). Maintain this strip to the tip of the mitten.

Dec this way every second rnd once, then every rnd. Where a 2-st dec is shown on the chart, k2tog twice in the MC areas on both sides, both front and back, in every rnd while continuing to dec on the edges as before.

Check measurements against finished measurements at beg of directions. If you are satisfied, break yarn leaving a 6" (15cm) tail. With yarn needle, thread one end through the remaining sts and draw up firmly.

Draw other end to inside of mitten. Thread first end through drawn-up sts again, darn a few sts to secure and draw it to inside of mitten.

Working the thumb

Needles 1 and 2: Pick up 17 sts from waste yarn.
Needle 3: Pick up 7 sts at top of thumb hole.
Pick up and twist 2 sts onto needle in each corner of thumb hole in the CC marking sts. Total: 28 sts.

Join both yarns by sewing (p. 20) into back of fabric starting at the right side of the thumb hole.

Needles 1 and 2: Continue Fleur-de-lis pattern from thumb gore following Chart C.
Needle 3: Alternate CC and MC, continuing the CC marking sts up the sides of the thumb and working 1-st-wide vertical stripes on the inside of the thumb.

Work even in patterns until thumb measures 2½" (6.5cm).

Mrs. Montague striped the palm side of the thumb on all her mittens to give them greater durability. She laughed when she saw a Maine striped mitten. "She knitted it all like a thumb," she said.

Closing the tip of the thumb

Following Chart C, dec as on hand until 10 sts remain.

Break yarn, leaving a 6" (15cm) tail. With yarn needle, thread one end through the remaining sts and draw up firmly. Draw other end to inside of thumb. Thread first end through drawn-up sts again, darn a few sts to secure and draw it to inside of thumb.

Finishing the mitten

Turn mitten inside out and darn all ends into the back of the fabric. Repair any holes at corners of the thumb hole with nearby tails. Trim ends closely.

This mitten is a right- or a left-handed mitten. Make another, being careful that it is for the opposite hand!

Double Irish Chain and Newfoundland Palm and Finger Stitch

This page offers two additional bits of mitten tradition—the chart and commentary for the traditional Double Irish Chain pattern for the backs of Newfoundland mittens or gloves and a curious and effective palm and finger pattern from Newfoundland. These can be applied as you wish to the other mittens and fingermitts in this part of the book.

Double Irish Chain

Double Irish Chain Mittens come from Conception Harbour, near St. John's, Newfoundland. Newfoundland folklorist Jerry Pocius reports that it's a beloved pattern there and is also hooked into rugs and worked into patchwork quilts as well as knitted into mittens. There is no way of knowing which came first, as the pattern works equally well in all three media, and we can only guess from the name that an Irish woman may have brought it to this continent.

Double Irish Chain can also be knitted with the diamond 7 sts wide with a little dot in the center. I liked the look of the dark diamonds and the white chains and so opted for the 5-st diamond. The color of the chains (CC on this chart) should be carried ahead to bring out the pattern.

Double Irish Chain can be substituted for the back pattern on Labrador Diamonds Mittens (page 156), as both patterns have an 8-st rep. Substitute it for the back pattern on Mrs. Martin's Finger Mitts (p. 164) too, but adjust the number of sts on Needle 1 to a multiple of 8 by taking sts from the palm needle on the little-finger side, then redistributing the palm sts so the two palm needles are more or less balanced.

Like much double-knitting in Newfoundland and Labrador especially, Double Irish Chain is often made with gray and white homespun (really homespun) yarns. I've knitted it here in denim and sheep's white medium weight yarn from Briggs & Little Woollen Mills in New Brunswick. Consider reversing light and dark on this pattern for a different look, but always carry the contrast color ahead to emphasize the narrow lines.

It might be fun to cover a whole mitten with this simple geometric pattern in the New Brunswick/Nova Scotia/Maine tradition. Remember your total sts must be a multiple of eight for the pattern to wrap seamlessly around the mitten.

Double Irish Chain Mitten made from Labrador Diamonds Mitten directions (p. 156)

Double Irish Chain

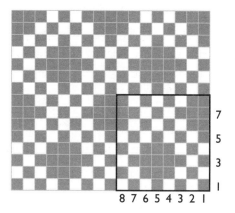

7
5
3
1

8 7 6 5 4 3 2 1

Key

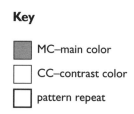

MC–main color

CC–contrast color

pattern repeat

Newfoundland Palm and Finger Stitch

The palm and thumb of the Double Irish Chain mitten and the little mitten beside it in the color photo are worked in a version of Salt and Pepper peculiar to Newfoundland. To create a pull-up effect like that in Stripes and Checkerboard patterns, Newfoundland knitters carry alternate *stitches* ahead (p. 16) in every rnd, regardless of color. The textured effect is said to make the mitten thicker on the palm and to give a better gripping surface. That is, in every rnd, say, all the odd sts (1, 3, 5, 7, and so forth) are carried ahead, while all the even sts (2, 4, 6, 8, and so forth) are carried behind.

The surprising visual effect of this alternation of carrying ahead by stitches is jagged horizontal stripes of color. This is why it does what it does (if you are interested): The color carried ahead always lies vertically beneath the other color. In Salt and Pepper, then (for example), the dark color lies above the light color in Rnds 1 and 3 and 5 and lies below the light color in Rnds 2 and 4 and 6. This puts the dark sts of two rnds close together in Rnds 1 and 2 and Rnds 3 and 4, while the light sts of two rnds lie close together in Rnds 2 and 3 and Rnds 4

and 5. (If that makes no sense to you, give it a try and see for yourself. Allow at least 6 rnds for the effect to develop.)

Neither of the two Labrador knitters I have oral accounts from do this, and Harriet Pardy Martin even says *not* to do it "or you gets a ridge in your knitting," but many mittens from Newfoundland (the island) have this effect, which is too tricky not to be deliberate. Try it on your second, third, or fourth pair

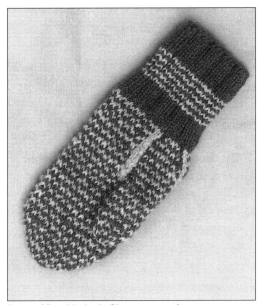

Palm of Double Irish Chain mitten showing Newfoundland palm and finger stitch

of Newfoundland mittens, but not on your first. It's a fun effect, and looks great in close colors, but is time-consuming to get right the first time. If you carry the wrong color ahead in one rnd, or even for two sts, the error will be quite obvious.

Knitting Salt and Pepper this way makes a darling all-over pattern for a child's mitten as well. You may need to use knitting needles one size larger than given in the Salt and Pepper directions to get the correct tension.

**Salt and Pepper Chart
for Newfoundland Palm**

2 Carry CC ahead in Round 2.
1 Carry MC ahead in Round 1.
2 1

Key

■ MC—main color

☐ CC—contrast color

☐ pattern repeat

PART FIVE

Baby Foxes and Goslings: Double-Knits for Babies and Small Children

Here are some of the same traditional patterns knit with a gentler yarn for babies and children up to four years old. The two layers of yarn and the tightness of the knit make a very warm but light mitten. I include directions for a little helmet that buttons under the chin that can be worked with most of the patterns in this book in colors to match the little one's mittens.

For babies, these can also be made of synthetic yarn, as it's unlikely that babies will spend much time in wet snow or fishing on icy waters.

All these patterns are worked on sizes 2, 3, and 4 double-pointed needles and are quickly made. The yarn is a medium-weight fingering—sport yarn—a little thicker than baby yarn.

These sizes overlap the sizes of the medium weight yarn mittens at size 2–4. The medium weight yarn is more quickly knit and heavier, but is also bulkier, like new denim blue jeans in baby sizes. Take your pick.

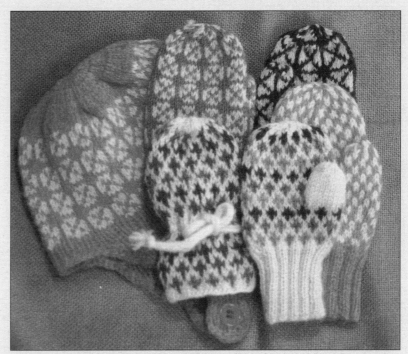

Mittens and a cap for babies and small children. *(From 12 o'clock)* Baby Foxes and Goslings; Compass Mittens for Small Mariners; Wee Checkerboard; Petites Mitaines en Fleur-de-lis with thumb and ribbed cuff; the same with a wide, patterned cuff, a tie, and no thumb; patterned baby helmet knitted from the top in Fox and Geese.

Baby Foxes and Goslings

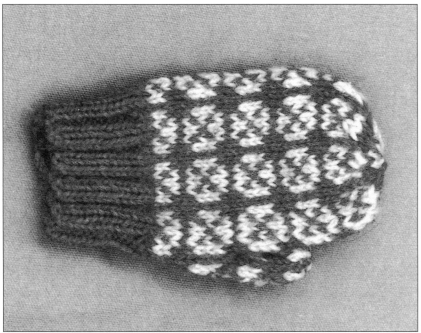

Baby Foxes and Goslings Mitten in two colors

Yarn Brunswick Yarns Pomfret, used for mitten in the photo, no longer exists, but we have had good luck with Jaggerspun 2/8, Halcyon Yarn's Victorian, and Raumagarn Hifa. Any sport weight yarn that knits to correct tension will work. Baby yarn or fingering is usually too fine. It is fine to use Superwash™ treated wool for babies, although it is not quite as warm when wet.

• MC (dark) ¾ oz or 21.5g sport weight yarn, preferably wool
• CC (light) ½ oz or 14.25g sport weight yarn, preferably wool

Equipment 1 set Size 2 (2.75mm, Can. Size 12) double-pointed needles, or size you need to knit in pattern at correct tension • 1 set Size 1 (2.25mm, Can. Size 13) double-pointed needles for ribbing • 6" (15 cm) length of contrasting waste yarn • Blunt-tipped yarn needle

Tension 9 sts and 9½ rnds = 1" (2.5 cm) in pattern

ABBREVIATIONS beg: beginning • CC: contrast color • dec(s): decrease(s) • inc(s): increase(s) • k: knit • k2tog: knit 2 together • M1: make 1 stitch • M1L: make 1 stitch left • M1R: make 1 stitch right • MC: main color • p: purl • rep: repeat • rnd(s): round(s) • SSK2tog: slip, slip, knit 2 sts together • st(s): stitch(es) • twisted M1: twisted make 1 cast-on

Measurements—inches and *centimeters*

	6–12 mos	2 yrs	3 yrs	4 yrs
Hand length	3	3½	3¾	4⅛
	7.5	*9*	*9.5*	*10.5*
Hand circumference, incl. tip of thumb	4½	5	5½	6
	11.5	*12.75*	*14*	*15.25*
Mitten hand length	3¼	3½	4	4¼
	8.25	*9*	*10.25*	*10.75*
Mitten thumb (⅓ mitten hand)	1⅛	1¼	1⅜	1½
	3	*3.25*	*3.5*	*3.75*
Mitten width	2¼	2½	2¾	3
	5.75	*6.5*	*7*	*7.5*

Pattern

Fox and Geese is a multiple of 6 sts and 6 rnds and, because of the single-color rnd, is not easily knitted flat. These mittens are knit circularly and, unlike the adult version, without a third color for the horizontal lines.

Incs and decs are made in the first pattern rnd only, with an inc of 6 sts—one pattern rep—at once. Challenging, but then there's only one inc rnd.

Off the Cuff

A simple k2, p2 ribbing in one color works well for these small mittens.

Chart 1: Baby Foxes and Goslings

Key

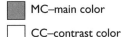

▓	MC–main color
☐	CC–contrast color
m	make 1
↗	knit both colors into 1 st

Chart 2: Thumb Gore Increase

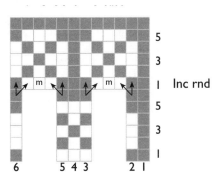

Inc rnd

Chart 3: Decrease

Making the cuff

With MC, smaller needles, and using the Maine method (p. 13), cast on

			6–12 mos	2 yrs		3 yrs	4 yrs
			40 sts	48 sts		52 sts	60 sts
Distribute sts:		Needle 1:	12 sts	16 sts		16 sts	20 sts
		Needle 2:	16 sts	16 sts		20 sts	20 sts
		Needle 3:	12 sts	16 sts		16 sts	20 sts

Join into a triangle, being careful not to twist sts around the needles.

		6–12 mos	2 yrs		3 yrs	4 yrs
K2, p2 in MC for	(inches)	1¼	1¼		1⅜	1½
	(cm)	*3.25*	*3.25*		*3.5*	*3.75*

Change to larger needles and stockinette.

		6–12 mos	2 yrs		3 yrs	4 yrs
K1 rnd MC, inc on Needle 2		2 sts	—		2 sts	—
	Total (a multiple of 6):	42 sts	48 sts		54 sts	60 sts

Six sts from end of rnd, join CC (p. 18). Finish rnd in MC.

Starting the pattern and the thumb gore

Note: Carry MC (dark color) ahead throughout (p. 16). Check after the first rnd that the rep comes out even. A mistake here can throw everything else off and take the fun out of the project.

	6–12 mos	2 yrs		3 yrs	4 yrs
Start Chart 1 at lower right on and work chart through Line 6.	Line 3	Line 1		Line 1	Line 1

Start thumb gore, beginning with Line 1 of next pattern band (marked "Inc rnd" on Chart 2).

Note: Practically speaking, the mitten can be worn on either hand, and you *can* make two right or two left mittens, as you please, but directions follow for individual left and right mittens, too. This traditional arrangement places the "seam" between rnds in the center of the palm.

Right mitten: K in pattern up to St 1 of next-to-last pattern block on Needle 3.

Left mitten: K in pattern to St 1 of second pattern block on Needle 1.

Both mittens: Inc. K1 MC into St 1; k both colors (p. 21) into St 2—first

MC then CC; M1 CC (p. 20); k both colors into St 3—first CC then MC; k1 MC into St 4; k both colors into St 5—first MC then CC; M1 CC; k both colors into St 6—first CC then MC. You are now ready to k St 1 of the next pattern block.

You have increased 6 sts in the space of 5 sts. A miracle. This is the only thumb gore inc in this mitten.

Work 5 more rnds, completing Chart 2 to end of Line 6.

Taking off the thumb gore stitches

Right mitten: Work in pattern to 12 sts before end of Needle 3. Put next 11 sts on a piece of waste yarn. Using twisted M1 (p. 23), cast on 5 sts in pattern over the gap, k 1.

Left mitten: K1, put next 11 sts on a piece of waste yarn. Using twisted M1 (p. 23), cast on 5 sts in pattern over the gap, work Line 1 to end of rnd.

Both mittens: Work even in pattern until hand *above cuff* measures

ending with Line 6 of chart completed.

Closing the mitten tip

Note: Decs are within each block of pattern. Chart 3 shows this graphically. You will dec by k2tog (p. 24) and SSK2tog (p. 24).

Rnd 1: Dec: Work Line 1 of chart, but as you do so, *k2tog, k1; rep from * to end of rnd.

Rnd 2: Work even. *K1 MC, k1 CC; rep from * to end of rnd.

Rnd 3: Dec: *SSK2tog MC, K1 CC; rep from * to end of rnd.

Rnd 4: Work even. *K2 MC, K2 CC; rep from * to end of rnd.

Rnd 5: Dec: *SSK2tog MC, K2tog CC; rep from * to end of rnd.

Check measurements against finished measurements at beg of directions before breaking yarn. If you're satisfied, break yarn,

		6–12 mos	2 yrs	3 yrs	4 yrs
	Total:	48 sts	54 sts	60 sts	66 sts
	Total:	42 sts	48 sts	54 sts	60 sts
(inches)		2¾	3¼	3¾	3¾
(cm)		7	8.25	9.5	9.5
	Total:	28 sts	32 sts	36 sts	40 sts
	Total:	19 sts	21 sts	24 sts	27 sts
	Total:	13 sts	16 sts	16 sts	19 sts

leaving 6" (15cm) tails. With a yarn needle, thread one end through the remaining sts and draw up firmly. Draw other ends to inside of mitten. Thread first end through drawn-up sts once more, darn a few sts to secure end and draw end to inside of mitten.

Working the thumb

The thumb has the same girth in all four sizes. On Needles 1 and 2, pick up 11 sts from waste yarn. On Needle 3, pick up 5 sts from top of thumb hole and 1 st in each corner of thumb hole. 18 sts total.

		6–12 mos	2 yrs	3 yrs	4 yrs
Work even until thumb gore and thumb together measure	(inches)	$2\frac{1}{8}$	$2\frac{3}{8}$	$2\frac{5}{8}$	$2\frac{7}{8}$
	(cm)	5.5	6	6.75	7.25

Closing the tip of the thumb

Dec sharply: Rnd 1: *K2tog, k1 alternating MC and CC, rep from * to end of rnd.

Rnd 2: *K2tog, alternating CC and MC (avoiding the appearance of stripes), rep from * to end of rnd. Total remaining: 6 sts.

Check measurements against finished measurements at beg of directions before breaking yarn. If you're satisfied, break yarn leaving a 6" (15 cm) tail. With a yarn needle, thread one end through the remaining sts and draw up firmly. Draw other end to inside of thumb. Thread first end through drawn-up sts once more, darn a few sts to secure it and draw to inside of thumb.

Finishing the mitten

Turn mitten inside out and darn all ends into the back of the fabric. Repair possible holes at corners of the thumb hole with nearby tails. Trim ends closely.

Make another mitten for the opposite hand.

Wee Checkerboard Mittens

Here is a favorite Canadian mitten rendered in small sizes. The checkerboard pattern pulls up widthwise in thick corrugated ridges that make it puffy, thick, and warm. The ridges, surprisingly, also make it soft and flexible. Look at the finished mitten: Because of the pull-up, the center of every two-stitch pair is all that shows clearly. It almost looks as if the mitten were knitted from the tip of the fingers down. But it isn't.

Wee Checkerboard Mittens in two sizes

Yarn I used Jaggerspun 3/8 Heather Yarn for the mittens in the photographs, but any soft sport weight yarn that knits to the correct tension will be fine. • MC: 1 oz (28.5g) sport weight yarn, preferably wool • CC: ¾ oz (21.5g) sport weight yarn, preferably wool

Equipment 1 set Size 3 (3.25mm, Can. Size 10) double-pointed needles, or size you need to knit in pattern at correct tension • 1 set Size 1 (2.25mm, Can. Size 13) double-pointed needles for ribbed cuff • 6" (15cm) contrasting waste yarn • Small blunt-tipped yarn needle

Tension 9 sts and 8 rnds = 1" (2.5cm) in pattern

ABBREVIATIONS beg: beginning • CC: contrast color • dec(s): decrease(s) • inc(s): increase(s) • k: knit • k2tog: knit 2 together • M1: make 1 stitch • M1L: make 1 stitch left • M1R: make 1 stitch right • MC: main color • p: purl • rep: repeat • rnd(s): round(s) • SSK2tog: slip, slip, knit 2 sts together • st(s): stitch(es) • twisted M1: twisted make 1 cast-on

Measurements—inches and *centimeters*

	6–12 mos	2 years	3 years	4 years
Hand length	3 *7.5*	3½ *9*	3¾ *9.5*	4¼ *10.75*
Hand circumference, incl. tip of thumb	4½ *11.5*	5 *12.75*	5⅝ *14.25*	6 *15.25*
Length of mitten hand	3¼ *8.25*	3⅝ *9.25*	4 *10.25*	4½ *11.5*
Length of finished mitten thumb	1¼ *3.25*	1¼ *3.25*	1⅜ *3.5*	1½ *3.75*
Finished mitten width	2¼ *5.75*	2½ *6.5*	2¾ *7*	3 *7.5*

Pattern

Checkerboard is a multiple of 4 sts and 4 rnds. It has a strong tendency to pull up widthwise, which is not a fault, as it makes the knit thicker and more insulating as well as delightfully soft. Because of this trait, I used needles one size larger than for the other double-knit baby mittens to knit at about the same tension.

Off the Cuff

The cuff is a simple k2, p2 ribbing without stripes.

Wee Checkerboard Chart

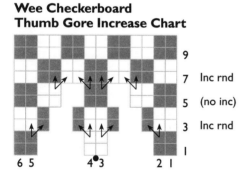

Key

◼ MC–main color

☐ CC–contrast color

⊡ place marker

↗↑ Knit both colors into 1 stitch

Wee Checkerboard Thumb Gore Increase Chart

Making the cuff

With MC, 3 smaller needles, and using the Maine method (p. 13), cast on
Join into a triangle, being careful not to twist sts around the needles.

	6–12 mos	2 yrs	3 yrs	4 yrs
	44 sts	48 sts	52 sts	56 sts.
Work k2, p2 ribbing for (inches)	1½	1¾	2	2¼
(cm)	3.75	4.5	5	5.75

Change to larger needles and stockinette. Work 1 rnd in MC. S
ix sts before end of rnd, join CC (p. 18).

Starting the hand and thumb gore

Start pattern at lower right corner of chart and rep to end of rnd.
Note: Check after the first rnd of pattern that the rep comes out even.
A mistake here can throw everything else off and take the fun out of
the project. Work 2 rnds in pattern.

Place a piece of contrasting waste yarn as a marker between Sts 3 and 4
on Needle 1. The thumb gore incs will branch out on both sides of this
marker, 4 incs close together every fourth rnd, starting with Rnd 3.
See the Thumb Gore Increase Chart for a visual representation.

Rnd 3: Work in pattern up to 2 sts before marker, a MC st; inc 4 sts in
the next 4 sts by knitting both colors into one st (p. 21), being careful to
keep the colors in the correct order, as shown in the inc chart.
Work the next st in CC and continue to end of rnd in pattern.

Rnds 4 through 6: Work even in pattern.

Rnd 7: Work in pattern up to 2 sts before marker, a CC st. Inc 4 sts in
the next 4 sts by knitting both colors into one st, being careful to keep the
colors in the correct order—the colors will be reversed from Rnd 3.
Work the next st in MC and continue to end of rnd in pattern.

Rnds 8 through 10: Work even in pattern.

Rnd 11: Rep Rnd 3 (first inc rnd).

Total added in all 3 inc rnds: 12 sts.

		6–12 mos	2 yrs		3 yrs	4 yrs

Rnd 15, *two largest sizes only:* Rep Rnd 7 (second inc rnd). Total added in all 4 inc rnds: 16 sts.

Rnd 15, *two smallest sizes:* Work even.

		6–12 mos	2 yrs	3 yrs	4 yrs
Total:		56 sts	60 sts	68 sts	72 sts
Work even in pattern until work *above cuff* measures	(inches)	1¼	1¼	1⅜	1½
	(cm)	*3.25*	*3.25*	*3.5*	*3.75*

Taking off the thumb gore stitches

		6–12 mos	2 yrs	3 yrs	4 yrs
K1, place on waste yarn the next		15 sts	15 sts	19 sts	19 sts

Using twisted M1 (p. 23), cast on 3 sts in pattern over the gap.

		6–12 mos	2 yrs	3 yrs	4 yrs
Total:		44 sts	48 sts	52 sts	56 sts
Work even until pattern above cuff measures	(inches)	2¾	3⅛	3½	3¾
	(cm)	*7*	*8*	*9*	*9.5*

Closing the mitten tip

Check that there are about the same number of sts on all 3 needles. If not, even them out, but don't move the first and last sts of the rnd.

On this fairly narrow mitten, the fit works best if the dec area is brief, producing a short, rounded tip. The decs are thus 6 to a rnd, every rnd, with a final 9- or 10-st dec. You will combine k2tog (p. 24) with SSK2tog (p. 24) in order to maintain the pattern.

Dec: K2tog in pattern, working to 2 sts from end of needle, SSK2tog in pattern.

Note: The pattern of the dec sts is the pattern on the needle you are knitting from. It's easy to be tempted to continue the pattern on, for example, the last or first st on the needle.

	6–12 mos	2 yrs	3 yrs	4 yrs
Rep this dec on all needles, every rnd	6 X	6 X	7 X	8 X
Total remaining:	8 sts	12 sts	10 sts	8 sts

Break yarn, leaving a 6" (15cm) tail. With yarn needle, thread one end through the remaining sts and draw up firmly. Draw other end to inside of mitten. Thread first end through drawn-up sts again, darn a few sts to secure it and draw to inside of mitten.

	6–12 mos	2 yrs	3 yrs	4 yrs

Working the thumb

Join both yarns by sewing (p. 20) into back of fabric starting at the right side of the thumb hole.

	6–12 mos	2 yrs	3 yrs	4 yrs
Needles 1 and 2: Pick up from waste yarn	15 sts	15 sts	19 sts	19 sts.
Needle 3: Pick up 3 sts over the thumb hole. Pick up and twist 1 st onto needle from each corner of thumb hole. **Total:**	20 sts	20 sts	24 sts	24 sts
Work even until thumb and thumb gore (from top of cuff) measure (inches)	1⅞	2	2⅛	2½
(cm)	*4.75*	*5*	*5.5*	*6.5*

Closing the tip of the thumb

	6–12 mos	2 yrs	3 yrs	4 yrs
Dec as on hand: In pattern, k2tog, work to 2 sts from end of needle, SSK2tog. Do this on all needles, every rnd	2 X	2 X	3 X	3 X
Remaining on 3 needles:	8 sts	8 sts	6 sts	6 sts

Break yarns, leaving 6" (15cm) tails. With yarn needle, thread one end through the remaining sts and draw up firmly. Draw other end to inside of thumb. Thread first end through drawn-up sts again, darn a few sts to secure it, and draw end to inside of thumb.

Finishing the mitten

Turn mitten inside out and darn all ends into the back of the fabric. Repair any holes at corners of the thumb hole with nearby tails. Thread the cast-on tail over and under along the p side of a k rib. Trim ends closely.

Make another identical mitten. This mitten can be worn on either hand.

Compass Mittens for Small Mariners

Baby Compass Mittens in two sizes

This pattern has many names. I first learned of it from Mrs. Viette Cruikshank in Liscomb, Guysborough County (Nova Scotia). Mattie Owl, an Indian woman, called one evening many years ago at the home of Mrs. Cruikshank's grandmother. Mattie Owl was wearing a ragged pair of double-knit mittens, which had been patched with scraps from other handknits, and the Liscomb woman's eye was caught by the double-knit pattern on one of the patches—this pattern.

She gave Mattie Owl a pair of new double-knit mittens then and there in trade for the ragged pair, and when Mattie Owl left, Mrs. Cruikshank must have promptly sat down and copied the pattern in new yarn, because her family has knit mittens in that pattern ever since, calling it Mattie Owl's Patch.

The pattern is not limited to the Cruikshank family, however, or even to Nova Scotia Indians. Other families in the Sherbrooke area knit it and call it Naughts and Crosses (the British name for tic-tac-toe). I learned that folkcraft writer Joleen Gorden found it knitted in the Barrington, Nova Scotia, area, where it is called Compass Work, and a woman in New Brunswick sent it to me under the name Spider's Web.

It seems to be an 8-stitch variant of Fox and Geese, a 6-stitch rep. —*Janetta Dexter*

My distant cousin Bertha York, of Harpswell, Maine, has childhood memories of her Aunt Esther Wilson knitting this pattern, which they called Compass Mittens or Compass Work. In spite of the local color of the Mattie Owl story, I still prefer the name "Compass Mittens," perhaps because that name comes from my own people, the Harpswell Islanders of 100 years ago. And I can always see compass needles pointing north in the design.

I knit this baby mitten in a navy blue and natural cream for people like myself, who want their babies to carry on the family's nautical tradition. Like many quilt designs, it offers young minds food for thought, directions to look to. —*Robin Hansen*

Compass Mittens for Small Mariners

Yarn MC (light color) 1 oz (28.5g) sport weight yarn • CC (dark color) 1 oz (28.5g) sport weight yarn, preferably wool •

It's fine to use Superwash™ for babies, although it's not as warm when wet. Brunswick Yarns Pomfret, used for mitten in the photo, no longer exists, but we have had good luck with Jaggerspun 2/8, Halcyon Yarn Victorian, and Raumagarn Hifa. Any sport weight yarn that knits to correct tension will work. Baby yarn or fingering is usually too fine.

Equipment 1 set Size 2 (2.75mm, Can. Size 12) double-pointed needles, or size you need to knit in pattern at correct tension • 1 set Size 1 (2.25mm, Can. Size 13) double-pointed needles for ribbing • 6" (15cm) length of contrasting waste yarn • Small blunt-tipped yarn needle

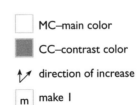

Tension 9 sts and 7 rnds = 1" (2.5cm) in pattern

ABBREVIATIONS beg: beginning • CC: contrast color • dec(s): decrease(s) • inc(s): increase(s) • k: knit • k2tog: knit 2 together • M1: make 1 stitch • M1L: make 1 stitch left • M1R: make 1 stitch right • MC: main color • p: purl • rep: repeat • rnd(s): round(s) • SSK2tog: slip, slip, knit 2 sts together • st(s): stitch(es) • twisted M1: twisted make 1 cast-on

Measurements—inches and *centimeters*

	6–12 mos	2 years	4 years
Hand length	3 *7.5*	3½ *9*	4⅛ *10.5*
Hand circumference, incl. tip of thumb	4½ *11.5*	5 *12.75*	6 *15.25*
Mitten hand length	3¼ *8.25*	3⅝ *9.25*	4¼ *10.75*
Mitten thumb (⅓ hand)	1¼ *3.25*	1¼ *3.25*	1½ *3.75*
Mitten width	2¼ *5.75*	2½ *6.5*	2¾–3 *7–7.5*

Pattern

Compass is a multiple of 8 rnds and 8 sts and is not easily knitted flat. Carry the darker color ahead (p. 16) at all times and weave in CC (p. 18) on Chart Lines 1 and 7.

In small children's sizes, the large 8-st pattern rep wraps perfectly around the hand only in the three sizes given here.

Chart 1: Baby Compass

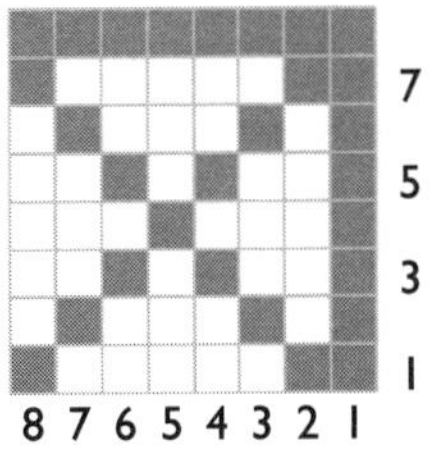
7
5
3
1
8 7 6 5 4 3 2 1

Key

MC–main color

CC–contrast color

direction of increase

m make 1

Chart 2: Thumb Increase

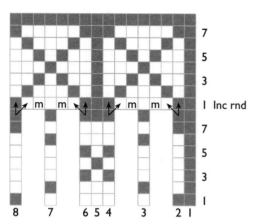

3-St Inside Thumb

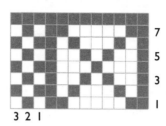

5-St Inside Thumb

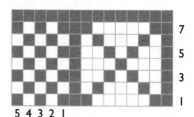

Decrease I

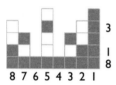

Decrease 2

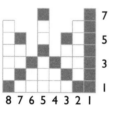

Off the Cuff

I have used a boldly striped cuff to offset the fine lines of the pattern. If you want other stripes, look at the adult Checkerboard Mittens or Maplewood Mittens patterns for ideas. Stripes on the cuff tend to balance the amounts of the two yarns used, in some cases making it possible to get two pairs of mittens from two contrasting skeins of yarn (not a problem in these sizes, of course).

Don't break the yarn at the end of its stripe. Carry it up to its next appearance.

This mitten has a longer than usual cuff—good to keep little wrists dry and warm.

Making the cuff

	6–12 mos	2 yrs	4 years

With MC, smaller needles, and using the Maine method (p. 13),
cast on

	39 sts	48 sts	54 sts

Distribute sts equally on 3 needles. Join into a triangle, being careful not to twist sts around the needles.

Work k2, p1 ribbing in MC for 10 rnds, CC for 4 rnds, MC for 2 rnds, CC for 4 rnds, and MC for 7 rnds. Twist the two yarns together at the beg of 3rd or 4th rnd of MC.

Change to larger needles and stockinette. K1 rnd CC, and inc by M1 (p. 20)

Total (a multiple of 8):

	6–12 mos	2 yrs	4 years
	1 st	—	2 sts
	40 sts	48 sts	56 sts

Starting the pattern and thumb gore

Note: Carry MC ahead throughout (p. 16). Check after the first rnd that the rep comes out even. A mistake here can throw everything else off and take the fun out of the project.

Start Chart 1 at lower right on
and work chart through Line 8.

	6–12 mos	2 yrs	4 years
	Line 4	Line 1	Line 1

Start thumb gore in next Rnd 1 of pattern. You will inc 8 sts all at once above 7 sts in established pattern, as shown in Chart 2.

This mitten can really be worn on either hand, if you wish to knit 2 mittens the same, but directions follow for making individual left and right mittens.

Right mitten: The first 9 sts of Needle 1 form the base of the thumb gore.

Left mitten: K, then slip, 1st st from Needle 1 onto Needle 3. The last 9 sts of the rnd (on Needle 3) form the base of the thumb gore.

Both mittens: Inc at thumb gore: K1 CC into St 1; k both colors (p. 21) into St 2—first CC then MC; M1 MC; k1 MC into St 3; M1 MC; k both colors into St 4—first MC then CC; k1 CC into St 5; k both colors into St 6—first CC then MC; M1 MC; k1 MC into St 7; M1 MC; k both colors into St 8—first MC then CC. You will have increased 8 sts in pattern in the space of 7 sts. Truly amazing. This is the only thumb inc in this mitten.

Total:

	6–12 mos	2 yrs	4 years
	48 sts	56 sts	64 sts

Work even until thumb gore measures

	6–12 mos	2 yrs	4 years
(inches)	1	1¼	1½
(cm)	*2.5*	*3.25*	*3.75*

Ideally for appearance, complete Rnd 8 or Rnd 3. If you are within 2 rnds of either of these rnds, make it so.

Taking off the thumb gore stitches

Right mitten: K2, put next 13 sts on waste yarn.
Left mitten: Work in pattern to last 15 sts on Needle 3. K2, put next 13 sts on waste yarn.
Both mittens: Using twisted M1 (p. 23), cast on 5 sts in pattern over the gap. Complete rnd in pattern.

		6–12 mos	2 yrs	4 years
Total:		40 sts	48 sts	56 sts.
Work even in pattern until hand above cuff measures	(inches)	2¾	3¼	3¾
	(cm)	7	8.25	9.5

End with Line 8 or Line 3 of chart completed.

Closing the mitten tip

Note: Decs are within each block of pattern. Consult Decrease Charts 1 and 2 (p. 196) for a visual representation of this.

	6–12 mos	2 yrs	4 years
Rnd 1, dec: *K2, SSK2tog (p. 24), k1, k2tog (p. 24), k1; rep from *, maintaining pattern (which will grow narrower, but should not lose its vertical lines).			
Rnd 2: Work even and maintain pattern on	30 sts	36 sts	42 sts
Rnd 3 (Line 3 or 6 on dec charts), dec: *K1, SSK2tog, k1, k2tog; rep from *.			
Rnd 4 (Line 4 or 7 on dec charts): Work even and maintain pattern on	20 sts	24 sts	28 sts
Rnd 5 (Line 5 or 8 on dec charts), dec: *SSK2tog, k2tog; rep from *.			
Remaining on 3 needles:	10 sts	12 sts	14 sts

Check measurements against finished measurements at beg of directions. If you are satisfied, break yarn leaving a 6" (15cm) tail. With a yarn needle, thread one end through the remaining sts and draw up firmly. Draw other end to inside of mitten. Thread first end through drawn-up sts again, darn a few sts to secure and draw it to inside of mitten.

Working the thumb

Join both yarns by sewing (p. 20) into back of fabric, starting at the right side of thumb hole.

Needles 1 and 2: Pick up 13 sts from waste yarn.
Needle 3: Pick up 7 sts at top of thumb hole. Pick up and twist 1 st onto needle in each corner of thumb hole. Total: 22 sts.

	6–12 mos	2 yrs	4 years

Note: Using only Compass pattern would make the thumb too wide or too narrow. Traditional knitters usually figure a way out of these problems skillfully and artistically, but I offer you a simpler solution: Work a smaller pattern on the inside of the thumb, as shown on the two charts on p. 196.

Starting at right corner of thumb hole, work Needles 1 and 2, matching pattern to that on thumb gore.

In the two smaller sizes, dec the circumference by 2 sts on Needle 3: SSK2tog CC, k1 MC, k1 CC, k2tog MC, k1 CC. Work the charted 3-st Inside Thumb pattern on Needle 3 and Compass pattern on Needles 1 and 2. Total: 20 sts.

In the largest size: Work the charted 5-st Inside Thumb pattern on Needle 3 and Compass pattern on Needles 1 and 2. Total: 22 sts.

		6–12 mos	2 yrs	4 years
All sizes: Work even in pattern until thumb and thumb gore together measure	(inches)	2¼	2⅜	2½
	(cm)	*5.75*	*6*	*6.5*

Closing the tip of the thumb

		6–12 mos	2 yrs	4 years
Dec Rnd 1: K2tog, k1, around, matching pattern as closely as possible.	Total:	13 sts	13 sts	15 sts
Dec Rnd 2: K2tog on all needles.	Total remaining:	7 sts	7 sts	9 sts

Break yarn, leaving a 6" (15cm) tail. With a yarn needle, thread one end through the remaining sts and draw up firmly. Draw other end to inside of thumb. Thread first end through drawn-up sts again, darn a few sts to secure it, and draw to inside of thumb.

Finishing the mitten

Turn mitten inside out and darn all ends into the back of the fabric. Repair any holes at corners of the thumb hole with nearby tails. Trim ends closely.

Make another mitten for the opposite hand.

Petites Mitaines
en Fleur-de-lis

Like Fox and Geese and Fences, the name of the Fleur-de-lis pattern is imagination at play. In some countries this pattern is called Netting, in others Diamonds. Look at the two-color pattern and you can see either, although not both at the same time.

Francophile knitters in Atlantic Canada and Maine look at the same pattern and see fleurs-de-lis, the lily-inspired symbol of both French royalty and the Boy Scout movement. You must hold the mitten cuff-side up for this image to be obvious. To emphasize the image, Franco-American knitters separate the "lilies" from the all-over pattern by knitting each band of lilies in its own color.

My children call this pattern Peeled Banana. For their image to work, you must again hold the mitten cuff-side up. Janetta Dexter's son Boyd looks at the pattern cuff-side down and says the figures look like devils' heads! With such a simple shape, imaging possibilities are almost limitless.

This mitten has no thumb gore, making it the simplest mitten in this book. Instead, there is an inc at the top of the cuff to accommodate the width of the thumb. In its simplicity, it can also be made without a thumb for babies too young to use their hands (left mitten

Petites Mitaines en Fleur-de-lis

in photo). Petite Mitaine is presented here with a choice of a ribbed cuff or—at the suggestion of young mothers in our family—a wide, patterned cuff with a tie at the wrist (center mitten in photo).

To make this mitten in adult sizes, you might want to inc eight sts around, rather than four, at the top of the cuff. (The adult mitten directions can be found in my book *Flying Geese & Partridge Feet*, Down East books, 1986).

Petites Mitaines en Fleur-de-lis

Yarn I used Jaggerspun 3/8 Heather Yarn for the mittens in the photographs, but any soft sport weight yarn that knits to the correct tension will be fine.

MC: 1 oz (28.5g) sport weight yarn, preferably wool • CC: ¾ oz (21.5g) sport weight yarn, preferably wool if you are working in only two colors. Otherwise CCa, CCb, CCc: ¼ oz (7g) each sport weight yarn, preferably wool • 12" (30cm) contrasting waste yarn • Small, blunt-tipped yarn needle

Equipment 1 set Size 3 (3.25mm, Can. Size 10) double-pointed needles, or size you need to knit in pattern at correct tension • 1 set Size 1 (2.25mm, Can. Size 13) double-pointed needles for ribbed cuff • 12" (30 cm) contrasting waste yarn • small, blunt-tipped yarn needle

Tension 9 sts and 8 rnds = 1" (2.5cm) in pattern

Measurements—inches and *centimeters*

	0–6 mos	6–12 mos	2 years	3 years	4 years
Hand length	2½	3	3½	3¾	4⅛
	6.5	*7.5*	*9*	*9.5*	*10.5*
Hand circumference, incl. tip of thumb	4½	4¾	5	5⅝	6
	11.5	*12*	*12.75*	*14.25*	*15.25*
Length of mitten hand	2¾	3¼	3¾	4	4¼
	7	*8.25*	*9.5*	*10.25*	*10.75*
Length of finished mitten thumb	—	1	1¼	1⅜	1½
	—	*2.5*	*3.25*	*3.5*	*3.75*
Finished mitten width*	2½	2⅝	2¾	3	3¼
	6.5	*6.75*	*7*	*7.5*	*8.25*

These widths seem a little wide because they include space for the thumb all the way up.

ABBREVIATIONS beg: beginning • CC: contrast color • dec(s): decrease(s) • inc(s): increase(s) • k: knit • k2tog: knit 2 together • M1: make 1 stitch • M1L: make 1 stitch left • M1R: make 1 stitch right • MC: main color • p: purl • rep: repeat • rnd(s): round(s) • SSK2tog: slip, slip, knit 2 sts together • st(s): stitch(es) • twisted M1: twisted make 1 cast-on

Pattern

Fleur-de-lis is a multiple of 4 sts and 6 rnds. If worked in 4 colors, it repeats every 18 rnds. It can be worked flat if desired, but be sure to allow an extra st on each side for the seam. The only incs come before the beg of the color pattern. Decs are in empty spaces between motifs at the tip. Carry the same color, preferably the darkest, ahead throughout (p. 16).

Off the cuff

The cuff is a simple k2, p2 ribbing without stripes.

Feur-de-lis A

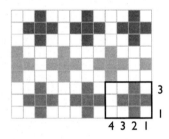

4 3 2 1

Key

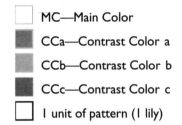

MC—Main Color

CCa—Contrast Color a

CCb—Contrast Color b

CCc—Contrast Color c

1 unit of pattern (1 lily)

Fleur-de-lis B

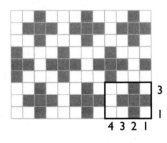

4 3 2 1

Final Decrease

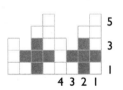

4 3 2 1

Making the ribbed cuff

		0–6 mos	6–12 mos	2 years	3 years	4 years
With MC, 3 smaller needles, and using the Maine method (p.13), cast on Join into a triangle, being careful not to twist sts around the needles.		40 sts	44 sts	48 sts	52 sts	56 sts
Work k2, p2 ribbing for	(inches)	1¼	1½	1¾	2	2¼
	(cm)	3.25	3.75	4.5	5	5.75
Change to larger needles and stockinette. Work 1 rnd in MC and, using M1 (p. 20), inc 4 sts spaced evenly around. This is the only inc in this mitten, and allows room for the thumb.	Total:	44 sts	48 sts	52 sts	56 sts	60 sts.

Six sts before end of rnd, join CCa (p. 18).

Making the alternative patterned cuff with tie or elastic

		0–6 mos	6–12 mos	2 years	3 years	4 years
Using MC, larger needles, and the Maine method (p. 13), cast on Join into a triangle, being careful not to twist sts around the needles.		44 sts	48 sts	52 sts	56 sts	60 sts

Work 1 rnd MC. Six sts before the end of rnd, join CCa (p. 18).

Start pattern at lower right corner of chart, always carrying ahead the darkest color in your hand. Check after the first rnd of pattern that the rep comes out even. A mistake here can throw everything else off and take the fun out of the project. If using 4 colors, twist all CC strands together behind your work at the end of each band of lilies.

		4 bands	5 bands	5 bands	6 bands	6 bands
Work in pattern of lilies, or about	(inches)	1⅝	1⅞	1⅞	2⅝	2⅝
	(cm)	4	4.75	4.75	6.75	6.75

Making holes for the tie:
Rnd 1: Work 1 rnd MC.
Rnd 2: *K2tog (p. 24), yarn over (bring the yarn forward as if to p, lift it over the needle and proceed to the next st). Rep from * to end of rnd.
Rnd 3: K 1 rnd in MC, knitting both sts and yarn-overs as sts. You should end with as many sts as you started with in Rnd 1 and all the yarn-overs will become neat holes to carry a MC tie.

Starting the pattern and the hand

Start pattern at lower right corner of chart, carrying the darker color ahead. Check after the first rnd of pattern that the rep comes out even. A mistake here can throw everything else off and take the fun out of the project. If using 4 colors, twist the CC strands together behind your work at the end of each band of lilies.

		0–6 mos	6–12 mos	2 years	3 years	4 years
Work even in pattern until hand above cuff measures	(inches)	1	1	1¼	1⅜	1½
	(cm)	*2.5*	*2.5*	*3.25*	*3.5*	*3.75*

The mittens for newborn babies have no thumb, so you will omit the next step for size 0–6 months. There will be plenty of room for a little fist in these.

Taking off stitches for the thumb

Because there is no thumb gore and the number of stitches above and below the thumb are the same, you can knit a waste-yarn thumb hole. At the beg of the rnd, K1 in pattern. Without joining yarn, k in waste yarn

	—	7 sts	8 sts	9 sts	10 sts

Replace the waste yarn sts on left needle and reknit them in pattern. (When you are finished with the mitten hand, you will pick out the waste yarn sts and have a line of sts along the bottom of a thumb hole and the bottoms of sts along the top—plenty of stitches for a little thumb.)

		0–6 mos	6–12 mos	2 years	3 years	4 years
Work even until mitten hand measures	(inches)	2¼	3	3½	3¾	4
	(cm)	*5.75*	*7.5*	*9*	*9.5*	*10.25*

Work in pattern to beg of the 3rd rnd of any band of lilies.

Closing the mitten tip

The dec on this mitten is abrupt, almost squared off at the end, with decs in every rnd.

		0–6 mos	6–12 mos	2 years	3 years	4 years
Dec Rnd 1: Refer to Dec Chart and dec: Starting at St 1 of a lily pattern, K1 MC, *SSK2tog (p. 24) in appropriate CC, K2 MC. Rep from * to end of rnd, ending with K1 MC. **Total remaining:**		33 sts	36 sts	39 sts	42 sts	45 sts

	0–6 mos	6–12 mos	2 years	3 years	4 years

Dec Rnd 2: Break all CC yarns with 6" tails and stuff them into the mitten. Following dec chart, *k1 MC, SSK2tog MC. Repeat from 8 to end of rnd.

Total remaining:	22 sts	24 sts	26 sts	28 sts	30 sts

Dec Rnd 3: K2tog MC to end of rnd.

Total remaining:	11 sts	12 sts	13 sts	14 sts	15 sts

Break yarn leaving a 6" (15cm) tail. With yarn needle, thread one end through the remaining sts and draw up firmly. Draw other ends to inside of mitten. Thread first end through drawn-up sts again, darn a few sts to secure it and draw to inside of mitten.

Working the thumb

Pick up one side of each stitch above waste yarn on one needle. Pick out waste yarn, taking care not to disturb the sts below. Put these sts on a second needle. (Because there are two colors, the bottoms of the sts from above the waste yarn will include floats between sts, which is confusing. Picking up the sides of these sts before you remove the waste yarn makes this step easier.)

	0–6 mos	6–12 mos	2 years	3 years	4 years
On top needle:	—	6 sts	7 sts	8 sts	9 sts
On bottom needle:	—	7 sts	8 sts	9 sts	10 sts

Transfer one-half the bottom stitches to a third needle and pick up 2 sts in each corner of thumb hole on Needles 2 and 3.

Total:	—	17 sts	19 sts	21 sts	23 sts

Join MC by sewing into back of fabric (p. 20), starting at the right side of the thumb hole. There is no color pattern on the thumb. Work even in MC until thumb and thumb gore together measure

(inches)	—	1⅞	2¼	2⅛	2¾
(cm)	—	4.75	5.75	5.5	7

Closing the tip of the thumb

K2tog, work to 2 sts from end of needle, SSK2tog. Do this on all needles, every rnd,

	—	2 X	2 X	3 X	3 X
Total remaining:	—	5 sts	7 sts	9 sts	11 sts

Break yarns, leaving 6" (15cm) tails. With yarn needle, thread one end through the remaining sts and draw up firmly. Draw other end to inside of thumb. Thread first end through drawn-up sts again, darn a few sts to secure it, and draw end to inside of thumb.

Finishing the mitten

Turn mitten inside out and darn all ends into the back of the fabric. Repair possible holes at corners of the thumb hole with nearby tails. Thread the cast-on tail over and under along the p side of a k rib. Trim ends closely.

If you made a patterned cuff, braid, twine, or crochet a MC cord about 12" (30cm) long. With a yarn needle or small safety pin, thread the cord in and out of the holes, starting at the center of the back of the hand. (Size 0–6 months has no front or back, so you can begin anywhere.) Tie the ends in a pretty bow, then knot the ends at a reasonable length and trim just outside the knots.

Alternatively, thread the holes with light round elastic. Tie the elastic with a square knot or other nonslip knot so that it sits comfortably on Baby's wrist without squeezing.

Make another identical mitten. This mitten can be worn on either hand.

| 0–6 mos | 6–12 mos | 2 years | 3 years | 4 years |

A Patterned Helmet
to Match Baby's Mittens

This cap, with a button at the chin and ear flaps, is based on a little Danish helmet belonging to my children. It can be made in Fox and Geese or any of the other double-knit patterns in this section. The helmet can either have a smooth crown or be topped with a little knot of I-cord as a cute finishing touch. (However, this does make the helmet less convenient under a hood.)

Although the numbers below may look scary, this is a simple pattern with no increases or decreases in the color-patterned portion. The seeming excess of numbers makes it possible to knit the helmet with any color pattern in this book.

The examples shown are in Chipman's Check and Fox and Geese.

This cap can be made in any of the patterns in this section. There are no increases or decreases in the patterned portion, so the trick is to get the correct multiple for the pattern you wish to use. The examples shown here are in Chipman's Check and two-colored Fox and Geese.

A Patterned Helmet
to Match Baby's Mittens

Measurements—inches and *centimeters*

	0–6 months	6 months–1 year	2–4 years
Head circumference	14	16	18
	35.5	*40.5*	*45.75*

Yarn MC 1.5 oz (42.75g) sport weight yarn • CC .75 oz (21.5g) sport weight yarn • CCa (for 3-colored Fox and Geese only) about 6 yards.

Equipment 1 set Size 2 (2.75mm, Can. Size 12) double-pointed needles for ribbing • *For Fox and Geese, Salt and Pepper, and Sawtooth:* 1 set Size 4 (3.5mm, Can. Size 9 or 10) double-pointed needles, or size you need to knit in pattern at correct tension • *For Stripes, Spruce, or Checkerboard:* 1 set Size 5 (3.75mm, Can. Size 9) double-pointed needles, or size you need to knit in pattern at correct tension

Size E or F crochet hook • 12" (30cm) contrasting waste yarn • Small, blunt-tipped yarn needle • One ⅜" (9.5mm) button

Tension 8.5 sts = 1" (2.5cm) in pattern

Pattern

See the mitten directions for the pattern you wish to use and read the accompanying pattern notes. This cap is knit from the top down.

ABBREVIATIONS beg: beginning • CC: contrast color • dec(s): decrease(s) • inc(s): increase(s) • k: knit • k2tog: knit 2 together • M1: make 1 stitch • M1L: make 1 stitch left • M1R: make 1 stitch right • MC: main color • p: purl • rep: repeat • rnd(s): round(s) • SSK2tog: slip, slip, knit 2 sts together • st(s): stitch(es) • twisted M1: twisted make 1 cast-on

Top of crown

	0–6 months	6 months–1 year	2–4 years
For a smooth crown, cast on	15 sts	17 sts	20 sts

Distribute sts evenly on 3 smaller double-pointed needles.
K 1 rnd even.

For an I-cord on top, cast on 5 sts. K even around until work measures 1½" (3.75cm).
Inc: K1, M1 (p. 20) on all needles. Total 10 sts. Work 1 rnd even.
Inc: K2, M1 on all needles. Total: 15 sts.
Work 1 rnd even.

Work 1 rnd and inc, evenly spaced		—	2 sts	5 sts
	Total:	15 sts	17 sts	20 sts

Body of cap

Both versions: Rnd 2: Inc by k1, M1 to end of rnd.	Total:	30 sts	34 sts	40 sts

Rnds 3 through 5: K1, p1 ribbing.

Rnd 6: Inc in every st.	Total:	60 sts	68 sts	80 sts

Rnds 7 through 11: K1, p1 ribbing.

Rnd 12: Inc in every st until there are	120 sts	136 sts	156 sts

or the closest number that works for the rep of the pattern you have chosen.
(Divide pattern rep into number of sts and add or subtract sts as necessary to
come out even.)

For patterns based on a multiple of 6 sts, add 2 more sts in the next
rnd *for Size 6 months–1 year only.*

Rnds 13 and 14: K1, p1 even.

Change to larger needles and stockinette. K 1 rnd MC (or CCb for Fox and
Geese pattern).

Start pattern, reading chart from lower right. Work pattern for	(inches)	2⅝	3	3½
	(cm)	6.75	7.5	9

or as near as possible while completing a band of pattern. Finish with 1 rnd
MC (or CCa for Fox and Geese pattern).

Change back to smaller needles and k1, p1 for 6 rnds (the edge of the cap).

Bind off for face and back of cap

Think of the cap as divided in 7 equal pie slices, 2 for the face, 1 for the back and 2 for each ear flap. You will bind off all but the 4 parts for the ear flaps.

	0–6 months	6 months–1 year	2–4 years
At beg of rnd, bind off for the back	17 sts	19 sts	22 sts
For first ear flap, k1, p1 for	34 sts	39 sts	45 sts
For front, bind off	35 sts	39 sts	44 sts
For second ear flap, k1, p1 for	34 sts	39 sts	45 sts

Note: For Fox and Geese pattern, add 1 more st to each ear tab *in Size 6 months–1 year only.*

On second ear flap, continue ribbing back and forth, decreasing 1 st at beg of every row until the flap, below the bound-off edge, measures	(inches)	2	2¼	2½
	(cm)	*5*	*5.5*	*6.5*

Dec 1 st both ends every row until		8 sts	10 sts	10 sts
remain. Continue to rib back and forth an additional	(inches)	1½	1¾	2
	(cm)	*3.75*	*4.5*	*5*

Bind off, leaving a 6" (15cm) tail.

Rep on the other ear flap, but do NOT break yarn after binding off.

Button loop and edging

Using tail left over from knitting, crochet a button loop on the end of the second ear flap. Single crochet around the edge of the entire cap. When you reach the button loop, single crochet around this too, making it stronger. Sew button on the other ear flap.

Finishing the cap

Turn cap inside out and darn all ends into the back of the fabric. Using the tail from casting on and a yarn needle, catch up all the cast-on sts and draw them up firmly so there's no hole in the top of the cap. Darn invisibly and smoothly back and forth over the top. If you started with an I-cord, sew its end closed and hide the cast-on tail inside. Tie the I-cord in an overhand knot. Trim ends closely.

Acknowledgments

Any collection of traditional processes must be the work of more than one person. It takes generations of craftspersons to carry a tradition into the present. It takes people like me and Down East Books to see the need to present the process to the wider public in a book, and it takes people hungry for roots to sink deeper into a native soil to read the book and make the mittens. Most of all, it takes the willingness of living tradition-bearers to share what amounts to privileged family craft techniques and lore with thousands of people they will never see or know.

To thank the knitters of the past and present for maintaining traditional knitting designs is superfluous, as their reward is in the pleasure of knitting and the love of those who wear their creations.

I thank those in the present generation who shared family knitting traditions: Ruth Claxton, formerly of Harpswell, Maine, for local information on Compass Mittens and Fox and Geese Mittens; Harriet Pardy Martin of Happy Valley, Labrador, for the basic instructions used for all the Newfoundland mittens; and Phyllis Montague of Northwest River, Labrador, for sharing her mother's Big Waves pattern; Albert Miller of Turner, Maine, for Mittens Hooked on a Dowel; Edna Mower of Merrimack, New Hampshire, and Beulah Moore of Kingfield, Maine, for Double-Rolled Mittens; Margaret Richard and Annie Pettipas of Charlos Cove, Nova Scotia, for Fleur-de-lis Mittens; Erin Pender for helping me to figure out Mittens with Shag on the Inside. These are only those whose family traditions contributed to this book. There are too many more of different traditions to mention.

In Maine, I thank Laura Ridgewell of West Point who gave me the idea for publishing a book of traditional Maine mittens when she asked me to find her a fishermen's wet mitten pattern. Jackie Trask, Diane Calder, and Elizabeth Bergh, all of Chebeague Island, Marge Creaser of Boothbay, and Mary A. Chase of South Brooksville provided much of the information on wet mittens. The instructions were written by Elizabeth Bergh, based on a pair of mittens knit by Jackie Trask's late grandmother, Minnie Doughty.

In Labrador, Judith McGrath, a crafts researcher for *Them Days* magazine, and Peggy Lough, both of Happy Valley, helped me with instructions for Fleece-Stuffed Mittens. Laura Jackson, also formerly of Happy Valley, showed me more Labrador "mitts" and introduced me to local knitters. Thank you!

In Atlantic Canada, I thank the women who shared with Janetta Dexter the patterns she has passed on in this book, particularly Mrs. Viette Cruikshank of Liscomb, Nova Scotia, for the Mattie Owl story and pattern (Compass Mittens), and Mrs. Murdock Hollingsworth of Truro, Nova Scotia, for information about Flying Geese Gloves.

I also thank the Nova Scotia Museum for letting me use the Flying Geese and Maplewood patterns that appeared in Janetta Dexter's book, *Traditional Nova Scotian Double-Knitting Patterns* (Halifax, 1985); *Them Days* magazine and Doris Saunders of Happy Valley, Labrador, for permission to reprint the interview and photos of her mother, Harriet Pardy Martin; the Maine State Museum for permission to print their photos and information on Double-Rolled Mittens.

Joan Waldron of the Nova Scotia Museum became a good friend. She put me in touch with knitting traditions in her province and introduced me to Janetta Dexter. Jane Nylander, formerly textile curator at Old Sturbridge Village, and Jane Radcliffe, formerly textile curator at the Maine State Museum, both helped by giving me access to their collections and expanding my general knowledge of traditional mitten knitting in their areas. Many thanks!

Thanks to the late Elizabeth Zimmermann and her daughter, Meg Swanson, the *doyennes* of American knitting design, for advice on publication, for contacts, for providing many books on British,

Scandinavian, and German knitting—and most of all, for saying nice things about my books in the knitting world.

Thanks to Professor Anthony Barrand of the University Professors Program at Boston University, for putting up with my slightly bizarre field of study, for teaching me better ways of documenting interviews and new (to me) methods of observation, and for general encouragement. Thanks to the University Professors Program for taking me in and allowing me to deepen my study of traditional handcraft processes.

I would also like to thank Nora Johnson, formerly of Five Islands, Maine, my mentor and best friend in traditional knitting, who was the first traditional knitter willing to talk to me about Maine double-knit patterns. She taught me my first three patterns and commented on and reviewed all the mittens I found in various corners of New England and Canada. As a seasoned knitter, she checked some patterns for readability. Her insistence on high quality workmanship and technique in mitten knitting continues to guide my eyes and hands. Nora died at age 97 in March 2004. I will miss her more than I can say.

I would like to thank my family for their patience, particularly my daughter, Hanne Orm Tierney of Palmyra, Maine, who produced many of the sample mittens while testing the directions for accuracy, my daughter-in-law Michele Orm Hansen of Troy, Maine, and my niece Adrienne D'Olimpio of Lyndonville, Vermont, for knitting samples and trial mittens for this book. My husband, Erik, a naval archi-tect, helped me devise formulas for the proportions of mittens and caps, and patiently checked my math and the metric conversions. He has also been a pleasant companion and driver on mitten and woolly tours of the Maritime Provinces—while I knit in the passenger seat!

I thank knit-technical editor Dorothy Ratigan. Her earnest work and insistence on a set format for the directions may make these the most complete and correct directions I have ever written. I do hope nothing's left out—or anything unnecessary is added!

Thanks also to Megan Richardson, summer intern at Down East Books, who added the metric conversions to make this book accessible for knitters who think in grams and centimeters. Down East Books editor Karin Womer demonstrated her patience in waiting for Dot and me to get the directions and the photos in order. Thanks, Karin! They are now finished.

Thanks also to you, dear knitters and readers, for remembering the stories of these mittens and making the mittens, thereby becoming tradition-bearers yourselves for new generations. The best reward for writing these books has been to see "my" mittens on children sliding at the Bath Golf Course, a woman shopping in Portland, Maine, and on the hands of a student waiting for a trolley on Commonwealth Avenue in Boston.

—*Robin Hansen*
West Bath, Maine

Read More about Traditional Mittens

100 Landskapsvottar (100 Mittens from the Countryside), ICA, (1980s). In Swedish.

Folk Mittens, Marcia Lewandowski, Interweave Press, 1997.

Knit in the Nordic Tradition, Vibeke Lind, Lark Books, 1984.

Mostly Mittens: Traditional Knitting Patterns from Russia's Komi People, Charlene Schurch, Lark Books, 1998.

Nova Scotian Double-Knitting Patterns, Janetta Dexter, Nova Scotia Museum, 1985.

The Swedish Mitten Book, Inger and Ingrid Gottfridsson, Lark Books, 1984. Translated from Swedish.

Textile Traditions of Eastern Newfoundland, Gerald Pocius, Canadian Centre for Folk Culture Studies paper no. 29, National Museum of Man Mercury Series, 1979.

Vottar från När och Fjärran (Mittens and Gloves from Near and Far), Eva Marie Leszner, LTs forlaget, 1981. Translated and adapted by Eva Trotzig from the original German: *Handschuhe, Mützen und Schals farbig gestrickt* (Gloves, Mittens, Caps, and Mufflers, Color-knitted), Rosenheimer Verlagshaus, 1980.

Votten i Norsk Tradisjon (The Mitten in Norwegian Tradition), Ingebjørg Gravjord, Landbruksforlaget, 1985. In New Norwegian.

Sources for Yarns Used in This Book

Medium (Worsted Weight) and Double-Knitting (DK) Weight Yarns

Bartlettyarns, Inc. *Fisherman's 2-ply, Rangeley 2-ply, Homespun 2-ply (heavy medium weight 100% wool yarns)*

Briggs & Little Woollen Mills Ltd. *2/8 (DK weight) and 3/8 (medium)*

Cottage Crafts Tweeds and Yarn. *2-ply medium weight wool yarns. 100% wool yarn in heathery colors and tweeds from the New Brunswick coastal landscape.*

McAusland's Woollen Mill. *2/8 and 3/8 medium (DK and medium weight, respectively), 3/8 fine (medium weight)*

Nordic Fiber Arts. *Rauma 3-ply Strikkegarn (DK weight, 100% wool yarn)*

Peace Fleece. *2-ply medium and DK weight, wool yarns from Maine island sheep and international sources*

Sport and Fingering Weight Yarns

Cottage Crafts Tweeds and Yarn. *Single-ply sport weight wool yarns. 100% wool yarn in heathery colors and tweeds from the New Brunswick coastal landscape.*

Halcyon Yarn. *Halcyon Yarn Victorian, a lovely 2-ply wool sport yarn.*

Jaggerspun. *The Maine Line 2/8 (fingering) and 3/8 (sport weight), 1 lb (.45kg) cones only. Soft, 100% wool, many colors.*

Nordic Fiber Arts. *Rauma Hifa Superwash Yarn and Finullgarn (sport weight yarns), Babygarn (fingering). Norsk Husflid's 100% wool yarn with a rich palette of Scandinavian colors.*

Fleece, Pencil Rovings and One-inch Rovings

Bartlettyarns, Inc. *Pencil rovings in natural sheep's colors. Order in 4-ounce (114g) wheels.*

Briggs & Little Woolen Mills, Ltd. *5-strand Country Roving (pencil roving), 12 natural and dyed colors*

Halcyon Yarns, Inc. *Many colors and breeds of rovings, tops, and loose fleece. Basic color palette. Minimum order one ounce (a yard). Write for a catalog.*

McAusland's Woollen Mill. *A selection of natural and dyed pencil rovings sold in 100-gram (3.5 oz) wheels*

Peace Fleece. *Loose wool in bright colors from Maine and international sources*

How to Go to the Source

Please note: Your local yarn store may carry some of these yarns or other wool yarns that will substitute nicely. You may even find skeins spun from local sheeps' wool there, and such yarns are usually ideal for traditional mittens.

Bartlettyarns, Inc.
20 Water Street
Harmony, Maine 04942
(207) 683-2341 • fax (207) 683-2261
www.bartlettyarns.com (order on-line)
sales@bartlettyarns.com

Briggs & Little Woollen Mills Ltd.
Harvey Station, NB E0H 1H0 Canada
(506) 366-5438
www.briggsandlittle.com/wool

Cottage Crafts Tweeds and Yarn
In Canada: 209 Water Street
St. Andrews By-the-Sea, NB E0G 2X0 Canada
(506) 529-3190 • (800) 355-9665 • fax (506) 529-3933

In the US: PO Box 1275, Calais ME 04619

www.townsearch.com/cottagecraft
cottcraf@nbnet.nb.ca (order on-line)

Halcyon Yarn
12 School Street
Bath ME 04530
(207) 442-7909 • (800) 341-0282
www.halcyonyarn.com (order on-line)

Jaggerspun
PO Box 188
(5 Water Street)
Springvale ME 04083
(207) 324-5622 • fax (207) 490-2661
www.jaggeryarn.com
wool@jaggeryarn.com

McAusland's Woollen Mill
Bloomfield, PEI C0B 1E0 Canada
(902) 859-3005 • fax (902) 859-1628
www.peisland.com/wool (no ordering capability on Web site
    as of May 2005)

Nordic Fiber Arts
4 Cutts Road
Durham NH 03444
(603) 868-1196
info@nordicfiberarts.com
 www.nordicfiberarts.com (order on line)

Peace Fleece
475 Porterfield Road
Porter ME 04068
(800) 482-2841
www.peacefleece.com
saw@peacefleece.com